M000106356

RENEWING THE EVANGELICAL MISSION

RENEWING THE EVANGELICAL MISSION

Edited by

Richard Lints

WILLIAM B. EERDMANS PUBLISHING COMPANY

GRAND RAPIDS, MICHIGAN / CAMBRIDGE, U.K.

© 2013 Richard Lints
All rights reserved

Published 2013 by
Wm. B. Eerdmans Publishing Co.
2140 Oak Industrial Drive N.E., Grand Rapids, Michigan 49505 /
P.O. Box 163, Cambridge CB3 9PU U.K.

Printed in the United States of America

19 18 17 16 15 14 13   7 6 5 4 3 2 1

Library of Congress Cataloging-in-Publication Data

Renewing the evangelical mission / edited by Richard Lints.
          pages   cm
Includes bibliographical references.
ISBN 978-0-8028-6930-2 (pbk.: alk. paper)
1. Missions.   2. Christianity — 21st century.
I. Lints, Richard, editor of compilation.

BV2061.3.R46   2013
270.8'3 — dc23
                                            2012047125

www.eerdmans.com

In honor of David F. Wells,
whose prophetic voice has exposed
the idols of the age in evangelicalism while
generously pointing the movement to the Living God
who alone will satisfy its deepest longings for truth and holiness

Contents

CONTENTS

Contributors

Os Guinness
Author and Social Critic
Senior Fellow, East/West Institute

Michael S. Horton
J. Gresham Machen Professor of Systematic Theology
Westminster Theological Seminary

Richard Lints
Andrew Mutch Distinguished Professor of Theology
Gordon-Conwell Theological Seminary

Bruce L. McCormack
Frederick and Margaret L. Weyerhaeuser Professor
    of Systematic Theology
Princeton Theological Seminary

Mark A. Noll
Francis A. McAnaney Professor of History
University of Notre Dame

J. I. Packer
Board of Governors' Professor in Theology
Regent College, Vancouver, B.C.

CONTRIBUTORS

GARY A. PARRETT
Professor of Educational Ministries and Worship
Gordon-Conwell Theological Seminary

RODNEY L. PETERSEN
Executive Director
Boston Theological Institute

CORNELIUS PLANTINGA JR.
President Emeritus
Calvin Theological Seminary

TITE TIÉNOU
Senior Vice President of Education and Academic Dean
Professor of Theology of Mission
Trinity Evangelical Divinity School

KEVIN J. VANHOOZER
Blanchard Professor of Theology
Wheaton College

ADONIS VIDU
Associate Professor of Theology
Gordon-Conwell Theological Seminary

MIROSLAV VOLF
Henry B. Wright Professor of Theology
Yale Divinity School
Founding Director, Yale Center for Faith & Culture

Introduction: Whose Evangelicalism? Which Renewal? The Task of Renewing a Renewal Movement

RICHARD LINTS

EVANGELICALISM MAY BE the most studied and least understood of the major modern religious movements in the West.[1] It has been well studied in the last 40 years because of its size and apparent influence over American religious sensibilities. It elicits such wide ranging confusion because of the sheer diversity and diffusion of the movement across an array of Protestant denominations and an almost infinite number of parachurch organizations functioning at different levels of the movement. For these reasons it is difficult to offer a fresh word of renewal to a movement which itself has been both overly analyzed and maintains such diverse identities.

"Who speaks for evangelicals?" is a question without a clear answer precisely because of the nature of the movement. It is a democratized coalition of diverse religious traditions built around a fragile consensus

---

1. The secondary literature on the history and nature of evangelicalism is enormous. A brief listing of major works on evangelicalism would include George Marsden, *Fundamentalism and American Culture* (New York: Oxford University Press, 1980); *The Variety of American Evangelicalism,* ed. Donald Dayton and Robert Johnston (Downers Grove: InterVarsity Press, 1991); Randall Balmer, *Encyclopedia of Evangelicalism* (Waco, TX: Baylor University Press, 2004); Robert Wuthnow, *The Restructuring of American Religion: Society and Faith Since World War II* (Princeton: Princeton University Press, 1988); James Davison Hunter, *American Evangelicalism: Conservative Religion and the Quandary of Modernity* (New Brunswick, NJ: Rutgers University Press, 1982); Christian Smith, *American Evangelicalism: Embattled and Thriving* (Chicago: University of Chicago Press, 1998); Mark Noll, *The Scandal of the Evangelical Mind* (Grand Rapids: Eerdmans, 1994). A helpful guide to primary sources of the movement is *Evangelicalism and Fundamentalism: A Documentary Reader,* ed. Barry Hankins (New York: New York University Press, 2008).

1

of the authority of Scripture, the personal nature of salvation, the unique work of Jesus Christ, and the manifest importance of the Christian life.[2] There is a common stereotype of evangelicalism as a thoroughly politicized movement, but with few exceptions, no confessional statement of the various movements of evangelicals contains any political statements. There are undoubtedly politically charged movements within the wider scope of evangelicalism, but reading all the various sub-groups of evangelicals through political eyes is to misread the vast majority of evangelicals, even with regard to their actions in the public sphere of culture.[3]

Evangelicalism is often referred to as a conservative religious movement, and in part this is surely accurate. Evangelicals of every stripe have been about the business of conserving the original meaning of the gospel of Jesus Christ. However, the means of conserving the message of the gospel has often been accomplished by throwing tradition to the wind, often disdainful of the establishmentarian impulses of religious traditions.[4] Being "relevant" and "contemporary" have been hallmarks of evangelicals over the last century or more. The all too popular perception that evangelicals are culturally significant because they provide a link to safer, more secure days in the American past does not fit the facts of evangelicals' wary relation to the religious traditions of the past. It has been a movement fascinated with youth culture and has steadfastly sustained a self-professed outsider status with relation to the religious establishment.[5]

It is therefore with some hesitation that the present collection of essays is offered toward the project of renewing the evangelical mission. Whose evangelicalism and which renewal? These are questions

2. These mirror in some respect David Bebbington's oft repeated four-fold description of evangelicalism: biblicism (the Bible as final authority), cruicentrism (atoning work of Christ), conversionism (salvation occurs through a personal faith in Christ), and activism (the gospel is actively expressed in a transformed life). See Bebbington, *Evangelicalism in Modern Britain: A History from the 1730s to the 1980s* (Grand Rapids: Baker Book House, 1989).

3. The recent *Evangelical Manifesto,* 2008 (http://www.anevangelicalmanifesto.com/), signed by a very wide array of evangelical religious leaders, is evidence of the push-back from many within the movement of being stereotyped as an essentially political movement.

4. Cf. Richard Lints, *Progressive and Conservative Religious Ideologies* (London: Ashgate, 2010).

5. Cf. Darryl Hart, "Same As It Ever Was: The Future of Protestantism in the Global North," *American Theological Inquiry* 1, no. 1 (2008): 38-53.

not easily answered in light of the diverse character of the movement, and yet the question of renewal has been near the center of the movement's identity from the beginning across its varied parts. Birthed in the Great Awakenings of the eighteenth and nineteenth centuries, evangelicals have always associated their mission with the project of spiritual renewal.[6] The battle with theological liberalism at the end of the nineteenth century and early into the twentieth century was a central cause for evangelicals precisely because of the perceived danger to the spiritual vitality of the church brought on by progressive theological forces.[7] The large evangelistic crusades in the middle of the twentieth century and the sizeable new ministries to youth in the 1960s and 1970s worked on the premise that evangelical faith could be renewed by reaching out to popular culture in its own vernacular.[8] Each of these eras of American evangelicalism thought in terms of the renewal of the church's mission rather than as a replacement for it.

The present collection of essays emerged from a symposium reflecting back on a peculiarly important collaborative project in the early 1990s distinctively aimed at renewing the theological character of evangelicalism. That original project enjoined David Wells, Mark Noll, and Cornelius Plantinga with the task of addressing the revitalization of evangelical theology at the end of the twentieth century. The project resulted in three significant and influential books: *No Place For Truth,* David Wells (Eerdmans, 1993), *The Scandal of the Evangelical Mind,* Mark Noll (Eerdmans, 1994), and *Not the Way It's Supposed to Be,* Cornelius Plantinga (Eerdmans, 1995).

That original project was aimed at giving voice to the renewal of the life of the mind in evangelical circles. It was primarily a theological voice that was envisioned by Noll, Wells, and Plantinga. Noll chronicled the unfortunate history of anti-intellectualism among evangelicals, be-

---

6. The best recent treatment of the Great Awakening and its connection to early evangelical renewal movements is Thomas Kidd, *The Great Awakening: The Roots of Evangelical Christianity in Colonial America* (New Haven: Yale University Press, 2007).

7. A brief but helpful overview of this period in evangelicalism can be found in Mark Noll, *American Evangelical Christianity: An Introduction* (Malden, MA: Blackwell Publishers, 2001). The best lengthy treatment of this era remains George Marsden, *Fundamentalism and American Culture: The Shaping of Twentieth Century Evangelicalism, 1870-1925* (New York: Oxford University Press, 1980).

8. On this point see Garth Rosell, *The Surprising Work of God: Harold John Ockenga, Billy Graham, and the Rebirth of Evangelicalism* (Grand Rapids: Baker Academic, 2008).

moaning the present state of serious evangelical scholarship, but also pointing the way forward with renewed attention to the internal intellectual resources of the movement. Wells chronicled the serious loss of a theological center in the evangelical movement and also pointed the way forward in part by recovering parts of the Protestant heritage which had been lost in popular evangelical circles. Plantinga took the unusual tact in his book of trying to renew a more fully orbed and more fully realistic notion of human corruptions in an evangelical movement far too naïve and far too optimistic about human nature. All of them drew attention to the influence of the contemporary cultural location of American evangelicals.

Standing a generation removed from the renaissance of the neo-evangelical mind of the post-war period of John Stott, Carl Henry, and J. I. Packer, the 1990s was a decisive time in American evangelicalism. The power of the populist "popes" of evangelicalism (Falwell, Robertson, Dobson, etc.) was at its zenith, but some like Wells, Noll, and Plantinga saw the day coming when that power would wane. There would come a time when the evangelical voice would no longer simply be a partisan one in the culture wars but rather a distinctively theological one in the public square.

In the last 15 years and more there has been a wealth of literature detailing the gaining cultural significance of evangelicals in America along with a remarkable renaissance of scholarly writings by evangelicals. There were major grant projects in the 1980s and 1990s encouraging young evangelical scholars to go into diverse sections of the academic guild.[9] The resulting significance of evangelical voices in the academy has been well chronicled in the disciplines of history, sociology, philosophy, and literature, as well as religious studies.[10] This has pointed at a larger revival of interest in the evangelical mind(s) in the public square and apart from politics. The movement is beginning to produce public intellectuals not driven by a partisan political agenda. Evangelicals are today much more diverse, much more intellectually ro-

9. The best known of these was the Pew Younger Scholars Grant Program, which ran from the late 1980s to the early 2000s.

10. See especially Michael Lindsay, *Evangelicals in the Halls of Power* (New York: Oxford University Press, 2007). Mark Noll's retrospective essay, "The Evangelical Mind Today," *First Things,* no. 146 (October 2004): 34-39, offers a thoughtful summary of the intellectual gains by evangelicals in the period after the writing of *The Scandal of the Evangelical Mind* (1994).

bust, and much less uniformly partisans of the culture wars. The time is surely ripe to think about challenges facing the renewal of the evangelical mind in a manner far different from the culture war challenges of the 1970s-1990s.

With David Wells's retirement as the Andrew Mutch Distinguished Professor of Systematic and Historical Theology at Gordon-Conwell Theological Seminary, the symposium took the occasion to honor the legacy of David Wells and his constructive and critical voice for global evangelicalism as well as to revisit the questions which the original project of Wells, Noll, and Plantinga sought to address. The completion of Wells's five-volume cultural theology provided the symposium with the occasion to consider the renewal of evangelicalism in the period after their cultural captivity to late modernity had been exposed.[11] It allowed the essayists in this volume to look beyond the culture narrative toward a different set of challenges in the coming decades.

Wells's work over the last decade and a half has largely been devoted to the task of understanding the captivity of American evangelicalism by the narratives of consumerism and technology. Because the contours of that story are by now familiar to many, the present essays sought to turn the page and think about the theological mission of evangelicalism and its role as one of the important dialogue partners of global Christianity. The hope of this collection of essays is to take stock of the significant changes in the cultural location of American evangelicals, and to stimulate thinking about key questions of evangelical identity(ies) in the relationship to the public square of a diverse, global, technologically advanced, consumer-saturated, and post-partisan culture.

The essays center around three key themes — the global mission of evangelicalism, the theological mission of evangelicals, and the ecclesial mission of evangelicals. The essays do not represent all the strands of evangelicalism, nor do the authors speak representatively even from their own traditions within evangelicalism. They intend to provoke strategic thinking about the challenges that face American evangelicals

---

11. David F. Wells, *No Place for Truth; or, Whatever Happened to Evangelical Theology?* (Grand Rapids: Eerdmans, 1993); *God in the Wasteland: The Reality of Truth in a World of Fading Dreams* (Grand Rapids: Eerdmans, 1994); *Losing Our Virtue: Why the Church Must Recover Its Moral Vision* (Grand Rapids: Eerdmans, 1998); *Above All Earthly Powers: Christ in a Postmodern World* (Grand Rapids: Eerdmans, 2005); and *The Courage to Be Protestant: Truth-lovers, Marketers, and Emergents in the Postmodern World* (Grand Rapids: Eerdmans, 2008).

and thereby to aid in the effort of renewing the unique renewal movement of American evangelicalism.

The Essays

In the first essay of the first section, Miroslav Volf addresses the critique that Christianity does not have the conceptual resources to underwrite the global yearning for human flourishing beyond the bounds of its own sectarian impulses. In many contemporary accounts of human flourishing, experiential satisfaction plays the key role in determining success, and satisfaction in turn is most often deemed a matter of individual preference. However, Volf argues that it is a mistake of significant proportions not to worry about how well our cultural notions of human flourishing fit the nature of reality. That's what the evangelical tradition must insist and the Christian tradition has always insisted. Most especially accounts of human flourishing have to cohere with ideas about God as the source and goal of all reality. If God is redemptive and we are created for love, evangelicals ought to reject the notion that human flourishing consists in being experientially satisfied, instead affirming that flourishing occurs when we love God with our whole being and when we love neighbors as we (properly) love ourselves. In this respect, Volf claims, the tradition of Christianity to which evangelicals belong uniquely has resources to tackle the perplexing global issue of human flourishing.

The African evangelical theologian Tite Tiénou probes the idea that evangelical theology ought be thoroughly missiological and missiology ought to be profoundly and distinctly theological. The renewal of the global character of evangelical mission requires fidelity to the Divine mission as it is refracted in the Scriptures. The breadth and depth of the Divine mission will not be understood unless and until there is patient and careful listening to Christians from the margins, in Africa, Asia, and Latin America. It is therefore a deeply theological development that the population center of Christianity has shifted from the West to those on the social and cultural margins. The challenge is to see the case for this influence not on demographic grounds but as centered in the very logic of the gospel. The argument must begin therefore with a clear explication of the gospel in light of its missiological demands. It is from these missiological demands that the vocation of theology naturally emerges.

6

Introduction

In the next essay, Mark Noll explores resources for evangelical theology that may be found in a dialogue with contemporary Roman Catholicism. He does so by drawing significantly on two aspects of David Wells's own contributions to contemporary evangelicalism. Noll claims that Wells was one of the very few evangelicals early on to write seriously about the Second Vatican Council. Against the backdrop of Wells's sharp critiques of contemporary Western evangelicals, Noll investigates whether some relief for the malaise that Wells has identified in contemporary evangelicalism might be found in appropriating the features he had identified early on as flowing from Catholic theology after Vatican II. The essay examines the extent to which evangelicals in the twenty-first century might be a more thoughtful voice globally by means of selectively appropriating theological moves from other Christian traditions that have faced the challenge of modernity from a different vantage point than American evangelicals.

Rodney Petersen's essay serves as a thoughtful bridge from Noll's ecumenical concerns to the wider global context of ecumenicity for evangelicals in the decades ahead. Petersen highlights the challenges facing evangelicals if they are to enter seriously into global ecumenical discussions. He notes in particular the troublesome embrace of American exceptionalism by evangelicals. He then maps the missional imperatives of the gospel onto the millennium development goals of the United Nations, arguing in effect that evangelicals need to learn to be good citizens of this world as a reflection of their citizenship in God's kingdom.

In the final essay in this section, Os Guinness offers an impassioned plea for a more thoughtful engagement of evangelicals with emerging global realities. At a time when the American republic has gone through a series of crises American evangelicals have been put on the defensive. The movement has too often lacked integrity, credibility, and civility sufficient to have a meaningful voice in the crisis. Guinness charts seven challenges to evangelical mission in light of the dangerous times in which the West finds itself. The challenges not only pose great threats to evangelical mission but also provide fresh opportunities to rethink the mission in a more faithful and biblically centered fashion.

The opening essay of Part Two of the collection is a collaborative piece, whose first part was penned by J. I. Packer and whose second part was written by Gary Parrett. They share a mutual interest in the significance of catechesis for evangelical churches and have coauthored several works in this general area, including a forthcoming evangelical cat-echism. In the essay in this volume the authors call for a return to a rigorous and robust ministry of evangelical catechesis illuminated in and by the Great Tradition. Catechesis is a pastoral, didactic discipline that is grounded in the claim that Christianity has to be *learned.* The Christian faith is not primarily a matter of a climactic decision of the will evangelicals refer to as conversion. It is also a set of theologically in-formed habits grounded in the life of the church, framed by the confes-sions of the church. Packer and Parrett explore the biblical data that compels us toward this vision of catechesis that ought to be embraced by "people of the Book." They also provide an honest assessment of the hindrances to restoring catechesis against the backdrop of the cultural captivity of American evangelicals. Importantly the authors offer a catechetical syllabus that could be taught, and a fistful of proposals for moving toward implementation in contemporary evangelical churches in diverse cultural settings.

In Michael S. Horton's essay, he reiterates the Wellsian conclusion that evangelicalism in the United States has become all too comfort-able with the goal of experiential satisfaction in the culture of moder-nity. This is manifest in a cultural captivity that is not primarily doc-trinal in character, but rather of its own ecclesial identity. It too often reduces the church's mission to that of creating comfortable and con-venient spaces for human interaction. He argues that American evan-gelicals at least since the First Great Awakening have separated the marks of the church from its mission in the world. In this regard, evan-gelicalism has never been a church but a movement that acts like a church — and too often substitutes itself for actual churches to which one might belong. The church too often is incidental to one's evangeli-cal identity. Though it may be appropriate in some contexts to speak of a broadly "evangelical ecclesiology," it is important to recognize the embedded evangelical animus to actual ecclesial communities. He ex-plores some of the ways in which evangelicalism's unofficial working ecclesiology reflects deeper theological assumptions and gives rise to the propensity to adopt cultural habits that are corrosive of concrete church community. The essay concludes with an appeal to recover a more robustly Trinitarian and "covenantal" ecclesiology.

In my contribution to the collection, I connect the "cultural captiv-ity" thesis to the conclusion that evangelicalism is too often a "least-common-denominator" ecclesial movement — securing evangelical identity by appeal to a smaller and yet smaller set of confessional essentials. The unintended consequence has been the surfacing of a larger and yet larger set of confessional differences among the diverse evangelical streams. It has left many in the pews and in the evangelical academy with a sense that evangelicals are deeply fractured — their unity is too thin and their differences too significant. The solution on this side of eternity is not reaching for a utopian final unity, but rather more squarely embracing a sufficiently rich conceptuality to deal with differences. The central argument of the essay is that traditions of democracy have both borne too much weight and borne too little weight upon evangelical ecclesial polities. They bear too much weight when they provide the sole instrumental structures for sustaining tolerance. They bear too little weight when the impulse toward the "old hierarchies" is not sufficiently resisted. I argue that a theologically invested notion of democracy may help evangelical Protestants learn to deal with differences respectfully and humbly, viz., as a reflection of the logic of the gospel.

Cornelius Plantinga's essay opens up the third section in the volume. He traces the legacy of Wells's cultural critique of evangelicalism along with Wells's theological embrace of evangelicalism. Wells's voice has become increasingly significant as American evangelicals wrestle with their identity in the context of global Christianity. Using the work of Wells over the last fifteen years as a case study, the essay argues that there is evidence that evangelicals may be awakening from their dogmatic slumbers at the very moment when their mission is under siege by many fierce critics. It also highlights how significant the stakes are for evangelicals in late modernity. Situating the critique of Wells inside the contemporary evangelical narrative manifests the potential for theological renewal within a movement not ordinarily prone to serious theological reflection. Unless and until Wells's deep and profound sense of loss is embraced by American evangelicals, they will inevitably miss the possibility of being a prophetic voice in the wider global Christian movement. The essay closes with some suggestions for the continuing renewal of evangelical identity in the light of the friendly but prophetic critique of North American evangelicalism by one of its preeminent cultural theologians.

Kevin Vanhoozer's essay examines how evangelicals speak about the Bible not in the public square, but in the academic quad. Specifically, it examines the so-called *ugly ditch* between biblical exegetes

9

and systematic theologians. Is there indeed a divide within evangelicalism over what it means to be biblical? If so, what might be the symptoms? Vanhoozer explores the analogy between systematic *federalists* who stress the need for a unifying theology and exegetical *republicans* who resist centralizing principles of interpretive authority. Attention is given to how Roman Catholics and Protestant postliberals cope with similar tensions in order to determine whether evangelicals have a distinct solution. Vanhoozer closes by considering how the theological interpretation of Scripture may be the best way forward in healing the wound between biblical studies and theology and hence in renewing the evangelical mission to be biblical in life and thought at all times and places.

Adonis Vidu's essay starts with a brief survey of recent evangelical work on the status of theological knowledge and language. He notes in particular the drift toward apophatic traditions by some evangelical theologians in their rejection of foundationalism and propositionalism. In these strands of evangelicalism Vidu charts the claim that the ontological difference between God and human beings places serious limitations on the reference of God-talk. While affirming these limitations in part, Vidu nonetheless argues that theological realism properly understood is not an attempt at epistemic mastery but at epistemic access. The consequence of Vidu's argument is the ongoing validity of traditional "talk-about-God" in a significantly chastened and humbled fashion.

In the final essay (fittingly) to the collection, Bruce McCormack issues a defense of the full and robust confession of the atonement as both penal and substitutionary. The prime obstacle to the doctrine according to McCormack in our day is the Chalcedonian definition of Christ's two natures, and in particular its affirmation that the divine nature of Christ cannot suffer. Penal substitution is rightly understood as the payment of a penalty which humans otherwise deserve. The experience of hell (as the payment) must be both a fully human experience of Christ at the cross but also thereby an event in God's own life. In this manner McCormack has sought to make our understanding of the person of Christ derivative from our understanding of the work of Christ. In the process an evangelical Christology will have become more concrete, more historical, and more relational.

PART ONE

Renewing the Global Mission

Human Flourishing

Miroslav Volf

Hope, in a Christian sense, is love stretching itself into the future. When I hope, I expect something from the future. But I don't hope for everything I expect. Some anticipated things — like a visit to the dentist — I face with dread, rather than welcoming them in hope. "I speak of 'hope,'" wrote Josef Pieper in his *Hope and History,* "only when what I am expecting is, in my view, *good.*"[1] And yet, even all good things that come my way are not a matter of hope. I don't hope for a new day to dawn after a dark and restful night; I *know,* more or less, that the sun will rise. But I may hope for cool breezes to freshen up a hot summer day. In our everyday usage, "hope" is, roughly, the *expectation of good things that don't come to us as matter of course.*

Christian faith adds another layer to this everyday usage of "hope." In *Theology of Hope* Jürgen Moltmann famously distinguished between optimism and hope. Both have to do with positive expectation, and yet the two are very different. Optimism has to do with good things in the future that are latent in the past and the present; the future associated with optimism — Moltmann calls it *futurum* — is an unfolding of what is already there. We survey the past and the present, extrapolate about what is likely to happen in the future, and, if the prospects are good, become optimistic. Hope, on the other hand, has to do with good things in the future that come to us from "outside," from God; the future associated with hope — Moltmann calls it *adventus* — is a gift of something

---

1. Josef Pieper, *Hope and History: Five Salzburg Lectures,* trans. David Kipp (San Francisco: Ignatius Press, 1994), p. 20.

new.[2] We hear the word of divine promise, and because God is love we trust in God's faithfulness, and God brings about "a new thing" — aged Sarah, barren of womb, gives birth to a son (Gen. 21:1-2; Rom. 4:18-21); the crucified Jesus Christ is raised from the dead (Acts 2:22-36); a mighty Babylon falls and a New Jerusalem comes down from heaven (Rev. 18:1-24; 21:1-5); more generally, the good that seemed impossible becomes not just possible but real.

The expectation of good things that come as a gift from God — that is hope. And that is love, too, projecting itself into our and our world's future. For love always gives gifts and is itself a gift; and inversely every genuine gift is an expression of love. At the heart of the hoped for future, which comes from the God of love, is the flourishing of individuals, communities, and our whole globe. But how is the God of love, "who gives life to the dead and calls into existence things that do not exist" (Rom. 4:17), related to human flourishing? And how should we understand human flourishing if it is a gift of the God of love?

Human Flourishing

Consider with me a prevalent contemporary Western understanding of human flourishing, how it differs from some previous understandings, and what its consequences are.

Satisfaction

Many people in the West today have come to believe — to feel in their gut, might be a colloquial but more accurate way of putting it — that a flourishing human life is an experientially satisfying human life. By this they don't mean only that the experience of satisfaction is a desirable aspect of human flourishing, so that, all other things being equal, people who experience satisfaction flourish in a more complete way than people who do not. Energetic and free of pain, for instance, we flourish

2. Jürgen Moltmann, *Theology of Hope: On the Ground and the Implications of a Christian Eschatology,* trans. Margaret Kohl (San Francisco: HarperSanFrancisco, 1991). For a brief summary see also Jürgen Moltmann, *The Coming of God: On Christian Eschatology,* trans. Margaret Kohl (Minneapolis: Fortress Press, 1996), p. 25.

more than enveloped in sadness and wracked with pain (even if it may be true that pain can be a servant of the good and exhilaration can be deceptive). Though some ancient Stoics believed that one can flourish equally well on the torture rack as in the comfort of one's home, most people from all periods of human history have thought that experiencing satisfaction enhances flourishing.

In contrast, for many in the West, experiential satisfaction is what their lives are all about. It does not merely enhance flourishing: it defines it. Such people cannot imagine themselves as flourishing if they do not experience satisfaction, if they don't feel "happy," as the preferred way of expressing it goes. For them, flourishing *consists* in having an experientially satisfying life. No satisfaction, no flourishing. Sources of satisfaction may vary, ranging from appreciation of classical music to the use of drugs, from the delights of "haute cuisine" to the pleasures of sadomasochistic sex, from sports to religion. What matters is not the source of satisfaction but the fact of it. What justifies an activity or a given life-style or activity is the satisfaction it generates — the pleasure. And when they experience satisfaction, people feel that they flourish. As Philip Rieff noted in *The Triumph of the Therapeutic* some decades ago (1966), ours is a culture of managed pursuit of pleasure, not a culture of sustained endeavor to lead the good life, as defined by foundational symbols and convictions.[3]

Love of God and Universal Solidarity

Contrast contemporary Western culture and its implicit default account of human flourishing with the two dominant models in the history of the Western tradition. Fifth-century church father Augustine, one of the most influential figures in Western religion and culture, represents well the first of these two accounts. In his reflections on the happy life in his major work on *The Trinity*, he writes: "God is the only source to be found of any good things, but especially of those which make a man good and those which will make him happy; only from him do they come into a man and attach themselves to a man."[4] Conse-

---

3. See Philip Rieff, *The Triumph of the Therapeutic: Uses of Faith After Freud* (New York: Harper and Row, 1966), pp. 232-61.

4. Augustine, *The Trinity* XIII, 10.

quently, human beings flourish and are truly happy when they center their lives on God, the source of everything that is true, good, and beautiful. As to all created things, they too ought to be loved. But the only way to properly love them and fully and truly enjoy them is to love and enjoy them "in God." Now, Augustine readily agrees with what most people think, namely that those are happy who have everything they want. But he adds immediately that this is true only if they want "nothing wrongly,"[5] which is to say, if they want everything in accordance with the character and will of their Creator whose very being is love. The supreme good which makes human beings truly happy — in my terminology: the proper content of a flourishing life — consists in love of God and neighbor and enjoyment of both. In the *City of God,* Augustine defines it as a "completely harmonious fellowship in the enjoyment of God, and each other in God."[6]

Around the eighteenth century, a different account of human flourishing emerged in the West. It was connected with what scholars sometimes describe as an "anthropocentric shift" — a gradual redirection of interest from the transcendent God to human beings and their mundane affairs and a birth of new humanism. This new humanism was different "from most ancient ethics of human nature," writes Charles Taylor in *A Secular Age,* in that its notion of human flourishing "makes no reference to something higher which humans should reverence or love or acknowledge."[7] For Augustine and the tradition that followed him, this "something higher" was God. Modern humanism became exclusive by shedding the idea of human lives centered on God.

And yet, even as the new humanism rejected God and the command to love God, it retained the moral obligation to love neighbor. The central pillar of its vision of the good life was a universal beneficence transcending all boundaries of tribe or nation and extending to all human beings. True, this was an ideal which could not be immediately realized (and from which some groups, deemed inferior, were de facto exempt). But the goal toward which humanity was moving with a steady step was a state of human relations in which the flourishing of each was tied to the flourishing of all and the flourishing of all tied to the flour-

---

5. Augustine, *The Trinity* XIII, 8.

6. Augustine, *City of God* XIX, 17.

7. Charles Taylor, *A Secular Age* (Cambridge, MA: Harvard University Press, 2007), p. 245.

ishing of each. Marx's vision of a communist society, encapsulated in the phrase "from each according to his abilities, to each according to his need,"[8] was historically the most influential and most problematic version of this idea of human flourishing.

In the late twentieth century another shift occurred. Human flourishing came increasingly to be defined as experiential satisfaction (though, of course, other accounts of human flourishing remain robust as well, whether they derive from religious or secular interpretations of the world). Having lost earlier reference to "something higher which humans should reverence or love," it now lost reference to universal solidarity, as well. What remained was concern for the self and the desire for the experience of satisfaction. It is not, of course, that individuals today simply seek pleasure on their own, isolated from society. It is also not that they don't care for others. Others are very much involved. But they matter mainly in that they serve an individual's experience of satisfaction. That applies to God as well as to human beings. Desire — the outer shell of love — has remained, but love itself, by being directed exclusively to the self, is lost.

Hope

One way to view the three phases in the conception of human flourishing — love of God and neighbor, universal beneficence, experiential satisfaction — is to see them as a history of diminution of the object of love: from the vast expanse of the infinite God, love first tapered to the boundaries of the universal human community, and then radically contracted to the narrowness of a single self — one's own self. A parallel contraction has also occurred with the scope of human hope.

In the book *The Real American Dream,* written at the turn of the millennium, Andrew Delbanco traced the diminution of American hope. I am interested in it here because America may be in this regard symptomatic: it would be possible trace an analogous diminution of hope in most societies or their elites, which are highly integrated into globalization processes. A glance at the book's table of contents reveals the main point of his analysis. The chapter headings read: "God," "Nation,"

---

8. Karl Marx, *Critique of the Gotha Program,* in *Essential Writings of Karl Marx* (St. Petersburg, FL: Red and Black, 2010), p. 243.

"Self." The infinite God and the eternal life of enjoying God and one's neighbors (at least some of them!) was the hope of the Puritans who founded America. American nationalists of the nineteenth century, notably Abraham Lincoln, transformed this Christian imagery, in which God was at the center, into "the symbol of a redeemer nation." In the process, they created a "new symbol of hope."[9] The scope of hope was significantly reduced,[10] and yet there still remained something of immense importance to hope for — the prospering of the nation which itself was a "chosen people," called upon to "bear the ark of the Liberties of the world," as Melville put it.[11] In the aftermath of the 1960s and 1980s, as a result of the combined hippy and yuppie revolutions, "instant gratification" became "the hallmark of the good life." It is only a minor exaggeration to say that hope was reduced "to the scale of self-pampering."[12] Moving from the vastness of God down to the ideal of a redeemer nation, hope has narrowed, argues Delbanco, "to the vanishing point of the self alone."[13]

Earlier on I noted that when the scope of love diminishes, love itself disappears; benevolence and beneficence mutate into the pursuit of self-interest. Something similar happens to hope. This is understandable if hope is love stretching itself into the future of the beloved object, as I have suggested at the beginning of this text. So when love shrinks to self-interest, and self-interest devolves into the experience of satisfaction, hope disappears as well. As Michael Oakeshott rightly insisted,

9. Andrew Delbanco, *The Real American Dream: A Meditation on Hope* (Cambridge, MA: Harvard University Press, 1999), p. 77.

10. The claim that the scope of hope was reduced when it was directed away from God and toward the nation can be contested. Delbanco himself maintains that the national ideal is lesser than God. In his review of Delbanco's book, Richard Rorty protests: "Why, one can imagine Whitman asking, should we Americans take God's word for it that he is more vast than the free, just, utopian nation of our dreams? Whitman famously called the United States of America 'the greatest poem.' He took narratives that featured God to be lesser poems — useful in their day, because suitable for the needs of a younger humanity. But now we are more grown up" (Richard Rorty, "I Hear America Sighing," *New York Times Book Review*, November 7, 1999, p. 16). The dispute about which dream is bigger — the dream of a nation or of God — must be decided in conjunction with the question of whether God in fact exists or not. For only under the assumption of God's nonexistence can God be declared lesser than the nation, however conceived.

11. Melville, *White-Jacket; or, The World in a Man-of-War* (1850), ch. 36.

12. Delbanco, *Real American Dream*, pp. 96, 103.

13. Delbanco, *Real American Dream*, p. 103.

hope depends on finding some "end to be pursued more extensive than a merely instant desire."[14]

Unsatisfying Satisfaction

Love and hope are not the only casualties of placing the experience of satisfaction at the center of human striving. As many have pointed out, satisfaction itself is threatened by the pursuit of pleasure. I don't mean simply that we spend a good deal of our lives dissatisfied. Clearly, we are dissatisfied until we experience satisfaction. Desire is aroused, and striving begins, goaded by a sense of discontentment and pulled by the expectation of fulfillment until satisfaction is reached. Dissatisfied and expectant striving is the overall state, fulfillment is its interruption; desire is eternal, satisfaction is fleetingly periodic.[15]

More importantly, almost paradoxically, we remain dissatisfied in the midst of experiencing satisfaction. We compare our "pleasures" to those of others, and begin to envy them. A fine new Honda of our modest dreams is a source of *dissatisfaction* when we see a neighbor's new Mercedes. But even when we win the game of comparisons — when we park in front of our garage the best model of the most expensive car — our victory is hollow, melancholy. As Gratiano puts it in Shakespeare's *Merchant of Venice,* "All things that are, are with more spirit chased than enjoyed."[16] First, marked as we are by what philosophers call self-transcendence, in our imagination we are always already beyond any state we have reached. Whatever we have, we want more and different, and when we have climbed to the top, a sense of disappointment clouds the triumph. Our striving can therefore find proper rest only when we find joy in something infinite. For Christians, this something is God.

---

14. Michael Oakeshott, "Political Education," in Michael Oakeshott, *Rationalism in Politics and Other Essays* (Indianapolis: Liberty Press, 1991), p. 48.

15. Offering a particularly bleak version of this point, Arthur Schopenhauer writes that in human existence, there is only "momentary gratification, fleeting pleasure conditioned by wants, much and long suffering, constant struggle, *bellum omnium,* everything a hunter and everything hunted, pressure, want, need and anxiety, shrieking and howling, and this goes on in *secula seculorum* or until once again the crust of the planet breaks" (*The World as Will and Representation,* trans. E. F. J. Payne [New York: Dover Publications, 1969], II, p. 354).

16. Act II, scene VI.

Second, we feel melancholy because our pleasure is truly human and therefore truly pleasurable only if it has meaning beyond itself. So it is with sex, for instance. No matter how enticing and thrilling it may be, it leaves an aftertaste of dissatisfaction — maybe guilt, but certainly emptiness — if it does not somehow refer beyond itself, if it is not a sacrament of love between human beings. It is similar with many other pleasures.[17]

When we place pleasure at the center of the good life, when we decouple it from the love of God, the ultimate source of meaning, and when we sever it from love of neighbor and hope for a common future, we are left, in the words of Andrew Delbanco, "with no way of organizing desire into a structure of meaning."[18] And for meaning-making animals as we humans ineradicably are, surd desire to satisfy self-contained pleasures will always remain deeply unsatisfying.

Accounts of Reality, Conceptions of Flourishing

For the sake of the fulfillment of individuals, the thriving of communities, and our common global future, we need a better account of human flourishing than experiential satisfaction. The most robust alternative visions of human flourishing are embodied in the great faith traditions. It is to them — and the debates between them as to what human flourishing truly consists in — that we need to turn for resources to think anew about human flourishing. In the following, I will suggest contours of human flourishing as contained in the Christian faith (or rather, one strand of that faith).

17. This observation fits with one of the central conclusions of the Grant Study — a study of well-adjusted Harvard sophomores begun in 1937, which, after more than 70 years of following its subjects, remains one of "the longest running, and probably most exhaustive, longitudinal studies of mental and physical well-being in history." In an interview in 2008, its longtime director, George Valliant, was asked, "What have you learned from Grand Study men?" His response was that "the only thing that really matters in life are your relationships with other people" (Joshua Wolf Shenk, "What Makes Us Happy?" *The Atlantic*, June 2009, p. 36). Applied to the question of satisfaction, this suggests that relationships give meaning to pleasure; pleasure hollows itself out without them.

18. Delbanco, *Real American Dream*, p. 103.

Centrality of Human Flourishing

Concern with human flourishing is at the heart of the great faiths, in-cluding Christianity. True, you cannot always tell that from the way faiths are practiced. When surveying their history, it seems on occasion as if their goal were simply to dispatch people out of this world and into the next — out of the veil of tears into heavenly bliss (Christianity), out of the world of craving into nirvana (Buddhism), to give just two exam-ples. And yet, for great religious teachers, even for the representatives of highly ascetical and seemingly otherworldly forms of faith, human flourishing has always remained central.

Take Abu Hamid Muhammad al-Ghazzali, one of the greatest Sufi Muslim thinkers, as an example. "Know, O beloved, that man was not created in jest or at random, but marvelously made and for some great end," he begins one of his books. What is that great end for a being whose spirit is "lofty and divine," even if its body is "mean and earthly"? Here is how Ghazzali describes it:

> When in the crucible of abstinence he [man] is purged from carnal passions he attains to the highest, and in place of being a slave to lust and anger becomes endued with angelic qualities. Attaining that state, he finds his heaven in the contemplation of Eternal Beauty, and no longer in fleshly delights.

These lines come from the introduction to Ghazzali's book which is all about "turning away from the world to God." As a consequence you may not think that it is about human flourishing. And yet its title is *The Al-chemy of Happiness.*[19] Precisely by talking about turning away from the world to God and purging oneself from carnal passions, the book is about flourishing, in this world and the next.

Or take one of the greatest Jewish religious thinkers, Moses Mai-monides. At the beginning of *The Guide of the Perplexed* he writes that the image of God in human beings — that which distinguishes them from animals — is "the intellect which God made overflow into man."[20]

19. Abu Hamid Muhammad al-Ghazzali, *The Alchemy of Happiness,* trans. Claud Field (Armonk, NY: M. E. Sharpe, 1991), p. xii.

20. Moses Maimonides, *The Guide of the Perplexed,* trans. Shlomo Pines (Chicago: University of Chicago Press, 1963), I, 2 (p. 24).

To underscore this point, Maimonides ends his work by stating that intellect is "the bond between us and Him."[21] True human perfection consists

> in the acquisition of the rational virtues — I refer to the conception of intelligibles, which teach true opinions concerning divine things. This is in true reality the ultimate end; this is what gives the individual true perfection, a perfection beonging to him alone; and it gives him permanent perdurance; through it man is man.[22]

The nature of ultimate reality, the character of human beings, the meaning of their lives, and the most worthy of their pursuits all cohere. The whole religious system is connected with human flourishing.

Contemporary fellow Muslims or Jews might quarrel with Ghazzali's or Maimonides' account of human flourishing, most likely deeming them too ascetical or intellectual. Indeed many internal debates within a religious tradition concern the question just what it is that constitutes properly understood human flourishing. Christians might do so as well (though many Christian sages and saints have understood flourishing in strikingly similar ways).[23] They might also disagree with them about the best means to achieve it (noting especially the absence of Jesus Christ in their accounts). My point in invoking Ghazzali and Maimonides is not to offer a Christian assessment of their thought, though a respectful critical conversation among great faiths about human flourishing is important. It is rather to illustrate that the concern for human flourishing is central to great religious traditions, one of their defining characteristics.

21. Maimonides, *The Guide* III, 51 (p. 621).

22. Maimonides, *The Guide* III, 54 (p. 635). Though prevalent, this "intellectualist" reading of Maimonides' account of human perfection has not remained unchallenged. For an alternative reading which emphasizes not just human apprehension of God but human love of God as well as human "return" to the world as a being transformed by the knowledge of God "to participate in the governance of one's society according to the principles of loving-kindness, righteousness, and judgment," see Menachem Kellner, "Is Maimonides' Ideal Person Austerely Rationalist?" *American Catholic Philosophical Quarterly* 76, no. 1 (2002): 125-43 (quote on p. 134).

23. Indeed, it has been a widespread Christian *critique* of Islam in the Middle Ages and Renaissance that it is "founded on pleasure" as Pope Pius II expresses in his letter to the Ottoman Sultan Mehmed II (Aeneas Silvius Piccolomini, *Epistola ad Mahomatem II* [*Epistle to Mohammed II*], ed. and trans. Albert R. Baca [New York: Peter Lang, 1990], p. 91).

Not so long ago human flourishing was also central to the institutions of higher learning in the West. They were largely about exploration of what it means to live well, to lead a meaningful life. They were less about how to be successful at this or that activity or vocation, but about how to be successful *at being human.* In my terms, they were about human flourishing. This is no longer so. In *Education's End* Anthony Kronman tells a compelling story of how the ideal of a "research university" and fascination with "postmodernism" in culture and theory colluded in making colleges and universities give up on exploring the meaning of life.[24] Today, he writes, "if one wants organized assistance in answering the question of life's meaning, and not just the love of family and friends, it is to the churches that one must turn."[25]

As a self-confessed secularist, Kronman is critical of the way religious traditions go about giving answer to the meaning of life. He believes — wrongly, I think — that faiths are inherently inhospitable to responsible pluralism and always demand a sacrifice of intellect. As a person of faith, I think that a secular quest for the meaning of life is very likely to fail, and that the viable candidates for the meaning of life are all religiously based. But whatever position one takes in the debate between secular humanism and religious traditions, both share a concern for human flourishing and stand in contrast with a pervasive cultural preoccupation with experiential satisfaction in Western societies today.

Fit

Ghazzali's *The Alchemy of Happiness* and Maimonides' *The Guide of the Perplexed* do not only illustrate the centrality of human flourishing to religious traditions. They also highlight one significant way in which religious accounts of human flourishing differ from the contemporary propensity to see flourishing as experiential satisfaction. The difference concerns a fit between how the world, including human beings, is constituted and what it means for human beings to flourish. The central chapters of Ghazzali's book, for instance, deal with the knowledge of the self, of God, of this world, and of the next world.[26] To know what

24. Anthony T. Kronman, *Education's End: Why Our Colleges and Universities Have Given Up on the Meaning of Life* (New Haven: Yale University Press, 2007).

25. Kronman, *Education's End,* p. 197.

26. See Ghazzali, *The Alchemy of Happiness,* pp. 1-26.

it means to reach happiness, you need to know who you are and what your place is in the larger household of reality — created and uncreated.

In this regard, Ghazzali is not unusual. As illustrated by Maimonides, most religions and most significant philosophies are based on the idea that there is a fit — maybe a loose fit, but some kind of fit nonetheless — between an overarching account of reality and a proper conception of human flourishing. And most people in most places throughout human history have agreed that there should be such a fit. They have done so mainly because their lives were guided by religious traditions. Let me flesh out this notion of a fit by stepping away for a moment from religious figures such as Augustine and Ghazzali and looking briefly at two philosophers, one ancient and one modern: Seneca and Nietzsche.

Seneca and the ancient Stoics (who have benefited from something of a comeback in recent years) coordinated their convictions about the world, about human beings, about what it means to live well, and about the nature of happiness.[27] They believed that god is Cosmic Reason, spread throughout creation and directing its development completely. Human beings are primarily rational creatures; they live well when they align themselves with Cosmic Reason. They are happy when, in alignment with Cosmic Reason, they achieve tranquil self-sufficiency and are not subject to emotions such as fear, envy, or anger, no matter what the outward circumstances might be. Thus, Stoic accounts of the world and of human flourishing cohere.

My second example, Friedrich Nietzsche, was a modern thinker radically opposed not just to Christianity but also to the ancient Stoics.[28] Even he, an anti-realist thinker suspicious of all systems, seems not to have been able to abandon the idea of a fit between an intellectually responsible understanding of the world and what it means for human beings to flourish within that world. The whole Western tradition of morality should be rejected, he believed, not just because it is to blame if "man, as a species, never reache[s] his highest potential power and splendor."[29] The Western tradition of morality is inappro-

---

27. For the purposes of this essay, I am following the discussion of Seneca and Stoics in Nicholas Wolterstorff, *Justice: Rights and Wrongs* (Princeton: Princeton University Press, 2008), pp. 146-79.

28. See Friedrich Nietzsche, *Beyond Good and Evil,* ed. Rolf-Peter Horstmann and Judith Norman, trans. Judith Norman (Cambridge: Cambridge University Press, 2002), p. 9.

29. Friedrich Nietzsche, *On the Genealogy of Morality,* ed. Keith Ansell-Pearson, trans. Carol Diethe (Cambridge: Cambridge University Press, 1994), Preface, p. 6.

priate primarily because it does not fit who human beings actually are. Contrary to the assumptions of Western moral traditions, human beings are (1) not free in their actions but governed by necessity, (2) not transparent to themselves and others in their motivations, but opaque, (3) not similar to each other and therefore subject to the same moral code, but each different. Conversely, Nietzsche's own advocacy of the "will to power" of "higher humans" fits precisely these features of human beings and makes possible the maximization of the excellence of "higher humans."[30] His "will to power" is simply the tendency of all beings — humans included — not just to survive, but to enlarge and expand — to flourish, so to speak, even at the expense of others. In a way completely different from the Stoics, Nietzsche's account of human flourishing also fits his account of reality as a whole.

Absence of Fit

In contrast, those among our contemporaries who think that flourishing consists in experiential satisfaction tend not to ask about how this notion of flourishing fits with the character of the world and of human beings. The reason is not simply that, for the most part, they are ordinary people, rather than philosophers (like Seneca or Nietzsche) or great religious thinkers (like Augustine, Ghazzali, or Maimonides). After all, over the centuries and up to the present, many ordinary people have cared about aligning their lives with the character of the world and of ultimate reality. No, the primary reasons have to do with the nature of the contemporary account of flourishing and the general cultural milieu prevalent in today's Western world.

First, as I have noted already, satisfaction plays the key role in many contemporary accounts of human flourishing. Satisfaction is a form of experience, and experiences are generally deemed to be matters of individual preference. Everyone is the best judge of their own experience of satisfaction. To examine whether a particular experience fits into a larger account of the world is already to risk relativizing its value as an

30. This last point stands even if it is true that Nietzsche cannot give rational reasons for preferring his noble morality to Western slave morality because he did not believe that there are objective facts about what is morally right and what morally wrong. See Brian Leiter, http://plato.stanford.edu/entries/nietzsche-moral-political/.

experience. If those who understand human flourishing as experiential satisfaction happen to be religious, their faith will shed its power to orient people, and will be reduced to a servant of experiential satisfaction — which is a major malfunction of faith. From being revered as the "Creator and the Master of the Universe," who by that very identity defines who human beings are and how they should live, God is then transformed into something like a combination of "Divine Butler" and "Cosmic Therapist."[31]

This sort of transformation of faith is in line with the pervasively anti-metaphysical tenor of contemporary Western culture. "In post-Nietzschean spirit," writes Terry Eagleton, "the West appears to be busily undermining its own erstwhile metaphysical foundations with an unholy mélange of practical materialism, political pragmatism, moral and cultural relativism, and philosophical skepticism."[32] In his book, *The Meaning of Life,* he notes that many contemporary intellectuals, unsurprisingly, tend to dismiss serious reflection on "human life as a whole as disreputably 'humanist' — or indeed as the kind of 'totalizing' theory which led straight to the death camps of the totalitarian state." In their view, there is "no such thing as humanity or human life to be contemplated";[33] there are only various culturally conditioned and individually inflected changing life projects. If each person is an artist of her own life, aiming to achieve experiential satisfaction unconstrained by moral norms reflective of a common human nature, then it seems superfluous to ask how the stream of ever new artistic self-creations aimed at experiential satisfaction fit within the larger account of reality.

My point is not that it would be impossible to offer a plausible interpretation of reality — "plausible," I write, not "true"! — into which an account of human flourishing as experiential satisfaction could be nestled comfortably. My point is that many today would not care

31. On God as Divine Butler and Cosmic Therapist among American teenagers, see Christian Smith with Melissa Lundquist Denton, *Soul Searching: The Religious and Spiritual Lives of American Teenagers* (New York: Oxford University Press, 2009), p. 165.

32. Terry Eagleton, "Culture and Barbarism: Metaphysics in a Time of Terrorism," *Commonweal* 136, no. 6 (2009): 9.

33. Terry Eagleton, *The Meaning of Life* (Oxford: Oxford University Press, 2007), p. 35. For a parallel critique of the impact of post-modernism on the engagement with the question of the meaning of life in educational institutions of higher learning, see Kronman, *Education's End,* pp. 180-94.

whether they live with or against the grain of reality. They want what they want, and that they want it is a sufficient justification for wanting it. Arguments about how their desires fit with the more encompassing account of reality — how they relate to "human nature," for instance — are simply beside the point.

Creator and Creatures

It is a mistake — a major mistake — not to worry about how well our notion of flourishing fits the nature of reality. If we live against the grain of reality, we cannot experience lasting satisfaction, let alone be able to live fulfilled lives. That's what the Christian tradition, along with other great religious and philosophical traditions, has always insisted. The great Christian saints, theologians, and lay leaders of the past believed that accounts of human flourishing had to cohere with ideas about God as the source and goal of all reality. But how should they be made to cohere?

At the very outset, we can eliminate one possible option. We cannot start with a preferred account of human flourishing and then construct an image of God to go with it, designing the fit between God and human flourishing the way we might look for a jacket to match our slacks. We would then be consciously enacting Nietzsche's devastating critique of the emergence of Christian morality and Christian faith as a whole. According to Nietzsche, Christians had designed false beliefs about God in order to legitimize their preferred values. If we were to start with an idea of human flourishing and then "build" God to match our values, then the only difference between Nietzsche's version and ours would be Nietzsche's dismissal of those values themselves as being perverse, as opposed to our upholding of them as healthy. More importantly, by constructing an image of God so as to fit already given notions of human flourishing, we would be enacting one of the most troubling malfunctions of faith — divesting faith of its own integrity and making it simply an instrument of our own interests and purposes.

Let's return once more to Augustine. We may sum up his convictions about God, the world, human beings, and human flourishing in four brief propositions, tailored to highlight the relation of his position to that of Stoics, Nietzsche, and many of our contemporaries. First, he believed that God is not an impersonal Reason dispersed throughout the world, but a "person" who loves and can be loved in return. Second, to be human is to love; we can choose *what* to love but not *whether* to love. Third, we live well when we love both God and neighbor, aligning ourselves with the God who loves. Fourth, we will flourish and be truly happy when we discover joy in loving the infinite God and our neighbors in God.

For Augustine, convictions about God, human beings, and human flourishing all cohered. That's the positive side of the fit: it specifies what is in, so to speak, when it comes to human flourishing. But the fit also specifies what is out. If we share Augustine's convictions about God and human beings, we have to reject some interpretations of reality and some accounts of human flourishing. Consider once again, now from an Augustinian perspective, Stoic, Nietzschean, and contemporary Western accounts of flourishing.

If we believe that God is love and that we are created for love, the Stoic ideal of tranquil self-sufficiency will not do. Instead of caring for our neighbor's well-being to the extent that we care about leading our lives well, as Stoics did, we will care for our neighbors' well-being — including their tranquility — for their own sake, not just our own. Our concern will then be not just to lead life well ourselves. Instead, we will strive for life to go well for our neighbors and for them to lead their lives well, and acknowledge that their flourishing is tied deeply to our flourishing.[34]

Similarly, if we believe that God is love and that we are created for love, we will be disinclined to believe that the Nietzschean noble morality designed to further the excellence of the "higher humans" is a proper road to human flourishing. Compassion and help for those whose lives do not go well — for the vulnerable, the weak — will then be an essential component of leading *our* lives well.

Finally, if we believe that God is love and that we are created for love, we will reject the notion that flourishing consists in being experientially satisfied. Instead, we will believe that we will be experientially satisfied when we truly flourish. When is it that we truly flourish? When is it that we lead our lives well, and our lives are going well? We lead our lives well when we love God with our whole being and when we love neighbors as we (properly) love ourselves. Life goes well for us when our

---

34. I owe the idea that human flourishing consists formally in a combination of life being lived well and life going well to Wolterstorff, *Justice: Rights and Wrongs*, p. 221.

basic needs are met and when we experience that we are loved by God and by neighbors — when we are loved as who we are, with our own specific character and history and notwithstanding our fragility and failures. Echoing Augustine's comment on the contrast between Epicurean and Christian visions of happiness, instead of our slogan being, "Let us eat and drink" (or a more sophisticated version of the same that privileges "higher pleasures"), it should be "Let us give and pray."[35]

Loving God, Loving Neighbor

What I have written about the relation between God and human flourishing is but a theological echo of two central verses from the Christian Scriptures: "God is love" (1 John 4:8) and "You shall love the Lord your God with all your heart, and with all your soul, and with all your strength, and with all your mind; and your neighbor as yourself" (Luke 10:27). In conclusion, let me apply this notion of human flourishing, together with its undergirding convictions about God, to the proper functions of faith in human life.

Every prophetic religion, including the Christian faith, has the following two fundamental movements: the ascent to God to receive the prophetic message, and the return to the world to bring the received message to bear on mundane realities. Both movements are essential. Without ascent, there is nothing to impart; without return, there is no one to impart to.

Most malfunctions of faith are rooted in a failure to love the God of love or a failure to love the neighbor. Ascent malfunctions happen when we don't love God as we should. We either love our interests, purposes, and projects, and then employ language about God to realize them (we may call this "functional reduction"); or we love the wrong God (we may call this "idolatrous substitution"). Return malfunctions happen when we love neither our neighbor nor ourselves properly; when faith either energizes and heals us but does not shape our lives to our own and our neighbor's benefit, or when we impose our faith on our neighbors irrespective of their wishes.

The challenge facing Christians is ultimately very simple: love God

35. Augustine, *Sermons for Christmas and Epiphany,* trans. Thomas Lawler (Westminster, MD: Newman Press, 1952), p. 35.

and neighbor rightly, so that we may both avoid malfunctions of faith and relate God positively to human flourishing. And yet, the challenge is also complex and difficult. Let me highlight three aspects:

First, we need to *explicate* God's relation to human flourishing with regard to many concrete issues we are facing today — from poverty to environmental degradation, from bioethical issues to international relations, from sex to governing. Without showing how Christian notions of God and human flourishing apply to concrete issues, these notions will remain vague and inert, with little impact on the way we actually live.

Second, we need to *make plausible* the claim that the love of God and of neighbor is the key to human flourishing. For centuries, non-believers have not just called into question God's existence, but railed against God's nature, against the way God relates to the world, and consequently against theistic accounts of how humans ought to live in relation to God. Sometimes it feels as if they would not have minded God existing if they could have just believed that God is good for us. And this just underscores how difficult it is to make plausible to non-believers the connection between God and human flourishing. For the notion of what is "good for us" — and not just the existence and character of God — is highly contested.

Finally, maybe the most difficult challenge for Christians is to actually *believe* that God is fundamental to human flourishing. And it is not sufficient for us to believe it as we might believe that there may be water on some distant planet. We must believe it as a rock-bottom conviction that shapes the way we think, preach, write, and live. Charles Taylor tells the story of hearing Mother Teresa speak about her motivation for working with the abandoned and the dying of Calcutta. She explained that she did the hard work of tending them because they were created in the image of God. Being a Catholic philosopher, Taylor thought to himself, "I could have said that, too!" And then, being an introspective person and a fine philosopher, he asked himself, "But could I have *meant* it?"

That, I think, is today's most fundamental challenge for theologians, priests and ministers, and Christian lay people: to *really mean* that the presence and activity of the God of love, who can make us love our neighbors as ourselves, is our hope and the hope of the world — that that God is the secret of our flourishing as persons, cultures, and interdependent inhabitants of a single globe.

Review: overly simplistic. What does it look like to love God and neighbor? That is the more important question as it relates to human flourishing.

Renewing Evangelical Identity from the Margins

Tite Tiénou

THE GROWTH OF EVANGELICAL FAITH around the world indicates the significance of mission, however it is defined, for evangelicalism as a movement. Evangelicals know the crucial role of mission for their identity. The relationship between mission and evangelical identity requires attention at this time of increased awareness to the global nature of the evangelical movement. This essay argues that the renewing of evangelical mission must involve an examination of how evangelical identity can be renewed within the context of the polycentric nature of the Christian faith and from the margins. Today, one need not expend much energy on providing evidence for the "polycentric nature of Christianity" (Tiénou, 1993) to academic and non-academic readers. Polycentric Christianity is Christian faith with many cultural homes. The fact that Christianity is at home in a multiplicity of cultures, without being permanently wedded to any one of them (Tiénou, 1993), presents for Christians everywhere a unique opportunity for examining Christian identity (Choong, 1998; Shenk, 2001), Christian scholarship and theology, as well as Christian mission. In this essay I want to focus my attention on the implications of the reality of world Christianity for Christian mission, especially the potential for renewing evangelical mission.

Leaders in theological education have acknowledged for some time the need to attend to the implications of the demographic changes in Christianity around the world. During the last two decades of the twentieth century the Association of Theological Schools in the United States and Canada examined the effect of globalization on theological education in North America through its Task Force on Globalization.[1] In June 1999 the Association of Theological Schools adopted its "Guidelines for Evaluating Globalization in ATS Schools." Globalization is currently an aspect of the Characteristics of Theological Scholarship of the General Institutional Standards of the ATS Standards of Accreditation (2002, p. 54). Yet, as Donald M. Lewis notes, globalization "appears to have become all things to all theologians" (1998, p. 37). Indeed, in spite of the attention paid to "Globalization and the Classical Theological Disciplines" (1993), Christian theology does not seem to be greatly affected by globalization. This may be due, in part, to the four meanings of globalization the Association of Theological Schools considers acceptable: "the church's universal mission to evangelize the world"; "ecumenical cooperation between the various manifestations of the Christian church throughout the world"; "dialogue between Christianity and other world religions"; and "the mission of the church in its social and political dimensions" (1999; Browning, 1986, pp. 43-44). There is nothing, in these four meanings of globalization, which suggests any significant change for theological education in the United States or Canada. Theological schools in these two countries have been able to conduct "business as usual" with minor adjustments.

The Association of Theological Schools is not alone in its experience with globalization. Let me illustrate with what took place at the International Congress on World Evangelization, called Lausanne II, in Manila, in 1989. During this Congress an international group of educators met to consider ways of making Christian higher education a global network. In his presentation to the group, David McKenna, then president of Asbury Seminary, lamented the fact that "our definition [of Christian higher education has] the tendency to identify [it] with the American system, perhaps with stringers in Europe and a few adopted institutions in other parts of the world" (1989, p. 1). He then made the plea to make Christian higher education truly global. To the best of my knowledge, not much has happened with his idea in the Lausanne movement. Now, twenty years later and on the eve of another Lausanne gathering, with

1. The Association of Theological Schools in the United States and Canada devoted four issues of its journal, *Theological Education,* to globalization and theology: "Globalizing Theological Education in North America" (Spring 1986); "Global Challenges and Perspectives in Theological Education" (Autumn 1986); "Globalization and the Classical Theological Disciplines" (Spring 1993); and "Globalization and the Practical Theological Disciplines" (Autumn 1993).

clear indications that major changes are still happening in world Christianity and with some of our elders like Andrew Walls warning us that "[t]he Western academy is sick" (2003, p. 14), can we afford business as usual in theological education and evangelical mission?

With the foregoing in mind, I will examine the implications of globalization and polycentric Christianity for renewing evangelical identity and mission. My purpose is to provide a framework for renewing evangelical mission. I will first offer a brief review of the status of contemporary world Christianity. Then I will examine the challenges and opportunities for renewing evangelical identity and mission.

Contemporary World Christianity

Let us first consider the reality of world Christianity. My contention is that in evangelical identity, mission and theology are inextricably linked. Consequently I want to probe the idea that, in the future, our theology will have to be missiology and missiology firmly rooted in theology. This requires careful listening to God's Scriptures as well as patient listening to Christians from the margins, that is, Christians from Africa, Asia, Latin America, the Caribbean, and the Pacific world. With this, we now turn our attention to the reality of world Christianity.

Today the people who should participate in the renewing of the evangelical mission form a Christian community, which is ever wider since "the new reality of the Christian community can be fully appreciated only from a global perspective" (Shenk, 1996, p. 56). We know, thanks to the works of numerous scholars (mostly missiologists and historians of world Christianity) that the Christian faith is no longer the faith of white Western people alone. David Barrett, Dana Robert, Wilbert Shenk, Lamin Sanneh, Andrew Walls, Kwame Bediako, and Philip Jenkins (to name only these) have taught us that the center of gravity of world Christianity has shifted to the South.

Missiologists have known this fact for a long time even though it may surprise the general population as well as many Christians. Indeed, in his 1989 *Friends of St. Colm's Public Lecture* Professor Andrew F. Walls stated that "the twentieth century has seen the most staggering development in the church for at least a millennium" (1989, p. 2).[2] For

---

2. It is worth noting that before Jenkins's *Next Christendom* was published in 2002

Professor Walls this "most staggering development" is the result of two major changes: the de-Christianization of the West and the Christianization of the non-Western world. Walls provides the following statistical evidence. "In 1900, 83% of the world's Christians lived in North America and Europe. Today [in 1989], something approaching 60% live in Africa, Asia, Latin America and the Pacific" (1989, p. 3). Note that this change occurred in less than a century. No wonder Walls could only come to the conclusion that "we have seen a massive change in the centre of gravity of the Christian faith, so that Africa has become one of its heartlands" (1989, p. 3). According to Walls, "[t]he Western missionary episode in Christian history is almost over, and Christianity is now predominantly a non-Western religion" (2002b, p. 272). I sometimes refer to the change in world Christianity as the literal darkening of Christianity's complexion.

The published literature on the southward shift of Christianity's center of gravity (including statistical documentation) tells only *part* of the story. For the darkening of Christianity's complexion cannot be fully documented in published form. For one thing, some of the documentation will remain inaccessible to scholars who read European languages exclusively. This is the case for documentation on grassroots Christianity in Africa written in African languages or on Chinese Christianity written in Chinese. Moreover, much of the story of Christianity around the world remains untold. Commenting on the African situation specifically, Kwame Bediako suggests that "African Christianity must be distinguished from the literature on African Christianity" (n.d., pp. 1-2). Similarly, world Christianity must be distinguished from the literature on world Christianity. Nevertheless, the literature on Christianity around the world provides sufficient information that things have changed dramatically. The change implies an increasing non-Western imprint on the Christian religion. We must, for this reason, keep in mind that "what at first glance appears to be the largest world religion is in fact the ultimate local religion" (Robert, 2000, p. 56). We may therefore have to consider the adoption of a new vocabulary

---

readers of non-academic publications have had similar information available. For instance *Christianity Today* featured the globalization of the Christian Church in its November 16, 1998, issue with several articles dedicated to the theme "Now that we are global." In the general press, *Time* (Europe) focused on the growth of Christianity in Africa (February 2000).

such as suggested by Lamin Sanneh: *world Christianity* instead of *global Christianity*. He writes:

> *World Christianity* is not one thing but a variety of indigenous re-
> sponses through more or less effective local idioms, but in any case
> without necessarily the European enlightenment frame. *Global
> Christianity,* on the other hand, is the faithful replication of Christian
> forms and patterns developed in Europe. (2003, p. 22)

Sanneh's distinctions may not persuade everyone but I think it is a
helpful description of these two ideas: (1) Christianity is a world religion because it is a local religion and (2) "Flexibility at the local level,
combined with being part of an international network, is a major factor
in Christianity's self-understanding and success today" (Robert, 2000,
p. 56). These two ideas provide a good framework for understanding the
reality of the Christian religion in the world today. You can now see why
world Christianity has been used in this chapter.

The shift of Christianity's center of gravity is good news because it
means that, as a global reality, the Christian faith is increasingly at home
in many cultures and will not be imprisoned by any single one. The good
news, in this case, is that since "people of color" now represent the majority of Christians in the world, the perception of Christianity as a Western religion can be corrected. Making the case for Christianity on the basis of its being a worldwide global religion can, especially in Africa, erase
the stigma of Christianity being a white man's religion. This will bring
about apologetic dividends not only for Christians in Africa, but also for
those in Asia and Latin America and the Pacific Islands. By apologetic dividends I mean that if Christianity is *de-Westernized*, Christians in Africa,
Asia, and Latin America are able to defend themselves when accused of
being agents of Westernization and puppets in the hands of foreigners
whose intention is the destruction of local cultures and religions.

The apologetic dividends of a non-European Christianity may also
apply to the United States and some European countries. Sociologist
R. Stephen Warner contends that the immigration of people of color
into the United States "represent[s] . . . the de-Europeanization of
American Christianity" (2004, p. 20), while Walter Hollenweger notes
that "in many European cities there are more black, yellow and brown
Christians coming together on a Sunday morning than white Christians" (2003, p. 94).

I am fully aware of the fact that many around the world continue to perceive Christianity as a Western religion. This perception does not, however, alter the reality that Christianity is now a local world religion. As Lamin Sanneh writes, "Christianity as a truly world religion [is] increasingly defined by the values and idioms of non-Western cultures and languages" (Sanneh, 1997, p. 296; see also Robert, 2000, and Walls, 1989).

Major changes have indeed occurred in world Christianity. These changes are known by missiologists and historians of world Christianity, less known by Christians who are not in missiology and similar disciplines in the West. The "southward shift" of Christianity's center of gravity is hardly noticed or seriously taken into account by other scholars who happen not to be Christian.

Non-Christian scholars may be able to afford ignoring the shift in Christianity's center of gravity. For Christian scholars (even those in the West), ignoring this "southward shift" has detrimental effects. Christian scholars, especially the theologians among them, need to be aware of the change in Christianity's center of gravity because

> [t]he faith of the 21st century will require a devout, vigorous scholarship rooted in the soil of Africa, Asia, and Latin America. [For] the majority of Christians are now Africans, Asians, Latin Americans, and Pacific Islanders. . . . Christianity is now primarily a non-Western religion and on present indications will steadily become more so. . . . The most urgent reason for the study of the religious traditions of Africa and Asia, of the Amerindian and the Pacific peoples, is their significance for Christian theology; they are the substratum of the Christian faith and life for the greater number of the Christians in the world. (Walls, 1997, p. 153)

In light of the foregoing, perhaps the question should be: Why has Christian scholarship paid so little attention to the majority of Christians? Is it because few Christian scholars, even the theologians, agree with Professor Andrew F. Walls that "the future of the Christian faith, its shape in the twenty-first and twenty-second centuries, is being decided by events which are now taking place in Africa, in Asia, and Latin America, or which will do so in the near future" (Walls, 1989, p. 3)? I wonder what would happen to Christian scholarship and theology if all Christian scholars and theologians (from Northern as well as Southern continents) really believed that the future of Christianity no longer depends on developments in the North?

Acknowledging the fact that *the majority of Christians* are no longer Westerners is one thing. One may even concede that the demographic future of Christianity belongs to Africa, Asia, and Latin America. Does this also mean that the future of Christian identity, mission, theology, and scholarship is being decided in these continents as well? One cannot presume a positive answer to this question in spite of the fact that Andrew F. Walls affirms that "the primary responsibility for the determinative theological scholarship for the twenty-first century will lie with the Christian communities of Africa Asia and Latin America" (2002a, pp. 221-22). Take Africa as an example. Kwame Bediako notes that "African Christianity has not attracted as much attention as its massive presence would appear to require" (1995, p. 263). Similar observations can be made about Asian and Latin American Christianities. Yet, Bediako is hopeful. In spite of the current Afro-pessimism and views on Africa's marginalization in today's world, Bediako believes that "in one particular respect, and perhaps others too, Africa will not be marginalized, and that is in the field of scholarship, and specifically Christian and religious scholarship" (1995, p. 253).

I do not share Bediako's optimism fully. For me, optimism must be tempered by the following observation made by Professor Walls in 1991:

> In the last three decades literally hundreds of Africans and Asians have qualified at doctoral or equivalent level in Western theological institutions. Many of them did work of high quality in the process, and not a few contributed substantially to knowledge by their research. The expectation was that these would be the standard-bearers of the theological scholarship in the Southern continents. Clearly there were among them those who are standard-bearers in any company, who exercise an impact throughout the world. But equally clearly, the impact on scholarship of this core of highly qualified people, taken as a whole, does not seem commensurate with their talents or training. . . . But the rule of the palefaces over the academic world is untroubled. The expected publications do not materialize; or they have little international effect. And this seems to hold even in studies specifically directed to regional questions. (1991, p. 152)

I realize that these words were written in the last decade of the twentieth century. Has there been no improvement? Is the Third World still marginalized in Christian scholarship and theology? What is the situation in evangelicalism? While one cannot honestly say that the situation remains as Professor Walls described it in 1991, it is also clear that Christian scholarship and theology are not yet endeavors in which scholars and theologians from Africa, Asia, Latin America, and the Pacific Islands participate fully. The theological scholarship from these new centers of Christianity still needs to make its mark in a substantial way if renewal from the margins is to occur. As Frans Wijsen writes,

> [o]ften European theologians eagerly take up contextual theologies from Africa, Asia and Latin America but they do not change their Western outlook and view of theology. They treat Third World theologies as if they are exotic fruit to supplement their traditional European dishes. (2004, p. 173)

As long as this situation remains, there will not be the full participation of the producers of these "exotic" theological creations.

Renewing Evangelical Identity and Mission from the Margins: Challenges and Opportunities

The full participation of theologians and scholars from the new centers of the Christian faith presents a number of challenges. It may, therefore, be useful to review some of these challenges by asking ourselves this question: why, to use Professor Walls's words, is "the rule of the palefaces untroubled" in Christian theology and scholarship? In my mind, "the rule of the palefaces" continues because of this paradox observed by Kenyan theologian John S. Mbiti: "The Church has become kerygmatically universal, but is still theologically provincial" (1976, p. 8). Perhaps this paradox helps explain why relatively few people realize that the change in Christianity's center of gravity "has not only statistical but theological implications as well" (Frostin, 1985, p. 127).[3] One may indeed acknowledge that the theological implications of this

---

3. This article, which was published in 1985, is an adaptation of a paper delivered at the 7th Nordic Systematic Theology Congress held in Copenhagen in 1983.

reality should lead to the development of Christian theologies from Africa, Asia, and Latin America (McGrath, 2001). Nevertheless the theologies of the Western "province" of the church continue their dominance even if today "Western theological leadership of a predominantly nonwestern church is an incongruity" (Walls, 2002a, p. 221). I note, in passing, that Andrew Walls has punctuated his more recent writings with statements such as the preceding.

I contend that Christian theology and scholarship will remain "provincial" as long as some major challenges continue unaddressed. I submit the following four challenges for your consideration: the West's "hegemony postulate" (Frostin, 1985), the West's self-perception as "the center," the perception of Third World scholars as "purveyors of exotic, raw intellectual material to people in the North" (Kalilombe, 1998, p. 19), and the "dialogue of the deaf" (Mazrui, 1990) between the West and the rest of the world.

The West's "hegemony postulate" is the first important challenge we must face. The expression "hegemony postulate" comes from Per Frostin. He explains it in these words:

> In discussing Third World Theologies with Scandinavian colleagues, I have frequently encountered arguments of the following character: It is interesting that Third World Christians create new types of theology, but I can dialogue with them only on the condition that they state their critique of Western theology in a manner understood by me as scientific. In other words, the prerequisite of a dialogue is that the other party accepts our rules, since only these rules are genuinely scientific. This prerequisite for dialogue is . . . the *hegemony postulate*. (1985, p. 131; italics in the original)

The West's "hegemony postulate" can be seen in other places. One may detect its presence in certain international gatherings. The 2001 Conference Against Racism held in Durban, South Africa, is an illustration. Writing in *The Chicago Tribune* Yvonne Scruggs-Leftwitch states the discord at the conference "was fueled by Western nations' determination to have their own way and to play by their own rules" (2001, Section 8, p. 6).

The "hegemony postulate" may also appear in statements about the West's contribution to the world. Consider, for example, this opinion expressed by Robert Royal, then vice president at the Ethics and Public Policy Center in Washington, DC:

Despite its many shortcomings and occasional atrocities, this Western dominance is providential. No better champion of justice, fair-
ness, liberty, truth, and human flourishing exists than the complex
and poorly known entity we call Western Civilization. The West, in
the broadest sense of the term, produced both the New Testament
and the Marquis de Sade, Francis of Assisi and Hitler. Yet, its rise has,
in the main, been a blessing to the human race. The West's weaken-
ing or demise would pose a threat to many human virtues. Recovering and extending Western principles remain our best hope for
a more humane world. For in these matters, there is no serious rival
to the West. (1998, p. 17)

How does this view of providential Western dominance affect the participation of the Third World in Christian scholarship in general and
theological scholarship specifically? In my opinion this view affects
Christian scholarship whether its proponents are Christian or non-
Christian. Can Third World Christian scholarship be taken seriously by
Christians, especially those in the West, who hold such a view? We may
find a clue in what happened at the 1998 Lambeth Conference. African
and Asian bishops were the majority at the 1998 Lambeth Conference
of the worldwide Anglican Communion. Yet, this did not prevent
Bishop Spong of Newark, New Jersey, from dismissing the views of Afri-
can bishops on human sexuality. As Lamin Sanneh reports, "he called
those who did not agree with his progressive view on the subject back-
ward and primitive in their reading of Scripture" (1998, p. 4). Bishop
Spong's attitude illustrates the "hegemony postulate" as well as the
West's self-perception as the center. So, despite Archbishop Henry
Luke Orombi's contention that "[t]he younger churches of Anglican
Christianity will shape what it means to be Anglican" (2007, p. 1), significant change has yet to take place in those who wield power. One can observe similar patterns in other world ecclesial communions.

The West's self-perception as the center is the second challenge we
will examine. It is a corollary of the "hegemony postulate." Here the assumption is that the West represents the center of scholarship and the
rest (usually Africa, Asia, and Latin America) fits in the margins. About
Africa, for example, Jonathan Bonk writes the following in his article
entitled "Ecclesiatical Cartography and the Invisible Continent": "Africa remains terra incognita, a blur on the margins of world Christianity's self-understanding" (2004a, p. 154). I see this assumption at work

in the reflex of dismissing Third World scholarship without real or adequate basis. So, for example, a seminary president in the United States can declare, with impunity, that an African seminary is "not a real seminary." I have encountered this on numerous occasions. One such encounter relates specifically to the West Africa Alliance Seminary, a seminary in Abidjan, Côte d'Ivoire. This is a seminary I helped establish in 1993. I was dismayed to hear that the president of a U.S. seminary made this remark about it: "This school they call seminary in Abidjan is not a real seminary." My immediate question was: How does he know? He had not visited the school at the time. As far as I know, he does not know French and is not acquainted with the details of academic life in the Francophone world. I find this remark puzzling. What is a "real seminary"? How does one determine its "reality" from a distance?

The West's self-perception as the center of scholarship is not limited to theology and Christian scholarship. It affects many academic disciplines. In his book on nationalism, *Imagined Communities,* Benedict Anderson notes how "an unselfconscious provincialism had long skewed and distorted theorizing on the subject" (2006, p. xiii). Commenting on literary studies, Christopher L. Miller writes: "the figure of the marginalized Africanist . . . is largely true to life. My contention is that Africa has been allowed to contribute almost nothing to the Western academy up to the present moment" (1993, p. 220).

Miller observes that "before the 1960s, Africa had been almost exclusively the province of anthropologists. Africans were seen more as cultural objects than producers of cultural interpretations" (1993, p. 219). We must not think that this view of Africans has disappeared completely. African scholars encounter it in Western academic institutions as they discover the contributions they are expected to bring. The nature of this contribution constitutes the third challenge.

Many Third World Christian scholars have experienced the frustration of realizing that their contribution to the Western academy is that of "purveyors of exotic, raw intellectual material to people in the North" (Kalilombe, 1998, p. 19). In seminaries this role fits more in mission studies or the practical disciplines. In the so-called theoretical disciplines of the theological academy Third World scholars often encounter "the hermeneutical strategy of negation at work" with the result that in biblical studies "Third World hermeneuts" see "the systematic editing-out of their work" (Sugirtharajah, 2003, p. 93). In this regard I have often wondered if the real value of an African theologian to a

Northern/Western seminary may not have more to do with his or her *Africanness* than with the person's expertise in a particular discipline! So, African scholars are forever asked to provide African comments and illustrations on all sorts of things. The Africans' scholarly expertise suffers in the long run. Consequently, "despite individual achievements and reputations, African scholarship is at best marginal, and at worst nonexistent, in the total intellectual and scientific endeavor in the world. . . . [W]e have no choice but to produce what is ultimately a derived discourse" (Irele, 1991, pp. 63-64). This is a case of inclusion by marginalization. As long as this persists in Christian circles, Christian theologizing cannot be a world endeavor.

The "rule of the palefaces" continues in Christian scholarship and in theology for a fourth reason: the "dialogue of the deaf" between the West and the rest. In his *Cultural Forces in World Politics,* published in 1990, Ali Mazrui observed that America and the Third World are engaged in a "dialogue of the deaf." I think that this characterization is applicable to the relationship between Western Christian scholars and those in Africa, Asia, and Latin America. Mazrui contends that in this "dialogue of the deaf" "Americans are brilliant communicators but bad listeners" (1990, p. 116). Today, America's "bad listening" skills prevent her from hearing the Third World. I am wondering if Western Christian scholars are better listeners than Mazrui's America? If they were, they would not continue the practice of marginalizing Third World theologies and Christian scholarship. I see bad listening from Western Christians and theologians when, for them, the rubric "Third World theologies" means that "the contextuality and historical process of their development are neglected and/or homogenized" (Sugirtharajah, 2003, p. 163).

Moreover, according to Mazrui the "dialogue of the deaf" between America and the Third World is the result of what he calls six languages of American policy toward the Third World. The sixth language, the English language (1990, p. 118), is the most relevant to our concerns here. English seems to be the language of global Christianity; it dominates international Christian conferences and international theologizing. According to Andrew Walls, "in 1910, English set out on its career as the successor to Latin as the international language of theology. The full implications of this for the world church remain to be faced" (2002b, p. 62). The present domination of English in international theologizing effectively closes the door to theologians who do not express their thoughts in that language. But, can Christian scholarship and theology be truly global with one language in control? The use of English as the de facto language for international theological scholarship can only reinforce the "dialogue of the deaf."

The "dialogue of the deaf" between the West and the rest is not limited to matters pertaining to theology. It is real, especially in scientific matters, and it prevents Westerners from listening to people from the Third World. Commenting specifically on Africa, Howard W. French (2004, p. 64) notes that "[i]n matters of knowledge, science and medicine in particular, the outside world has never grown accustomed to listening to Africans, or respecting their knowledge of serious matters."

We have seen that the changed center of gravity of Christianity is undeniable. We have also noted that the West continues to practice bad listening. These two realities create the overall context of Christian theologizing and scholarship in the world today. This context may be a partial explanation for the fact that in the West

> The adjectives Black, Asian and Latin American are more important than the quality of the theology they espouse. Assigning a collective identity enables the academy to view these theologies as a separate object to be studied and assessed. (Sugirtharajah, 2003, p. 163)

So, in spite of the theological works produced by Third World scholars, acknowledgment that Western theologians need "the experience and reflection of missionaries and missiologists" (Stackhouse Jr., 2000, p. 55; also Mouw, 1994), calls for "the validity of multiple perspectives in theology" (Poythress, 1987, p. 1), pleas for contextualization as a method in systematic theology (Davis, 1978, 1984), recognition of the necessity of missiological theology (Henry, 1988), missional theology (Hiebert and Tiénou, 2002), and intercultural theology (Hollenweger, 1986)[4] which is "the theology of intercultural encounter in the context of multicultural societies and a globalizing world" (Wijsen, 2004, p. 171), "the global domination of Western theology remains largely unaddressed" (Shenk, 2001, p. 98). Consequently, Third World theologians are either pushed to the margins (Fernandez and Segovia, 2001; Segovia, 2002) or their theologies are perceived as threats to orthodoxy

---

4. The expression "intercultural theology" was first proposed in 1979 by H.-J. Margull, R. Friedli, and W. Hollenweger (see Hollenweger, 2003, p. 90).

(Packer, 2000). It is a well known fact that "standard" textbooks of systematic theology either lack any reference to theologians of non-European descent or have only passing references to some without significant interaction with their ideas. When Third World theologies are given better treatment, they tend to be covered in an appendix (see Smith, 1992). We are then left with this: the West claiming to produce universal theology and the rest wanting "to articulate a fundamental theology that will make [them] equal partners in the theological circles that determine what is theologically normative" (García, 2001, p. 56). The net result of the "global domination of Western theology" is that we are prevented from wrestling with the fact that "any theology needs to attend both to its contextual and to its universal dimensions" (Schreiter, 1997, p. 3). We unwittingly perpetuate the idea that "at the theological banquet table, mission studies are roughly the equivalent of after dinner mints" (Walls, 2002b, p. 273) and we do not seriously grapple with the fact that "only through mission can theology be liberated from its otherwise cultural bondage" (Bonk, 2010, p. 194). This situation makes us unable to transcend provincialism.

Today authentic Christian theologizing and provincialism are incompatible. We can, therefore, ill afford to continue on a path where we have colliding "arrogant regionalisms" (Quéau, 2001, p. 14) as we seek to find ways of renewing evangelical mission and identity. Let us move forward as if we truly belong together. But how do we do so? Habits formed over years, and even centuries, cannot change overnight. Change will require specific actions. One such action may be for Northern (Western) theologians/scholars, and potential scholars, to learn Southern languages (even minority ones) well enough so that they engage in scholarship not from a position of strength and power. In order to do so, Westerners will have to "work hard at practicing the skills that distinguish a human being from a corporation: genuine listening, empathetic accompanying, and patient suffering" (Bonk, 2004, p. 97). Such "genuine listening" is complicated by what Nigerian writer Chinweizu calls "Colonizer's Logic":

These natives are unintelligent
We cannot understand their language. (1988, p. 32)

As long as this kind of attitude remains, evangelical identity cannot fully gain from the renewal potential of the margins.

Another way forward is for us to engage in sustained international and interdisciplinary scholarship on matters affecting all of us. Christian identity can be a matter worth our consideration. Now, more than ever, "the question of Christian identity is . . . a global one" (Choong, 1998, p. 225; see also Shenk, 2001). Reflection on Christian identity is urgent in light of the complex issues raised by the change in Christianity's center of gravity.

There are, no doubt, many other issues that can only be adequately addressed through international and interdisciplinary scholarship. True international and interdisciplinary Christian theology requires the kind of global linkages in Christian higher education envisioned by David McKenna in 1989. Ours is a day of alliances of all kinds, evidenced in many human endeavors, from airlines to car manufacturers; from churches to academic institutions, secular or religious. It is as if we now realize that our common future can only be secured through mutuality, interdependence, and partnership. Partnerships between academic institutions in the United States and Canada and ones in Africa, Asia, and Latin America can therefore be ways of renewing evangelical theological education and, thereby, evangelical mission and identity. For evangelical institutions, in particular, such partnerships can provide the context for renewal from the margins. Care must be taken to avoid asymmetrical partnerships because "genuine listening" can occur only in the context of true mutuality and interdependence.

REFERENCES

(1999) *Handbook on Accreditation, Section Seven: Guidelines for Evaluating Globalization in ATS Schools.* Pittsburgh: The Association of Theological Schools in the United States and Canada.

(2002) *Bulletin 45, Part 1.* Pittsburgh: The Association of Theological Schools in the United States and Canada.

Anderson, B. (2006) *Imagined Communities,* revised. London and Brooklyn, NY: Verso.

Bediako, K. (1995) *Christianity in Africa: The Renewal of a Non-Western Religion.* Maryknoll: Orbis Books.

———(No date) *Urgent Questions Concerning Christianity in Africa: Some Reflections on a Manifesto.* Unpublished paper.

Bonhoeffer, D. (1954) *Life Together,* E.T. John W. Doberstein. San Francisco: HarperSanFrancisco.

Bonk, J. J. (2004a) "Ecclesiastical Cartography and the Invisible Continent." *International Bulletin of Missionary Research* 28, no. 4 (October): 154.

———(2004b) "Orientalism, Occidentalism, and Christian Mission." *International Bulletin of Missionary Research* 28, no. 3 (July): 97.

———(2010) "Missions and the Liberation of Theology." *International Bulletin of Missionary Research* 34, no. 4 (October): 193-94.

Browning, D. S. (1986) "Globalization and the Task of Theological Education in North America." *Theological Education* 23, no. 1 (Autumn): 43-59.

Chinweizu (1988) "Colonizer's Logic." *Voices from Twentieth Century Africa: Griots and Towncriers,* edited by Chinweizu. London: Faber and Faber.

Choong, C. P. (1998) "Samuel Huntington's Clash of Civilizations and its Implications for Christian Identity in Asia." *A Global Faith: Essays on Evangelicalism and Globalization,* edited by M. Hutchinson and O. Kalu. Sydney: Centre for the Study of Australian Christianity.

Conn, H. M. (1984) *Eternal Word and Changing Worlds.* Grand Rapids: Zondervan.

Davis, J. J. (1978) "Contextualization and the Nature of Theology." *The Necessity of Systematic Theology,* 2nd edition, edited by J. J. Davis. Grand Rapids: Baker Book House.

——— (1984) *Foundations of Evangelical Theology.* Grand Rapids: Baker Book House.

Fernandez, E. S., and F. F. Segovia (2001) *A Dream Unfinished: Theological Reflections from the Margins.* Maryknoll: Orbis Books.

French, H. W. (2004) *A Continent for the Taking: The Tragedy and Hope of Africa.* New York: Alfred A. Knopf.

Frostin, P. (1985) "The Hermeneutics of the Poor: The Epistemological Break in Third World Theologies." *Studia Theologica* 39.

García, I. (2001) "The Future of Hispanic/Latino Theology: The Gifts Hispanics/Latinas Bring to the Table." *Journal of Hispanic/Latino Theology* 9, no. 1 (August): 46-56.

Garrett, W. R., and R. Robertson (1991) "Religion and Globalization: An Introduction." *Religion and the Global Order,* edited by Roland Robertson and William R. Garrett. New York: Paragon House Publishers.

Grenz, S. J. (2000) *Renewing the Center: Evangelical Theology in a Post-Theological Era.* Grand Rapids: Baker Academic.

Griffiths, M. C. (2004) "My Pilgrimage in Mission." *International Bulletin of Missionary Research* 28, no. 3 (July): 122-25.

Henry, C. F. H. (1988) *Twilight of a Great Civilization: The Drift Toward Neo-Paganism.* Westchester: Crossway Books.

Hiebert, P. G. (1994) *Anthropological Reflections on Missiological Issues.* Grand Rapids: Baker Books.

Hiebert, P. G., and T. Tiénou (2002) "Missional Theology." *Mission Focus: Annual Review* 10: 29-42.

Hollenweger, W. J. (1986) "Intercultural Theology." *Theology Today* 43, no. 1 (April): 28-35.

——— (2003) "Intercultural Theology: Some Remarks on the Term." *Towards an Intercultural Theology: Essays in Honor of J. A. B. Jongeneel,* edited by Martha Fredris, Meindert Dijkstra, and Anton Hontepen. Zoetermer: Uitgeverij Meinema.

Huntington, S. P. (1996) *The Clash of Civilizations and the Remaking of World Order.* New York: Simon and Schuster.

Irele, A. (1991) "The African Scholar." *Transition* 51: 56-69.

Jenkins, P. (2002) *The Next Christendom: The Coming of Global Christianity.* New York: Oxford University Press.

Kalilombe, P. (1998) "How Do We Share Third World Christian Insight in Europe?" *AFER: African Ecclesial Review* 40, no. 1 (February).

Lewis, D. M. (1998) "Globalization: The Problem of Definition and Future Areas of Historical Inquiry." *A Global Faith: Essays on Evangelicalism and Globalization,* edited by M. Hutchinson and O. Kalu. Sydney: Centre for the Study of Australian Christianity.

Lonergan, B. (1972) *Method in Theology.* New York: The Seabury Press.

Mazrui, A. A. (1990) *Cultural Forces in World Politics.* London: James Currey; and Portsmouth, NH: Heinemann.

Mbiti, J. S. (1976) "Theological Impotence and the Universality of the Church." *Mission Trends, No. 3,* edited by Gerald H. Anderson and Thomas F. Stransky. Grand Rapids: Eerdmans.

McGrath, A. (2001) *Christian Theology,* 3rd edition. Malden, MA: Blackwell.

McKenna, David L. (1989) *Christian Higher Education: A Global Network.* Unpublished paper delivered at Lausanne II in Manila.

Miller, C. L. (1993) "Literary Studies and African Literature: The Challenge of Intercultural Literacy." *Africa and the Disciplines: The Contribution of Research in Africa to the Social Sciences and the Humanities,* edited by Robert H. Bates, V. Y. Mudimbe, and Jean O'Barr. Chicago: University of Chicago Press.

Mouw, R. J. (1994) *Consulting the Faithful.* Grand Rapids: Eerdmans.

Orombi, H. L. (2007) "What Is Anglicanism?" *First Things: The Journal of Religion, Culture, and Public Life,* August/September.

Packer, J. I. (2000) "Maintaining Evangelical Theology." *Evangelical Futures: A Conversation on Theological Method,* edited by J. G. Stackhouse Jr. Grand Rapids: Baker Books; Vancouver, BC: Regent College Publishing; and Leicester, England: Inter-Varsity Press.

Poythress, V. S. (1987) *Symphonic Theology: The Validity of Multiple Perspectives in Theology.* Grand Rapids: Zondervan Academic Books.

Presler, T. (2010) "Mission Is Ministry in the Dimension of Difference: A Definition for the Twenty-first Century." *International Bulletin of Missionary Research* 34, no. 4 (October): 195-294.

Quéau, P. (2001) "Un mythe fondateur pour la mondialisation." *Le monde* (samedi 17 février).

Ranger, T. O. (2002) "Evangelical Christianity and Democracy in Africa." *Transformation* 19, no. 4 (October): 265-67.

Robert, D. L. (2000) "Shifting Southward: Global Christianity since 1945." *International Bulletin of Missionary Research* 24, no. 3 (April): 50-58.

Royal, R. (1998) "Who Put the West in Western Civilization?" *The Intercollegiate Review* 33, no. 2 (Spring): 3-17.

Sanneh, L. (1997) "Missionary Enterprise." *Encyclopedia of Africa South of the Sahara.* New York: Charles Scribner's Sons.

——— (1998) "The 1998 Lambeth: Conflict and Consensus." *Christians & Scholarship* 2, no. 3: 1-2, 4-5.

——— (2003) *Whose Religion Is Christianity? The Gospel Beyond the West.* Grand Rapids: Eerdmans.

Sayers, D. L. (1969) *Christian Letters to a Post-Christian World.* Grand Rapids: Eerdmans.

——— (1978) "Creed or Chaos." *The Necessity of Systematic Theology,* 2nd edition, edited by John Jefferson Davis. Grand Rapids: Baker Book House.

Schmetzer, U. (2001) "Leader Says Islam Is Inferior to West." *The Chicago Tribune,* September 28, section 1.

Schreiter, R. J. (1985) *Constructing Local Theologies.* Maryknoll: Orbis Books.

——— (1997) *The New Catholicity: Theology between the Global and the Local.* Maryknoll: Orbis Books.

Scruggs-Leftwitch, Y. (2001) *The Chicago Tribune,* September 26, section 8.

Segovia, F. (2002) "Racial and Ethnic Minorities in Biblical Studies." *Ethnic-*

ity and the Bible, edited by Mark G. Brett. Boston and Leiden: Brill Academic Publishers. [Originally published in 1996.]

Shenk, W. R. (1996) "Toward a Global Church History." *International Bulletin of Missionary Research* 20, no. 2 (April): 50-57.

——— (2001) "Recasting Theology of Mission: Impulses from the Non-Western World." *International Bulletin of Missionary Research* 25, no. 3 (July): 98-107.

Smith, D. L. (1992) *A Handbook of Contemporary Theology.* Wheaton: BridgePoint/Victor Books.

Stackhouse, J. G., Jr. (2000) "Evangelical Theology Should Be Evangelical." *Evangelical Futures: A Conversation on Theological Method,* edited by John G. Stackouse Jr. Grand Rapids: Baker Books; Vancouver, BC: Regent College Publishing; and Leicester, England: Inter-Varsity Press.

Sugirtharajah, R. S. (2003) *Postcolonial Reconfigurations: An Alternative Way of Reading the Bible and Doing Theology.* St. Louis: Chalice Press.

Tiénou, T. (1993) "Forming Indigenous Theologies." *Toward the 21st Century in Christian Mission,* edited by J. M. Phillips and R. T. Coote. Grand Rapids: Eerdmans.

Tshibangu, T. (1987) *La théologie africaine: manifeste et programme pour le développement des activités théologiques en Afrique.* Limete/Kinshasa: Editions Saint Paul Afrique.

Turner, H. E. W. (1952) *The Patristic Doctrine of Redemption.* London: A. R. Mowbray & Co.

Vanhoozer, K. J. (1995) "Exploring the World; Following the Word: The Credibility of Evangelical Theology in an Incredulous Age." *Trinity Journal* 16, NS: 3-27.

Walls, A. F. (1989) *The Significance of African Christianity.* Church of Scotland, St. Colm's Education Centre and College.

——— (1991) "Structural Problems in Mission Studies." *International Bulletin of Missionary Research* 13, no. 4 (October).

——— (1997) "Old Athens and New Jerusalem: Some Signposts for Christian Scholarship in the Early History of Mission Studies." *International Bulletin of Missionary Research* 21, no. 4 (October).

——— (2002a) "Christian Scholarship in Africa in the Twenty-first Century." *Transformation* 19, no. 4 (October): 217-28.

——— (2002b) *The Cross-Cultural Process in Christian History.* Maryknoll: Orbis Books; and Edinburgh: T&T Clark.

——— (2003) "Theology Is Moving South." *In Trust: The Magazine for Leaders in Theological Education* 14, no. 2 (New Year): 14-19.

Warner, R. S. (2004) "Coming to America." *The Christian Century* (February 8): 20-23.

Wijsen, F. (2004) "Intercultural Theology Instead of Missiology: New Wine in Old Wineskins?" *SEDOS Bulletin* 36, no. 718 (July-August): 171-80.

Williams, S. (2000) "The Theological Task and Theological Method: Penitence, Parasitism, and Prophecy." *Evangelical Futures: A Conversation on Theological Method,* edited by John G. Stackhouse Jr. Grand Rapids: Baker Books; Vancouver, BC: Regent College Publishing; and Leicester, England: Inter-Varsity Press.

Ecumenical Realities and Evangelical Theology

MARK A. NOLL

ECUMENICITY IN THE CONTEMPORARY WORLD has become an ever more complicated challenge. This chapter addresses one specific aspect of the ecumenical challenge for evangelicals, especially as that challenge is illuminated by what David Wells has written both more recently and very early in his professional career. But before we get to that specific issue, a lengthy detour tries to sketch the complexity of the current ecumenical situation.

For Protestant evangelicals in the United States, the recent rise of political activism, the recent increase in international social self-consciousness, and recent forays in academic life have opened doorways to new layers of ecumenical opportunity. In the political sphere, what Timothy George once called "the ecumenism of the trenches" has promoted a range of alliances that were inconceivable fifty years ago. In some political venues, evangelical initiatives on behalf of pro-life and pro-family causes are now regularly pursued in cooperation with Mormons, some Roman Catholics, some Jews, and even some Muslims. Such cooperation among moral conservatives will probably only become more common as the ethical certitudes of Western society continue to erode. Similarly, what might be called "the ecumenism of a hungry world" has created some of the same cross-religious alliances in support of the many programs — some very large like World Vision, but most smaller like the Rafiki Foundation (supported by David and Jane Wells) — that attack world poverty, address crises created by the HIV/AIDS epidemic, promote peace in war-torn regions, and oppose the international trafficking of women and girls. Likewise, in those parts of the academy where evangelicals have recently gained a toehold, but where reference to the deity is still mostly an embarrassment, an ecumenism of simple theism has resulted in surprising alliances among a wide range of Christians, Jews, Muslims, and even some secularists who realize how foolish it is to exclude God from serious attempts at understanding actually existing human beings.

The proliferation of ecumenical opportunities in political activism, international social service, and the intellectual life has certainly added to the complexity of more traditional ecumenical ventures in theology. This complication works in two ways. On the one hand, for an evangelical to share a figurative or literal trench with someone who is not an evangelical can open the evangelical to a more positive evaluation of the theology that leads to cooperation from the new partner. On the other hand, for evangelicals to find themselves deeply opposed to what other evangelicals are advocating in one of these practical areas can put pressure on the theological convictions that have defined evangelicals for each other. If on pro-life issues I am closer to my Mormon collaborators than to many in my own church, if in feeding the hungry I work most closely with a general service NGO, if as an evangelical I think creation science is nonsense — and if I consider that working for life, feeding the hungry, or doing science properly are matters of practical theology — then ecumenical relations with other evangelicals are at risk.

Further complexity is added to the ecumenical picture by the dramatic changes that have occurred in the Christian world over the last century. These changes have significantly altered the three most important domains of theological ecumenicity for evangelicals: the domain of historical evangelicalism itself, the domain of historical Christianity, and the domain constituted by new realities of world Christian adherence. In the evangelical world, long-existing efforts continue at promoting discussion between Arminians and Calvinists, Pentecostals and non-Pentecostals, pacifists and just-war advocates, confessionalists and Bible-only believers. Historical fissures between Caucasians and African Americans still frustrate ecumenical cooperation between these two conservative Protestant constituencies that share much in belief, much in moral practice, but almost nothing in social and political allegiance. To this already complex picture the recent proliferation of hyphenated evangelical sub-groups only adds further uncertainty. Finding a theological meeting place for young evangelicals, old evangelicals, emergent evangelicals, paleo evangelicals, right-wing evangelicals, post-evangelical evangelicals, green evangelicals, social justice evangelicals, egalitarian evangelicals, complementarian evangelicals, seeker evangelicals, conservative evangelicals, and so on has become a real problem in itself.

Adding to the ecumenical challenge for evangelicals trying to manage proliferating developments in groups closest to home are the dramatic changes that have recently occurred in the broader sweep of Western Christian history. A good case could be made that developments of the last half-century within both Eastern Orthodoxy and Roman Catholicism have moved more rapidly than at almost any other time in their history. For the Orthodox, the collapse of the Soviet Union ushered in a new day for all Eastern churches and, by extension, for the relationships between all Orthodox churches and their potential dialogue partners. For Catholics, the Second Vatican Council decisively changed the trajectory of the world's oldest and most numerous Christian communion, but changed it in ways that continue to be hotly contested more than forty years after the Council came to an end. With mainline Protestants the always fraught relationships with evangelicals have become ever more involved, as both modernist and confessional forces increase the tempo of deconstruction among what were once the theological agenda-setters of American Protestantism as a whole.

As wide-ranging as the changes among Western evangelicals and the Western Christian traditions have been, the most mind-stretching changes affecting ecumenical realities have occurred in the world at large. As all but the most soundly sleeping Rip Van Winkles have recognized, the universe of Christian adherence now differs dramatically from the situation only a century ago; within even the last fifty years a new map of world Christianity stares all believers in the face. Africa is now the most church-going continent. Anglicanism is primarily an African religion. The growth of Pentecostal and Pentecostal-like groups in Latin America since the end of the Second World War would constitute the most rapid expansion of a Christian movement in history were it not for an even more rapid expansion of Christian adherence in China over the same period. "Christendom" has come back to life on a few South Sea islands. While the old Western Christian heartlands struggle to manage demoralizing downsizing, the new non-Western heartlands struggle to manage chaotic expansion. David Barrett and his carefully enumerating colleagues have concluded that nearly a fourth of Christian believers today are independent — they exist with no self-conscious connection to the historic Orthodox, Catholic, or Protestant churches.

For whatever value a historian's predictions might have, my own sense is that this third domain of "world Christianity" will generate the most demanding ecumenical challenges in the future. Given the explosive growth of Christianity in the non-Western world and the difficulties of older traditions in former Christian heartlands, it seems almost inevitable that the future ecumenical agenda will be set first by the practical problems of Christian expansion in non-Western regions and then by the theological maturation of participants from the newer churches. Thus, by the middle of the century, if not before, the pressing ecumenical issues for evangelicals will probably be concentrated on issues that have occupied a small place, or none, in heretofore traditional ecumenical discussions. So, I would expect,

- less discussion on reconciling Eastern and Western, or Catholic and Protestant, varieties of historical Christianity, and more effort at drawing into conversation newer forms of belief and older formulations — in other words, less on debating differences among Augsburg, Trent, Heidelberg, and Westminster, and more in debating the relevance of any Western formula for the majority of the world's Christians;
- less on the interpretation of Paul's letters and more on the interpretation of the Book of Acts;
- less on debates about whether the Holy Spirit continues to speak directly in this age and more on how best to understand the Spirit's ongoing work;
- less on trying to understand the relationship of the Testaments to each other and more on how both Testaments relate to the present;
- less on defining a proper Christian stewardship of affluence and more on establishing Christian responses to poverty;
- less on divine healing understood in spiritual terms and more on healing as a physical as well as spiritual reality;
- less on traditional debates over how the original Semitic and koiné expressions of Christianity were translated into Hellenistic, Roman, Romance, and Germanic forms, and more on how they translate into Mandarin, Swahili, and Hindi.

If I am correct that such issues will dominate ecumenical discussions, it does not necessarily follow that trying to understand the current American situation in relation to historical Western Christianity is unimportant. Rather, these efforts continue to be important as they clarify Christian thinking at this stage in Western Christian history when Western believers are going forward to meet newer Christian communities from the rest of the world. The United States remains a significant center of Christian, especially evangelical, adherence; its schools, mission agencies, and publishing enterprises still exert a disproportionate influence in the world; its successes and failures receive the over-publicity that makes them trend-setters for the planet. Although it is dubious in the extreme to think that what evangelicals do or believe simply determines what happens in the world at large, it is not dubious to think that the conditions of evangelical Christianity in the United States still matter greatly at home and abroad.

Thus, the situation for theology among evangelicals in the United States remains ecumenically important — for those of us who live in this venue and, to some degree, for the world as a whole. It is, therefore, imperative to work seriously at assessing the quality of theology and Christian life among American evangelicals. It is likewise imperative to think soberly about which partners, given the state of evangelical life and theology, would be most profitable to engage in ecumenical discussion.

Which brings us to the argument to be developed in the rest of the chapter. The argument has three parts. First, the critique that David Wells has leveled against American evangelicals in five notable books published from 1993 to 2008 deserves to be taken with deadly seriousness. Second, if that critique is taken seriously, it follows that the ecumenical partners whom evangelicals need most for dialogue, discussion, mutual exhortation, and correction are those that display particular strengths where Wells has identified the greatest evangelical weaknesses. Third, for the weaknesses that Wells has identified most clearly, the most obvious source of help from ecumenical dialogue, discussion, mutual exhortation, and correction comes from the official teaching of the Roman Catholic Church. For this third part of my argument, David Wells's writing is again important, but this time his prescient study of the Second Vatican Council that was published more than twenty years before the first of his books assessing contemporary evangelicalism.

55

The Wellsian critique of contemporary American evangelicalism is telegraphed clearly by the titles: first in 1993 — and that date is important — *No Place for Truth; or, Whatever Happened to Evangelical Theology?;* then in 1994, *God in the Wasteland: The Reality of Truth in a World of Fading Dreams;* followed in 1998 by *Losing Our Virtue: Why the Church Must Recover Its Moral Vision;* and in 2005 by *Above All Earthly Pow'rs: Christ in a Postmodern World;* and finally in 2008, *The Courage to Be Protestant: Truth-lovers, Marketers, and Emergents in the Post-Modern World.*[1]

The critique developed in these five books can be summarized in traditional theological terms. Thus, American evangelicals are imperiled because they have relaxed their grip on historical Christian dogmas, including especially the character of God, the person and work of Christ, the ministry of the Holy Spirit, and the nature of godliness. They have betrayed their theological birthright by abandoning the *sola*s of the Reformation: "Scripture alone" as "God's authoritative truth," Christ alone" where "salvation [is] found," "by grace alone that we are saved," and "through faith alone" as the means by which salvation is received (p. 20). In particular, it has been a disaster for evangelicals to let slip the two anchors of their historical faith: belief in Scripture as the definitive revelation from God; and belief in Christ's saving work understood as a substitutionary atonement for human sinfulness.

Yet even from only the titles of David's books, it is clear that his critique grows out of a broad, comprehensive account of why these doctrinal defalcations have occurred. That account argues that "truth" has been compromised; "virtue" and "morality are under attack by forces from the "postmodern world"; and, as a result, evangelicals have fogged their own vision of God, Christ, and the church.

In the last volume of the series, Wells summarizes and expands the critique that he developed in the preceding books. Phrases from this book sketch his understanding of the problem, explain why the problem has developed, and show how the problem should be addressed. The diagnosis is dire: most or at least many evangelicals now lack "doctrinal seriousness" (p. 4), "intellectual integrity" (p. 6), and "strength, discipline, direction" (p. 6). Since "everything is about power" (p. 71), evangelicals have become "very leery about truth" (p. 59), and they display "an indifference toward much of the fabric of belief that makes up

1. All published by Eerdmans (Grand Rapids, MI). In what follows, parenthetical page numbers refer to *The Courage to Be Protestant.*

Christian faith" (p. 8). The sad result is that for many evangelicals "the church vanishes" (p. 10), and they now practice "a faith so cramped, limited, and minuscule as to be entirely unable to command our life, our energies, or . . . even much of our attention" (p. 14). Many evangelicals have "destroyed . . . the biblical doctrines of sin, of the incarnation, and of redemption" (p. 53). In addition, "the decline in Bible knowledge" that has been allowed to take place plays "a large factor in the disintegrating moral culture of Christian life today" (p. 46). Evangelical churches, moreover, are being led by "ecclesiastical free spirits who flit around a much smaller doctrinal center" (p. 17) In Wells's despairing query, he asks why, even if evangelical churches continue to point to Scripture as the truth, "the church that professes this truth [is] so untouched by it?" (p. 60).

The answer to his own question is that sometime after World War II "evangelicalism began to be infested by the culture in which it was living" (p. 8). This infestation involved accepting "the constant cultural bombardment of individualism" (p. 11). The problem was manifest particularly in the "stunning cultural naïveté" (p. 13) that accepted cultural individualism as an excuse for handing leadership in the churches over to "church marketers" (p. 14) who positively embraced "conquest by the market" (p. 11) as a desirable goal. "The marketing analogy," which "is deeply harmful to Christian faith" (p. 53), led to worship auditoria "stripped of all religious symbols such as the cross" (p. 27) and to a faith now crippled by its being "market-defined, market-driven, and market-sensitive" (p. 25). More recently, the new networks of "emergents" have only compounded the problem, since in being "skeptical of power and its structures" (p. 16), emergents only buy deeper into the postmodern retreat from truth, virtue, and moral certainty.

David Wells's antidote for the poisons he has identified is straightforward. "Absolute truth and morality are fast receding in society because their grounding in God as objective, as outside of our self, as our transcendent point of reference, is disappearing" (p. 61). The answer to evangelical decay is "an integrated, whole understanding of biblical truth" (p. 21); it requires remembering that "Christianity is not just an experience, . . . but it is about truth" (p. 45), that it involves "a revelation that is truthful" (p. 75). Evangelical churches desperately need to recall that "Gospel truth, biblically speaking, is not a formula, not simply a relationship, not just about spirituality. It is about the triune God acting in this world redemptively, in the course of time, in the fabric of history, and bringing all of this to its climax in Christ" (p. 52). Again, "Christian faith is about revealed truth, doctrine that is to be believed, moral norms that should be followed, and church life in which participation is expected" (p. 53). Thankfully, Wells concludes, the current scene is not entirely dismal, since "there are still many who think evangelicals should be doctrinally shaped, who love the Word of God, who value biblical preaching, who want to be God-centered in their thought and life, who do live upright lives, and who are not ashamed of their roots in the Reformation" (p. 6). Such ones are the increasingly lonely saints who understand aright that "Christianity . . . is from first to last all about *truth!* It is about he who is the Way, the *Truth,* and the life" (p. 76).

Using my own phrases, I summarize the Wellsian critique like this: forces from contemporary culture have been undermining specific Christian doctrines for several decades; even more damagingly, they have undermined the traditional Protestant trust in Scripture as God's true revelation and the traditional Protestant understanding of Christ as sacrifice for sin. But most of all they have undermined traditional Christian understandings of truth as given by God for human redemption and of the human self as lost in sin until rescued by the love of God in Christ. Wells himself defines the main themes of his five books as "truth, God, self, Christ, and the church" (p. xiii), and the books structure these themes in the following cause-and-effect sequence: because truth and self have been so corrupted by the forces of postmodernity, understanding of God and Christ has been corrupted with near fatal consequences, and these corruptions have had disastrous effects for the church.

To recognize the cogency and urgency of the Wellsian critique does not require complete agreement with its every particular. Some, like myself for example, do not think the evangelical grasp of theology — of truth — was ever as secure in the era of World War II as David has presented it. Evangelical churches in the 1930s and 1940s may well have been less contaminated by the worldly forces of modernity and postmodernity, fidelity to Scripture was certainly more secure, and classical views of the atonement were consistently reinforced wherever the hymns of Isaac Watts, Charles Wesley, Augustus Toplady, William Cowper, and John Newton were sung. Yet in evangelical and fundamentalist churches of this era, there were also very serious problems. Preaching from the Bible was regularly trivialized by wild eschatological speculation or a runaway mania for typology. Strong moral standards on sexual sins were constantly compromised by nonbiblical insistence on "the separated life" and nonexistent moral teaching on pressing social sins like racism. Even worse, evangelical congregations almost everywhere suffered from Gnostic notions of "holiness" that had more to do with romantic Victorian conventions than responsible biblical teaching. There was, in other words, as much harmful cultural conformity to these conventions as there has been conformity to postmodern values in contemporary churches.

In addition, I join others who think that recent efforts by many evangelicals to speak the gospel into the circumstances of contemporary cultures require more differentiation than the Wellsian critique allows. Some of these efforts have been corrupting; others have maintained considerable gospel fidelity. I do not, in other words, sign on to the critique in its entirety.

But even if David Wells is only partly correct, his critique amounts to a major problem for evangelical theology, and hence a major problem for the ecumenical relations of evangelical theology. Ecumenism that wallows in relativism, foregrounds therapeutic views of the self, trivializes scriptural accounts of human sinfulness and divine redemption, relativizes the Holy Spirit to the realm of the consumer's felt needs, and concentrates on discovering new marketing strategies aimed at populations swamped by endless choice — such ecumenism cannot be helpful for strengthening individual or corporate Christian life, no matter how many partners share in the discussion.

Instead, the payoff of the Wellsian critique for ecumenism must be to recognize the clear need for Christian conversation partners who agree about the necessity of truth, who agree that modern and postmodern forces have gravely distorted notions of the person, who agree about the need for clear and definitive scriptural teaching about God and Christ, and who agree on the definite need for a strong church where truth is upheld and where classically Christian norms challenge and comfort the self. In other words, to the extent that the Wellsian critique of evangelicals is valid, the desperate ecumenical need for evangelical theology is sustained, serious, and painstaking discussion with the Roman Catholic theologians who uphold the regnant theology of their church.

To develop this contention properly would require a much more extensive discussion of contemporary Roman Catholicism than I can offer. But this claim can be sketched briefly, and can begin by drawing on one of the very few evangelical efforts to assess the meaning of the Second Vatican Council. This effort was David Wells's book, *Revolution in Rome,* published by InterVarsity Press in 1972. Although only a slim volume of less than 150 pages, this study was remarkable in a number of ways. Its very presence was unusual since among evangelicals there existed almost no other sober analyses of the decisive event in modern Catholic history. *Christianity Today,* under its founding editor Carl F. H. Henry, for example, published only a handful of relatively lightweight articles on the subject.[2]

Revolution in Rome was also important, however, because it caught so insightfully how much had changed so rapidly in Catholic theology. Thus, Wells's careful assessment of the official documents of the Council and of general trends in the Catholic Church led him to conclude that "it is not entirely clear what direction the new thinking in Catholicism will take," but also that the church's altered position on matters as "fundamental as revelation, the relation of the natural and supernatural, salvation and the doctrines of the Church and papal authority has rendered the vast majority of Protestant analysis of Catholic doctrine obsolete."[3]

The book ended with well-grounded predictions about how Catholic theology might develop.[4] The first possibility was that the Council's new stress on human subjectivity could prompt a large exodus from the church as individuals rejected its teaching in favor of their own inner lights. Whether this is the exact explanation, later studies have in fact documented large numbers of baptized Catholics, especially in Canada, the United States, and Europe, who no longer practice their faith.

The second possibility that Wells foresaw was unification of Catholics and Protestants under the auspices of the World Council of Churches. While that exact scenario has not played out, there have been an unprecedented number of official dialogues between Catholics and other Christian churches, including two with general evangelical groups and several with largely evangelical denominational families. These dialogues have not resulted in church union, but they do testify to the greatly increased Protestant-Catholic contacts that Wells's prediction foresaw.

2. The ATLA Religious Index identified two articles in *Christianity Today* from 1962, four from 1963, one in 1964, four in 1966, three in 1967, and one in 1968.

3. David F. Wells, *Revolution in Rome* (Downers Grove, IL: InterVarsity Press, 1972), pp. 22, 117.

4. Wells, *Revolution in Rome,* pp. 120-25.

The third possibility that Wells offered was rapid growth of Marxist-oriented Catholicism, especially in Latin America. With the 1968 meeting of the Latin American bishops in Medellín, Colombia, and the appearance of landmark works like Gustavo Gutíerrez's *A Theology of Liberation,* published like Wells's book in 1972, this prediction was directly on target.

The fourth possibility that Wells foresaw was that the Council's changed "attitude" on Scripture might lead to a situation where "many Catholics will belatedly acknowledge that historic Protestant belief holds the key to their religious needs."[5] While this possibility has not taken place, it is nonetheless the case that a number of evangelical-type developments have taken place among Catholics since the Council. What might be called Rome's evangelical intimations include more lay Catholic study of Scripture, several instances where Catholic groups in various regions call themselves "evangelical" in the standard meaning of the term, much Catholic use of evangelical tools like the *Alpha* program, and wide prevalence of charismatic phenomena especially among majority-world Catholics. In addition, noticeably more positive attitudes toward Martin Luther, the Augsburg Confession, and Lutheran formulas of justification by faith are now commonplace in official Catholic teaching.

Much of Wells's discerning analysis of post-conciliar Catholicism hinged on his sense that there had occurred in the church a "shift towards subjective religious experience and away from objective Catholic allegiance."[6] This assessment was at once his most prescient conclusion and the part of his analysis that later events would show had been most incomplete. It came, at least in part, from historical conclusions that Wells developed in yet another early book, this one on the theology of George Tyrrell, one of the leading modernists condemned by the church in the very early years of the twentieth century. In his work on Tyrrell, which was carried out in conjunction with *Revolution in Rome,* but not published until 1981, Wells saw considerable continuity between Tyrrell's modernist views on the supernatural, Scripture, and religious experience and later views prominent in the documents of Vatican II.[7] That continuity supported his first three predictions for the

---

5. Wells, *Revolution in Rome,* p. 124.

6. Wells, *Revolution in Rome,* p. 118.

7. David F. Wells, *The Prophetic Theology of George Tyrrell* (Chico, CA: Scholars Press, 1981), with links between Tyrrell and the Council, pp. 78-81.

possible future of Catholicism, since in various ways these predictions foresaw the growth of a corrupting subjectivist trend that Wells would later excoriate among evangelicals. The problem with this assessment was that it registered only some of the theological influences coming to light during the Council and that it failed to see how strong would be re-actions within Catholicism itself to the subjectivist trends that Wells accurately perceived.

Still one more book of David Wells is pertinent to his analysis of the Council, the future of Catholic theology, and the ecumenical needs of evangelicals. In 1984, Wells published *The Person of Christ: A Biblical and Historical Analysis of the Incarnation,* which in my view has received far less attention than it deserved. In this study, Wells combined bibli-cal and historical materials in outlining a classically orthodox view of Christ's person and work; toward the end he also paused to assess the Christological opinions of three twentieth-century theologians. The three were Karl Barth, Norman Pittinger, and Edward Schillebeeckx. In explaining the Christologies of these figures Wells came down hard on the process theology of the Protestant Pittinger. He came down even harder on the views of Schillebeeckx, who represented the far left of post-conciliar Catholicism. In Schillebeeckx, Wells saw the same ram-pant subjectivism and the same compromises on biblical authority that he had documented in George Tyrrell and that he felt were pushing the Vatican Council dangerously close to theological modernism.

By contrast, the section on Barth was much different. In a relatively detailed analysis, Wells commended many aspects of Barth's Christol-ogy — especially its faithfulness to the Chalcedonian Definition and its rejection of Protestant liberalism — but also challenged Barth on what Wells described as his "concessions to Kantianism" and his over-reactions to the errors of Protestant liberalism.[8] In the pages of this book where Wells engaged Barth, we have bracing ecumenical dialogue in which Wells's historically orthodox position wrestled productively with Barth's neo-orthodox position.

The relevance of Wells's book, *The Person of Christ,* to his earlier study, *Revolution in Rome,* and also to the ecumenical tasks of evangeli-cal theology, lies in developments within the Catholic Church that al-

8. David F. Wells, *The Person of Christ: A Biblical and Historical Analysis of the Incarna-tion* (Westchester, IL: Crossway Books, 1984), p. 160; on Barth more generally, pp. 154-61; on Pittinger, pp. 161-65; and on Schillebeeckx, pp. 165-70.

most no one during or immediately after the Council saw clearly. Most early accounts of the Council described it as a venue in which "conservatives" vied with "progressives" for control of the church. Conservatives defended scholastic Thomism, defined the church as unchangeable, and condemned contemporary culture. Progressives advocated neo- or mystical-Thomism, embraced the possibility of beneficial historical development, and sought dialogue with contemporary culture. Pictured like this as a bi-polar contest — which was almost everywhere the standard early picture and still now a popular image — the Council witnessed a revival of the struggle between Leo XIII and the modernists of the early twentieth century, only this time with the modernists claiming at least a partial victory.

The reality that has become more apparent since the close of the Council is that the so-called "progressive" party was actually made up of two quite distinct groups. One was indeed modernist and described as such by David Wells in *Revolution in Rome* as well as in his account of Edward Schillebeeckx for the book *The Person of Christ*. But the other party, which flew under the radar screen for a decade or more, was not modernist. It was, in fact, the Catholic equivalent of neo-orthodoxy. In retrospect, as has been visible only in recent years, the struggle at the Council involved three contenders: traditionalists, modernists, and this third group which represented a *nouvelle théologie* along lines that had been anticipated in the nineteenth century by Cardinal John Henry Newman.[9]

This third party was represented at the Council by bishops and *periti* whose views resembled those of Henri de Lubac. De Lubac had found himself at odds with church traditionalists for much of his career — because of how he had emphasized Scripture, the early church fathers, and a historical appropriation of Thomism. But by the early 1960s his general viewpoint was gaining ground. After the Council a similar perspective informed the voluminous writings of Hans Urs von Balthasar. Later it would come to much greater visibility in the works of Cardinal Karol Wojtyla (later Pope John Paul II) and Cardinal Joseph

9. For orientation, see Fergus Kerr, *Twentieth-Century Catholic Theologians* (Malden, MA: Blackwell, 2007); and a series of perceptive articles reviewing the avalanche of books on the Council by Jared Wicks, S.J., "New Light on Vatican Council II," *The Catholic Historical Review* 92 (2006): 609-28; "More Light on Vatican Council II," *The Catholic Historical Review* 94 (2008): 75-101; and "Further Light on Vatican Council II," *The Catholic Historical Review* 95 (2009): 546-69.

Ratzinger (later Pope Benedict XVI). This point of view was progressive insofar as it saw historical development making a potentially positive contribution to Christian doctrine and as it defined dogma in relationship to human consciousness and the development of the person. But from a Protestant point of view, it could also be called conservative in stressing the scriptural foundation for dogma and for preferring the early church fathers over doctrinal formulations from Trent and the First Vatican Council. For ecumenical purposes, this group was also distinguished by its fruitful engagement with the theology of Karl Barth.

The reason that David Wells and almost all other observers of the Council for a long time missed the salience of this third Catholic option was the difficulty in distinguishing the two very different "progressive" emphases at work in the Council's deliberations, in the later exposition of its teaching, and in the more general direction of Catholic theology. To understand the great significance of this alternative progressivism, it is helpful to note that its perspective was largely dominant in crafting *The Catechism of the Catholic Church* that from its publication in 1994 has defined the official dogma of the church. With his research dating from the late 1960s and early 1970s, David Wells — along with most other commentators — missed the importance of this Catholic grouping. Had it been clearer at that earlier stage, it might have altered the shape of Wells's predictions about the future of Catholic theology and also the shape of his book on the person of Christ. If the latter volume, for instance, could have added an assessment of van Balthasar to those of Barth, Pittinger, and Schillebeeckx, it would have given David *two* ecumenical partners for constructive ecumenical dialogue.

The reason why this strand of Catholic *nouvelle théologie* is especially relevant for the theological needs of evangelical ecumenism — as defined by the Wellsian critique of contemporary evangelicalism — will be clear from a sketch of just a few historical signposts. A meeting in Cracow, Poland, from October 1975 provides a good starting point. In that month a French layman, Gérard Soulages, paid a visit to the Cardinal Archbishop of that city, Karol Wojtyla. As detailed in George H. Williams's *The Mind of John Paul II,* Soulages had come to Wojtyla's attention through Catholic circles that shared respect for St. John of the Cross and antipathy to Soviet communism. Soulages, who had once leaned in a modernist direction, was pulled back toward orthodoxy by his alarm at the Catholic radicals who claimed support for their radicalism from Vatican II. In particular, publication in 1966 of *The Dutch Catechism,* which reflected emphases aligned with Edward Schillebeeckx's modernist views, had spurred Soulages to action. Now in 1975 he was bringing Bishop Wojtyla a seven-point cry of alarm about trends in the French Catholic Church. Three of Soulages's points treated problems among French Catholics that roughly paralleled problems David Wells would later find among American evangelicals: they were suffering a crisis of authority because of uncertainties in the priesthood, they were beset by unseemly divisions, and they were hurt by extreme conservatives who took such marginal positions that they drove others away from Catholic belief and practice. But the other four of Soulages's points so closely anticipated David Wells's concerns that they might have served as rough drafts for the explicit criticisms he would publish almost twenty years later: young French Catholics adopted uncritically a "horizontalism" that substituted social action for Christian salvation, French Catholics in general were suffering "the degradation of morals" brought about by the modern sexual revolution, they suffered equally from the "horizontalism" coming from Holland that defined so much of the faith in humanistic terms, and they were crippled by "the semi-Modernist, post-Bultmannian disappearance of the main articles of faith in . . . Catholic scriptural exegesis."[10] This seven-point indictment exerted limited influence on Bishop Wojtyla, but only because his own thinking was already moving strongly in the direction represented by his French visitor.

The next signpost in this quick survey is an extensive interview given in 1985 by the then cardinal prefect of the Sacred Congregation for the Doctrine of the Faith at the Vatican. At the center of this book-length interview, Cardinal Joseph Ratzinger made two bold assertions that again intimated material that David Wells would later elaborate for evangelicals. First was the cardinal's belief that "in recent years theology has energetically dedicated itself to make faith and signs of the times accord with each other in order to find new ways for the transmission of Christianity." This effort, however, had aggravated rather than resolved the church's crisis. What the church needed was not "this subjective view of theology" in which "dogma is often viewed as . . . an assault on the freedom of the individual scholar." Rather, it needed the

10. George H. Williams, *The Mind of John Paul II: Origins of His Thought and Action* (New York: Seabury, 1981), p. 242 (and pp. 238-44 generally).

realization that "dogmatic definition is . . . a service to the truth, a gift offered to believers by the authority willed by God."[11] Second was the cardinal's statement about which Christian doctrine he would most like to expound if he were freed from his official duties: "I should like to devote myself precisely to the theme of 'original sin' and to the necessity of a rediscovery of its authentic reality." If, Ratzinger asserted, humans lose sight of their desperate state without God, they no longer can "understand . . . the necessity of Christ the Redeemer."[12] In this interview, Ratzinger was not announcing Protestant convictions, but he was advancing an argument very similar to what would come only a few years later from David Wells.

Then in 1993 the great conjunction took place. Even as the Wm. B. Eerdmans Publishing Company was shipping copies of *No Place for Truth* from Grand Rapids, the Vatican issued Pope John Paul II's encyclical, *Veritatis Splendor*. The rousing opening of this document led on to a sophisticated exposition of truth itself and an even more impassioned defense of where humans could find the truth. It began by asserting that "the splendor of truth shines forth in the works of the Creator and, in a special way, in man, created in the image and likeness of God (cf. Gen. 1:26)." Then within only a few paragraphs the encyclical became more explicit: "No one can escape from the fundamental questions: *What must I do? How do I distinguish good from evil?* The answer is only possible thanks to the splendor of the truth which shines forth deep within the human spirit." After quoting the psalmist's prayer for the light of God's face to shine upon us, the encyclical went on to affirm, "The light of God's face shines in all its beauty on the countenance of Jesus Christ, 'the image of the invisible God' (Col. 1:15), the 'reflection of God's glory' (Heb. 1:3), 'full of grace and truth' (Jn 1:14). Christ is 'the way, and the truth, and the life' (Jn 14:6). Consequently the decisive answer to every one of man's questions, his religious and moral questions in particular, is given by Jesus Christ, or rather is Jesus Christ himself."[13] While much in *Veritatis Splendor* was clearly not Protestant, its main themes offered a striking parallel in Catholic terms to the urgent plea that David Wells was making to evangelicals at just the same time.

11. Joseph Cardinal Ratzinger, with Vittorio Messori, *The Ratzinger Report: An Exclusive Interview on the State of the Church* (San Francisco: Ignatius, 1985), pp. 71-72.

12. *Ratzinger Report*, p. 79.

13. *Encyclical Letter of John Paul II: The Splendor of Truth, Veritatis Splendor* (Boston: Pauline, 1993), pp. 9, 10-11.

There is space for only one more signpost in this Catholic trajectory; it is the homily that Cardinal Ratzinger delivered at the Votive Mass on April 18, 2005, for the congregation of cardinals who convened to select a successor to the recently deceased John Paul II. In the course of expounding upon the day's gospel from Luke 4:21 ("today this scripture passage is fulfilled in your hearing"), Ratzinger paused to chart the "many winds of doctrine" that had blown upon the faithful in recent years. Included in these winds were blasts "from Marxism to liberalism, even to libertinism; from collectivism to radical individualism; from atheism to a vague religious mysticism; from agnosticism to syncretism, and so forth." The cardinal reported that "having a clear faith, based on the Creed of the Church," was often described as fundamentalism, while "relativism" seemed to be "the only attitude acceptable to today's standards." Yet the cardinal was obviously distressed by what he saw as an impending "dictatorship of relativism which does not recognize anything for certain and which has as its highest goal one's own ego and one's own desires." Against this relativist tide, Ratzinger held up "a different goal: the Son of God, true man. He is the true measure of true humanism."[14]

Shortly after delivering this homily, Cardinal Ratzinger became Pope Benedict XVI. In encyclicals and books published since his selection, the pope has continued to defend the vision of truth and the true self that he outlined in this homily. He has used these convictions as the foundation for his classically orthodox declarations on God and Christ; he has propounded those declarations in order to strengthen the Roman Catholic Church.

To the extent that David Wells has accurately defined evangelicalism as it actually exists, the most pressing task for evangelical ecumenicity is to talk seriously and at length with Catholics in the lineage of de Lubac, Balthasar, Soulages, Wojtyla, and Ratzinger.

In closing, it is important to spell out limits for my argument about the future of ecumenical theology for evangelicals.

- Except in a very few instances, Roman Catholics are not becoming more Protestant; even when Catholics employ evangelical language, use Scripture with complete confidence, or take advantage of evangelism tools like *Alpha,* they are doing so for purposes that cannot be easily conflated with Protestantism.

14. www.oecumene.radiovaticana.org/enl/Articolo.asp?id=33987 (Sept. 21, 2009).

- Official Catholic doctrine, as found in *The Catechism of the Catholic Church* as well as the encyclicals and books of the two most recent popes, is today much closer to classical Protestant theology than was the case before the Second Vatican Council, but by no means have the streams of classical Protestant theology and official Catholic theology flowed harmoniously together.
- If it is true that recent Catholic leaders have articulated a theology from which evangelicals can learn much, it is also true that Catholics have much to learn from evangelicals — especially as Catholics address serious problems in their own midst of rampant nominalism, formalism, syncretism, tribalism, and antinomianism.
- Moreover, contention within the Catholic Church over theological direction is by no means over. While official teaching from the Vatican and the popes is remarkable in its basic orthodoxy, the modernist, subjectivist, Marxist, and individualist varieties of Catholic theology that David Wells foresaw as possible directions for the church remain very much alive.
- In addition, while the two formal dialogues that have taken place between Catholics and evangelicals — from 1977 to 1984, and from 1993 to 2002 — yielded some positive results, they left many issues still unresolved, especially great differences over the role of the institutional church in the order of salvation.[15]

Yet with these qualifications carefully in place, the reality remains: if evangelicals seek constructive ecumenical dialogue with the Christian movement that is most strongly committed to truth and virtue, that dialogue must engage the Roman Catholic Church. If evangelicals seek constructive ecumenical dialogue with the Christian movement that is most strongly committed to classical doctrines of God and Christ, that dialogue must engage the Roman Catholic Church. And if evangelicals seek constructive ecumenical dialogue with the Christian movement that is most strongly committed to the necessity, the integrity, and the truth-telling character of the church, that dialogue must bring evangelicals and Catholics together who are committed to their contrasting understandings of the church.

15. Basil Meeking and John R. W. Stott, *The Evangelical-Roman Catholic Dialogue on Mission, 1977-1984: A Report* (Grand Rapids: Eerdmans, 1986); George Vandervelde, "Church, Evangelization, and the Bond of Koinonia," *Evangelical Review of Theology* 239 (April 2005): 100-130.

Mapping Evangelicalism:
For the Sake of Mission in the Twenty-first Century

RODNEY L. PETERSEN

EVANGELICALISM HAS REACHED its way into multiple sectors of American life and carried its message around the world. Transcending the pulpit, its insights and preachments have challenged the realms of public policy, shaped scientific research and academia, as well as having had a continuing impact upon popular culture. Evangelicalism is by far one of the most dynamic movements in contemporary America. It has, together with other social forces, helped to reshape the religious landscape not only in the United States, but globally from Boston to Bejing.[1]

The term "evangelical" is expansive. It is often inclusive of Pentecostals, progressive evangelicals, and conservative evangelicals. Each of these terms, in turn, is susceptible to an almost endless subcategorization such that the term "evangelical," as it becomes parsed out in many different communities, is particularized and called upon to defend many different sides of contemporary culture wars. Such defense often follows lines of debate identified by scholars like Donald Dayton and Ernest Sandeen. In earlier scholarship Dayton laid bare the roots of a progressive evangelicalism and found it often related to North American Holiness and Pentecostal movements throughout the nineteenth and early twentieth centuries. Later, Dayton concluded that this almost endless proliferation of the term and its location in a particular way of reading American church history is such as to make it almost meaningless. On

---

1. On the origin of the term, see David Wells and John Woodbridge, eds., *The Evangelicals* (Nashville: Abingdon Press, 1975). See my book with George Huntston Williams, *Evangelicals: Society, the State, the Nation, 1925-1975* (Nashville: Abingdon Press, 1975).

the other hand, Ernest Sandeen found evangelicalism a close cousin to American Protestant fundamentalism in its relation to conceptions of biblical inerrancy, pre-millennialism, and other social factors characteristic of late nineteenth-century Protestantism in the United States.[2]

More recently, Garth Rosell has laid out a moderate path definitive of both evangelical left and right, the tradition of American revivalism beginning with eighteenth-century New England Puritan Jonathan Edwards and carried through in Presbyterian revivalist Charles G. Finney. In keeping with his historical trajectory, Rosell describes evangelicalism's further movement beyond North America to worldwide missional reach, grounding this in eighteenth-century revivals and their nineteenth-century outcomes, e.g., 1806 Haystack Prayer Meeting, 1812 commissioning of America's first foreign missionaries, 1886 beginning of the Student Volunteer Movement at D. L. Moody's Mount Hermon, etc. Each of these movements carried an explicit vision for global witness and reach.

Despite its many divisions Rosell finds evangelicalism as a movement united around "a shared focus (the cross), a shared authority (the Bible), a shared experience (conversion), a shared mission (worldwide evangelization), a shared vision (the spiritual renewal of church and culture). . . ." Insofar as the term has taken on a certain normative definition in American religious and cultural life it can be said to be the defining experience of American Protestant Christianity.[3] But it was and is more than this, rooted as it is in a profoundly American setting.[4]

2. Donald Dayton, *Discovering an Evangelical Heritage* (New York: Harper & Row, 1976), and Ernest Sandeen, *The Roots of Fundamentalism: British and American Millenarianism, 1800-1930* (Chicago: University of Chicago Press, 1970); and see George Marsden, *Understanding Fundamentalism and Evangelicalism* (Grand Rapids: Eerdmans, 1991).

3. Garth M. Rosell, *The Surprising Work of God: Harold John Ockenga, Billy Graham, and the Rebirth of Evangelicalism* (Grand Rapids: Baker Academic, 2008). Rosell grounds contemporary evangelicalism in the biography of scholar/preacher Harold John Ockenga, focal figure in this analysis. Ockenga, described early on as a "lone wolf," is seen to be largely responsible for carving out what would become twentieth-century evangelicalism, a vision for American Christianity that was neither Protestant Liberalism nor Fundamentalism. The initial social setting for this would become Boston's Park Street Church, a "microcosm . . . of the larger evangelical movement," bearing the themes of the historic American Great Awakening(s) *"rebirthed"* in the twentieth century. This should be read against the more expansive, yet sympathetic study by Douglas A. Sweeney, *The American Evangelical Story: A History of the Movement* (Grand Rapids: Baker Academic, 2005).

4. This is not to deny the historical context of the term "evangelical" in the German

An explosive growth came to the evangelical movement in the years following the Second World War in what was to be an explicitly redefined neo-evangelicalism. This effort was part of a larger cultural endeavor to find a new post-war moral order in the face of the war's devastation — something also seen in the ecumenical movement for the larger Protestant and Orthodox worlds (1948-) as well as in the Second Vatican Council (1962-65) for Roman Catholicism. For evangelicalism in the United States this growth happened through youth movements such as Youth for Christ, the Inter-Varsity Fellowships, Navigators, and Campus Crusade. These prospered through associations of evangelists who promoted them, but particularly through the work of Billy Graham. The Boston Crusade (1949-50) began a "floodtide" of religious fervor to become structured by five initiatives identified by Rosell as central to the direction of evangelicalism or what might be more particularly called neo-evangelicalism: (1) biblical and theological illiteracy to be addressed by the Boston School of the Bible (1943); (2) scholarly advance fostered through Scholars Conferences (1944); (3) advancing theological education through the founding of Fuller Theological Seminary (1947), and then what would become Boston's Gordon-Conwell Theological Seminary, to "train people for our Lord's service" as a West Point for Military Science or a Caltech for engineering; (4) the launching of a new magazine (1956), *Christianity Today,* to be a focal point for evangelical scholarship; and (5) the vision, although scuttled, of a Christian University as the movement, significantly, rejected cultural or religious separatism and embraced Ockenga's idea of "infiltrating, penetrating and transforming the culture for Christ. . . ."

However, the very success of evangelicalism, whether measured since Edwards or as a post-war phenomenon, has brought about an infiltration of global culture into the movement such that today evangelical mission can be identified with contemporary global realities and a widening array of global agents. Precisely because of this success of evangelicalism's rooting in a particular interpretation of American history, as defined by Rosell and others, and its very susceptibility to American "exceptionalism" or conception of the nation's unique role in

---

evangelische understanding as rooted in the Lutheran reforms nor its understanding in aspects of British Anglicanism, specifically with eighteenth-century Wesleyans or later with the early nineteenth-century Clapham Sect and its reformist agenda. It is to say that these influences upon post-WWII American "neo"-evangelicalism have been diffuse at best.

God's plan for history, there develops a challenge if not contradiction in evangelicalism's deeper partnership with world Christianity.[5] Puritan and then Christian revival impulses built up a foundation of theological supercessionism, the idea that the people of the nascent United States were an elect people with a manifest destiny. This conception of the role of the American churches, a kind of "Roots Revival" in post-war neo-evangelicalism, is now called into deeper dialogue with the world church, certainly an issue caught up in post-colonial analysis. This dialogue can be expected in at least two areas. First, it will come through a deeper engagement with global ecumenism, the witness of the global church in all of its varieties — the liturgies, spiritualities, and traditions are a challenge to the Reformed and Holiness traditions and political sensitiveness that have shaped American evangelical churches. This is a dialogue that must happen for the health of the global church. American evangelicalism will also be challenged to the extent it has become synonymous with an American civil religion, often shaped by conceptions of American exceptionalism that define global geo-political realities. This issue lies at the heart of the identity of neo-evangelicalism. Its challenge is to the very ideology of the nation at a time of growing religious pluralism and religious non-affiliation.

Evangelicalism in Dialogue with Ecumenism

In the year of the centennial celebration (2010) of the Edinburgh Missionary Conference of 1910, the evangelical movement found itself in a deeper conversation with global ecumenism.[6] By ecumenism is meant the quest for church unity as it grew out of the context of European and global conflict in the mid-twentieth century.[7] Evangelicalism, suscepti-

---

5. See Walter Russell Mead, "God's Country: Evangelicals and Foreign Policy," *Foreign Affairs* (September/October 2006). The theme is well taken up by Geiko Müller-Fahrenholz, who draws attention to elements of American theology that have contributed to this "exceptionalism," *America's Battle for God* (Grand Rapids: Eerdmans, 2007).

6. See the website for Lausanne III and the Cape Town centennial celebration of the Edinburgh Missionary Conference of 1910. Also note inter-linkages with other centennial celebrations in Tokyo, Edinburgh, and Boston.

7. The history of the ecumenical movement is documented in the following three volumes: Ruth Rouse and Stephen Charles Neill, eds., *A History of the Ecumenical Movement*, vol. 1, *1517-1948* (Philadelphia: Westminster, 1967); Harold E. Fey, ed., *A History of*

ble to revival ecclesiology subsequent to nineteenth-century revivals, has seen many defections to Orthodoxy and Roman Catholicism — and often over the issue of ecclesiology. To his credit, Ockenga eschewed perfectionist separatism — and this has had a long-term positive impact upon American Christianity as evangelicals have largely remained in dialogue with other branches of Christian corporate expression.[8]

Our global reality since WWII has become something of a "new" Antioch, i.e., approximating for Christians for purposes of religious understanding and practice the pre-Constantinian age in which Christianity first found itself — and this has moved the question of ecclesiology increasingly to the fore. We live in the context of a demographic change that has occurred between the Antioch of Acts 11:26 and the present global "Antioch," bound together by such patterns of globalization as trade, technology, and organization. Missiologist Dana Robert argues that the Great Commission itself has been an intrinsic part of creating globalization. Missions are intertwined with this process through theological understanding, historical connections, demography, organizational structure, and technology and through mission personnel. She raises four points that give meaning and continuing validity to "the Great Commission" in the face of contemporary globalization and demography, mission that is Christ-centered and not grounded in economic self-interest, mission that rediscovers spiritual discipline, mission that is didactic in nature and that re-grounds the church in the simplicities of the New Testament. Robert reminds us that "the disciples witnessed across national and ethnic boundaries not because they were powerful, but because they were faithful to the vision of the Kingdom of God they had glimpsed in Jesus Christ."[9]

The expansion of global Christianity into every region of the world raises the question of who is promoting this expansion. Research by the Gordon-Conwell Center for Global Christianity under the direction of Todd Johnson illustrates that whereas in the early part of the twentieth

the *Ecumenical Movement,* vol. 2, *1948-1968* (Philadelphia: Westminster, 1970); and John Briggs, Mercy Amba Oduyoye, Georges Tsetsis, Ruth Rouse, and Harold E. Fey, eds., *A History of the Ecumenical Movement,* vol. 3, *1968-2000* (Geneva: WCC, 3rd ed., 2004).

8. This can be seen expressed in the work of the evangelical leader and president of Fuller Theological Seminary, Richard J. Mouw; see his *Uncommon Decency: Christian Civility in an Uncivil World* (Downers Grove, IL: InterVarsity Press, 2010).

9. See Dana Robert, *Christian Mission: How Christianity Became a World Religion* (Malden, MA: Wiley-Blackwell, 2009).

century the Christian faith was easily identifiable as a Western religion
— the vast majority of Christians were Europeans or North Americans
— by the end of the twentieth century the majority of Christians would,
as in the first days of the church, be African, Asian, and (now) Latin
American.[10] The center of gravity of the church is no longer in the West,
but is increasingly centered in the Southern Hemisphere.[11] In other
words, global mission is increasingly a global enterprise. The implications of this demographic shift for Christian self-understanding and
scholarship — and the training of church leadership — are drawn out
by historian Andrew Walls. This is a shift that he calls inspiring with its
fresh vision and energy and fresh excitement for academic study. Just as
Christians explored their faith in engagement with the Hellenistic culture, so Christian interaction with the cultures of Africa and Asia will
open us to new perspectives on the fullness of Christ, and in the process
find a renewal of scholarship itself.[12]

As the churches enter their third millennium, they must take
stock of their fundamentally different identity and mission from that
which was assumed at the beginning of the twentieth century. This demographic shift reminds us that however significant the modern mission movement, world Christianity is not simply the result of the
Western missionary effort, whether we mark this with such Catholic
missions as that of Bartolomé de Las Casas, OP (1484-1566), and his
advocacy of the rights of indigenous peoples of the Americas, with the
Puritan John Eliot and the translation of the Bible into Algonquin in
early New England (1661-63), or with the Royal Danish-Halle (Pietist)
Mission of Bartholomew Ziegenbalg and Henry Pluetschau to
Tranquebar, India (1706). It is both an older phenomenon as well as a
more complex modern movement, drawing upon the active missionary work of persons living throughout the world.[13] This will have its

10. Todd Johnson and Kenneth Ross, eds., *The Atlas of Global Christianity* (Edinburgh: University of Edinburgh Press, 2010).

11. Philip Jenkins, *The Next Christendom: The Coming of Global Christianity* (Oxford:
Oxford University Press, 2002).

12. Andrew F. Walls, *The Cross-Cultural Process in Christian History: Studies in the
Transmission and Appropriation of Faith* (Maryknoll, NY: Orbis Books, 2002). Walls's argument finds resonance in the work of Paul F. Knitter, *Without Buddha I Could Not Be a Christian* (Oxford: One World, 2009).

13. Dale T. Irvin and Scott W. Sunquist, eds., *The History of the World Christian Movement* (Maryknoll: Orbis Books, 2001).

challenges for evangelicalism insofar as evangelicalism is an American phenomenon.

Ever since the formation of the modern ecumenical movement there has been a growing consciousness of the interdependent nature of global Christianity. Following the World Missionary Conference, Edinburgh, 1910,[14] an International Missionary Council (IMC) was established at London (1921), meeting again at Jerusalem (1928) and Tambaram (1938), becoming associated with the World Council of Churches (WCC) movement in 1939. Following the founding WCC Assembly (1948), an International Missionary Council met at Whitby, Ontario, in 1947 where emphasis was laid on the need to overcome an "older church — younger church" dichotomy, one of patrons and senders.[15] At the next world meeting at Willingen (1952), emphasis was placed on understanding mission as God's mission to the world *(missio dei)* whereby the church, wherever it is found, is seen as the "sent" community, a theme that lies behind the work of Darrell Guder with his focus on the "missional" church.[16] At the International Missionary Assembly held at Achimota near Accra, Ghana (1958), the missiologist Lesslie Newbigin stressed the fact that "the church is the mission," going on to point out that "the home base is everywhere" since every Christian community is in a missionary situation.[17] The Assembly at Ghana is also known for the IMC decision to unite formally with the WCC, uninviting to some who feared that such integration of mission and church would be detrimental to mission effort. With the "integration" of the IMC to the WCC, effective in assemblies at New Delhi (1961), dissenting mission bodies participated with the Billy Graham Evangelistic Association in sponsoring a World Congress on Evangelism in Berlin in 1966. This led to the formation of a Planning Committee (1971) and Lausanne Congress on Evangelism (1974) of continuing impact through the Lausanne Covenant and Con-

---

14. T. V. Philip, *Edinburgh to Salvador: Twentieth Century Ecumenical Missiology* (Kashmere Gate, Delhi, India: ISPCK, 1999).

15. Margaret Guider, OFM, "From the Ends of the Earth: 'International Minister' or Missionary? Vocational Identity and the Changing Face of Mission in the USA. A Roman Catholic Perspective," in *The Antioch Agenda,* ed. Daniel Jeyaraj, Robert Pazmiño, and Rodney Petersen (New Delhi, India: ISPCK, 2007).

16. Darrell L. Guder and Lois Barrett, eds., *Missional Church: A Vision for the Sending of the Church in North America* (Grand Rapids: Eerdmans, 1998).

17. David Bosch, *Transforming Mission: Paradigm Shifts in Theology of Mission* (Maryknoll: Orbis Books, 1996), p. 370.

tinuation Committee with further Conferences on World Evangelization and inspiration for regional networks and mission conferences.[18]

Concurrently, mission councils affiliated to the IMC became affiliated to the Commission on World Mission and Evangelism (CWME) of the WCC, eventually the Division on World Mission and Evangelism (DWME), which, after Vatican II (1962-65), worked increasingly with Roman Catholic observers. With the entry into the WCC at this time of the Orthodox churches of Eastern Europe, prevented from doing so in 1948 because of the Cold War, something of a context for a proxy ideological war between Socialism and Capitalism was provided, but also deepened reflection on the nature of mission as the WCC began to move markedly beyond its earlier largely North Atlantic constituency. CWME meetings in Mexico City (1963), Bangkok (1972-73), and Melbourne (1980) stressed holistic and contextual mission issues.[19] Notable, too, were the efforts at Melbourne to re-center ecumenical mission theology around evangelization without loss to prophetic challenge, recognition of the significance of the Lausanne movement.[20]

The world mission conference of San Antonio (1989) was notable for its affirmation of salvation through Jesus Christ but refusal to categorically reject God's saving power wherever it might be discerned. After further WCC reorganization, the work of mission from 1992 to 1998 became the concern of WCC Unit II — Churches in Mission: Health, Education, and Witness. A further WCC conference on mission at Salvador da Bahía (Brazil, 1996) took up the theme of gospel and culture with attention to the effect of cultural and ethnic identity on violent conflict, more visible following the end of global bi-polar conflict (1918-89). Upon the reinstatement of the CWME following the meeting of the WCC General Assembly in Harare (1998), an assembly in Athens (2005) on the theme "Come, Holy Spirit, Heal and Reconcile!" raised the question of how the churches can better become agencies of the healing and reconciliation they proclaim: "The New Global Mission: The Gospel from Everywhere to Everyone."[21]

---

18. See Lausanne Occasional Papers, available on the web: www.lausanne.org.

19. The book by Ion Bria has been quite influential in this respect, *The Liturgy After the Liturgy: Mission and Witness from an Orthodox Perspective* (Geneva: WCC Publications, 1996).

20. See *Mission and Evangelism: An Ecumenical Affirmation* (New York: National Council of Churches, 1983).

21. The term is from the title of a book by missiologist Samuel Escobar, *The New*

Not only does evangelicalism face global realities that drive toward a deeper dialogue with ecumenism, but also global players who resist easy categorization. In order to see the context for this we might begin by turning back to the Book of Acts where we read the story of the first commissioning of missionaries out of Antioch (Acts 13:1). Strengthened with spiritual power, Barnabas and Saul (to be named Paul) were perceived through the Spirit to be called and set apart for a special mission, a first missionary journey to the dark continent of Europe. Strengthened with spiritual power, the three prophets and teachers remaining in Antioch, Simeon called Niger, Lucius of Cyrene, and Manaen, lay their hands on the two departing ones, indicating by their names that at least two of the three may have been African in origin.[22]

While the gospel is embedded in Judaism, this scene and the events it portrays in Acts 13–14 carry us to a first council of the church at which issues of gospel and culture are preeminent, the Jerusalem Council (Acts 15:1-35), to be the early church's first cultural crisis, occasioned by the Antioch mission and its aftermath. The decision reached: one did not have to become Jewish before becoming a follower of Jesus. We stand today on the point of another cultural crisis, a "clash of civilizations" — and we are learning that we do not need to become "Western" before becoming Christian. Charles Onyango Oduke, SJ, asks us to perceive, through the lens of the attack on the U.S. World Trade Center and Pentagon (September 11, 2001), a larger world, one in which local and international actions interpenetrate. In the language of contemporary political reference, use of antiquated or demeaning sociological terms such as "Third World" perpetuates historical myopia, lacks social realism, and conveys disrespect.[23] Mission requires global partnerships and networking toward the healing of the world. Christian mission requires, in Oduke's opinion, the perspectival outlook of "cosmopolis," an idea advanced by Bernard Lonergan, which rejects the "screening of memories . . . , the falsification of history. . . ." We are at an historical moment which requires us to listen to

Global Mission: The Gospel from Everywhere to Everyone (Downers Grove, IL: InterVarsity Press, 2003); and see C. René Padilla, *Mission between the Times: Essays on the Kingdom* (Grand Rapids: Eerdmans, 1985), pp. 129-41.

22. Mensa Otabil, *Beyond the Rivers of Ethiopia: A Biblical Revelation on God's Purpose for the Black Race* (Accra, Ghana: Alter International, 1992).

23. See debate on the term "Third World" in Vinay Samuel and Chris Sugden, *Sharing Jesus in the Two Thirds World* (Grand Rapids: Eerdmans, 1984).

the cry of the citizens of the world: "Listening to voices outside one's gate is a humble admission for the need for all cultures to complement one another."[24]

One way to listen to voices "outside one's gate" — whether this is Africa, Asia, Europe, the Americas, or the Pacific — is to recognize that God speaks all languages.[25] Using the work of the nineteenth-century Hindu convert to Christianity, Indian nationalist, journalist, and theologian Brahmabandhav Upadhyay (1861-1907), missiologist Timothy Tennent asks us to take note of not only the linguistic translatability of the Christian message, but its cultural translatable nature as well. Not only does the gospel come to us as an enscripturated text, but also as an encultured message. It must be made intelligible in specific, local contexts. Authentic theological work is "reflecting on the faith in the light of one's historical context." Upadhyay sought to use the language of advaitic Hinduism as an interpretive bridge to better communicate Christianity to inquiring Hindus. For Romanian Orthodox Marian Simion, this carries a political as well as general cultural implication, that the end of global bi-polar conflict has impacted the Orthodox churches in their encounter with society, particularly as European political theory experiences the end of the Grotian [Hugo Grotius] statist model. A challenge of globalization is the need to revisit the Kantian universalistic model, but in alliance with Christian universalism — "no more Jew or Greek" — in order to shape Europe's new identity and perhaps that of the wider family of nations; theologically, to make space for the churches to exercise their prophetic role within a strategy of "adaptability."[26] This is challenging not only for Europe but also for North America, as pointed out by African theologian John B. Kauta.[27]

In a post-Constantinian era the Apostle Paul's dialogue with soci-

24. Charles Onyango Oduke, SJ, "Listening to Voices Outside Our Gate," in *The Antioch Agenda*.

25. See Puritan linguist John Eliot's encounter with Chief Waban in *The Day-Breaking, if Not the Sun-Rising of the Gospell with the Indians of New-England* (London, 1647), in Massachusetts Historical Society Collections, 3 ser. IV (1834), cited by J. Tremayne Copplestone, *John Eliot and the Indians, 1604-1690* (Boston: Published by the estate of Eleanor D. Copplestone, 1998), pp. 71-72.

26. Marian Simion, "Beyond Huntington's Gate: Orthodox Social Thinking for a Borderless Europe," in *The Antioch Agenda*.

27. John B. Kauta, "Is North America a Mission Field? What Does the World Church Say?" in *The Antioch Agenda*.

ety, revealed in his Letters, is a critique of both the church of the right and of the left, asserts author and former *Christianity Today* editor Rodney Clapp, looking for a redefinition of liturgy, social ethics, and especially evangelism and missions for a postmodern church whose locus is not the individual but the faith community.[28] In this light American Baptist theologian Mark Heim documents four "conversations" drawn from the ethicist Orlando Costas that shape a methodology for mission in a new "Antioch" era, one whereby a renewed gospel might be heard again by the dominant European culture of North America by way of its interface with the North American Hispanic community and other racial minorities. These conversions include the internal horizons of universality, ecumenism, and world Christianity, and gave attention to three external horizons, "critical literacy" in religion, the scientific cast of culture, and the universality that is constituted by the world religions.[29] This methodology exemplifies what Miroslav Volf identifies as the crossing of boundaries of "exclusion and embrace."[30]

Listening "beyond the gates" takes each of us into the realm of the other, an important move toward the maturation of identity, an important step for an engaged evangelicalism as envisioned by Okenga. The gospel has long been in the thrall of European and North Atlantic culture, but for all the good that has come of this, it is not an unmitigated blessing. It has come with a price. That price has been increasingly set by the political and economic power residing in transnational corporations and in the technology that shapes perception, captivates the imagination, and offers legitimacy to current consumerist and other practices.[31] Listening "outside" and "beyond" our gates asks us to take up participation in global community, rejecting what Robert Bellah

28. Rodney Clapp, *A Peculiar People: The Church as Culture in a Post-Christian Society* (Downers Grove, IL: InterVarsity Press, 1996); see also Rodney Petersen, "Violence and the Church: Tales of Hope," in *Violence, Truth and Prophetic Silence: Religion and the Quest for a South African Common Good,* ed. C. W. du Toit (Pretoria: UNISA, 2000), pp. 102-28.

29. See Mark Heim, "Renewing Ways of Life: The Shape of Theological Education," in *Theological Literacy for the Twenty-first Century,* ed. Rodney Petersen (Grand Rapids: Eerdmans, 2002), pp. 55-67.

30. Miroslav Volf, *Exclusion and Embrace: A Theological Exploration of Identity, Otherness, and Reconciliation* (Nashville: Abingdon Press, 1996).

31. Howard J. Wiarda discusses the impact of "dependency" theory whereby development between a stronger and weaker partner may not always be synchronous but in favor of the stronger entity. See *Introduction to Comparative Politics: Concepts and Processes* (Belmont, CA: Wadsworth/Thomson, 2000), pp. 79-99.

identified as an "ontological individualism," a failure to see how we are embedded in a deeper social ecology where individual interests are linked to the common good.[32] The restoration of social ecology must be one of the goals of Christian mission, lending both meaning and authenticity to mission.[33] This happens as evangelicals take up a wider conversation with ecumenism, a movement itself interrelated with evangelicalism ever since the lineaments of the ecumenical movement were first laid out following the Edinburgh Missionary Conference of 1910.

Evangelicalism and American Exceptionalism

Another contemporary challenge for evangelicalism is its relation with its American past. The extent to which evangelicalism has given direction to the nation is well attested. Walter Russell Mead makes the case for religious and explicitly evangelical influence in the life of the nation and its foreign policy. He writes, "Religion explains both Americans' sense of themselves as a chosen people and their belief that they have a duty to spread their values throughout the world."[34] As he argues, this relationship is not necessarily to be lamented given the passionate interest in justice and human rights and record for improving the world evidenced on the part of evangelicals. But while this might have been an adequate expression for the America of the 1950s and the era which birthed the National Association of Evangelicals, the challenge is now greater: to remain with Mead is to become susceptible of fostering Christianity in a "Constantinian" mold, ever a tendency for evangelicals. The challenge for today has been articulated by Pentecostal theologian Amos Yong, to develop a "hospitable" Christianity in relation to

32. Robert Bellah et al., *Habits of the Heart: Individualism and Commitment in American Life* (Berkeley: University of California Press, 1996 updated ed.); and see Robert Putnam, *Bowling Alone: The Collapse and Revival of American Community* (New York: Simon and Schuster, 2001 ed.).

33. As the Willowbank Report puts it, such effort requires the renunciation of "a cultural imperialism which both undermines the local culture unnecessarily and seeks to impose an alien culture instead." See John Stott and Robert Coote, eds., *Gospel and Culture* (Pasadena: William Carey Library, 1979), p. 442.

34. Walter Russell Mead, "God's Country: Evangelicals and Foreign Policy," *Foreign Affairs* (September/October 2006).

the non-Christian "other" and a Christianity shaped by and attentive to global culture, not merely American culture.[35]

Global community requires that we see ourselves as global citizens. Few have been as tireless in promoting such an idea as Quaker peace activist Elise Boulding,[36] a cause taken up in his day by the former president of Notre Dame University, Theodore M. Hesburgh. There can be no place for discrimination or social and economic exclusion from the perspective of global citizenship, no priority given to corporatism, cultural dominance, or any perspective that promotes benign or lethal forms of dependency. This is the challenge faced by evangelicalism to the extent it continues to rely on forms of American exceptionalism.[37]

Global consciousness has been driven by mission, not just by corporatism and technology — and it is important to ask who has been in the driver's seat. Leslie Sklair and colleagues have argued that global capitalism driven by politically connected transnational corporations drive the culture.[38] This may be, but as the rise of global fundamentalism illustrates, the picture is not always so clear. Of the five categories of persons that political scientist Richard Falk identifies as engaged with global needs and networks — global reformers, elite global business people, global environmental managers, politically conscious regionalists, and trans-national activists — four of the five have grassroots activism at their core.[39] In his later discussion of globalization, Falk makes the distinction of globalization from above and from below, the former being economistic and often brutal in nature and the latter oriented to global human rights, often alive in relation to living religious traditions.[40] Legitimacy for such activism is not

35. Amos Yong, *Hospitality and the Other: Pentecost, Christian Practices, and the Neighbor* (Maryknoll, NY: Orbis Books, 2008).

36. Elise Boulding, *Cultures of Peace: The Hidden Side of History* (Syracuse: University of Syracuse Press, 2000); see "Ministry in the 21st Century: Building Cultures of Reconciliation," *Newsletter of the Boston Theological Institute* 32, no. 2 (September 18, 2002).

37. C. René Padilla and Lindy Scott, *Terrorism and the War in Iraq: A Christian Word from Latin America* (Buenos Aires: Ediciones Kairós, 2004): "Christians believe that identity does not depend on race or nationality, social or economic position, or status or gender, but that we all bear the image of God."

38. Leslie Sklair, ed., *Capitalism and Development* (New York: Routledge, 1994).

39. Richard Falk, "The Making of Global Citizenship," in *The Condition of Citizenship,* ed. Bart van Steenbergen (London: Sage Publications, 1994), pp. 127-40, esp. p. 138.

40. Richard Falk, *Religion and Humane Global Governance* (New York: Palgrave Macmillan, 2001).

drawn from any state, whether in areas of global economics, environ-mentalism, human rights, but from a kind of natural law although sel-dom identified as such.[41] The connection made between globaliza-tion and mission by Dana Robert earlier in this essay now becomes clearer.

If the Christian movement gains legitimacy from universalism as-sociated with a kind of grass-roots "natural law," it also finds this through its expression of local culture. Both are implied in Andrew Walls's work.[42] Local cultures become caught up in a larger Christian movement to the extent that they can be articulated through theology.[43] The International Missionary Council (Jerusalem, 1930) stressed that the Christian message must be expressed in national and cultural pat-terns, implying movement beyond Euro-North American cultures. This indigenization was furthered by the Theological Education Fund in the 1970s with its emphasis upon contextualization. Decolonization in po-litical and mental sovereignty, signaled by the liberation and then Pen-tecostal theologies of Latin America,[44] offered legitimacy to an array of theologies — water buffalo theology (Thailand), minjung theology (Ko-rea), and other national theologies throughout Asia[45] as well as to such rapidly growing movements as African Initiated Churches (AICs) and

41. Compare Rico Lie and Jan Servaes, "Globalization: Consumption and Identity — Toward Researching Nodal Points," in *The New Communications Landscape,* ed. Georgette Wang, Jan Servaes, and Anura Goonasekera (London: Routledge, 2000), pp. 307-32, and Margarett Scammell, "Internet Civic Engagement: Age of the Citizen-Consumer" [http://jsis.artsci.washington.edu/programs/cwesuw/scammell.htm] (2001), with Hans Küng, *A Global Ethic for Global Politics and Economics* (New York: Oxford University Press, 1998). Much of the work of the World Council of Churches in its efforts on "Justice, Peace, and the Integrity of Creation" has developed in relation to a natural law perspective.

42. Andrew F. Walls, *The Missionary Movement in Christian History: Studies in Trans-mission of Faith* (Maryknoll: Orbis Books, 1996).

43. Robert Schreiter, *Constructing Local Theologies* (Maryknoll: Orbis Books, 1999); see also John Parratt, ed., *An Introduction to Third World Theologies* (Cambridge: Cam-bridge University Press, 2005).

44. Enrique Dussel, ed., *The Church in Latin America, 1492-1992* (Maryknoll: Orbis Books, 1992); and *Mysterium Liberationis: Fundamental Concepts of Liberation Theology,* ed. Ignacio Ellacuría, SJ, and Jon Sobrino (Maryknoll: Orbis Books, 1993). On Pentecostal-ism: Andre Corten and Ruth Marshall-Fratani, eds., *Between Babel and Pentecost: Transna-tional Pentecostalism in Africa and Latin America* (Bloomington: Indiana University Press, 2001).

45. John C. England et al., *Asian Christian Theologies: A Research Guide to Authors, Movements, Sources,* 3 vols. (Maryknoll: Orbis Books, 2004).

indigenous theologies.[46] Examples such as these offer opportunities for debate as charges of syncretism, accommodation, situational fidelity, and biblical fidelity have vied with one another through phases of adaptation, incarnation, and self-conscious identity formation.

Local theologies have permitted the expression of suppressed identities through affirmation of an inherent human dignity.[47] Group consciousness, histories of privilege, and histories of deprivation — as well as local languages and folk ways — crowd together to shape these identities — and identity has political implications. The Christian movement, growing worldwide, struggles to find the way through these complexities of gospel and culture to "integral mission," affirming, perhaps, what Kwame Appiah calls "rooted cosmopolitanism."[48] We are told in the text to "fix our eyes on Jesus" (Heb. 12:2), yet we are more aware than ever of how differently he may be depicted.[49] But he is the one — prophet, priest, and king — who gives identity to the church and gives the church courage to be the body of Christ in the world.[50]

As each of the major lines of interpretation on the history of evangelicalism indicates, evangelicalism has been a major force in U.S. history, its identity, culture and politics. Evangelicalism has been immensely significant in defining the nation's character, its ideas about the world, and ways by which the United States interacts on a global stage. Religion provides a sense of identity, direction, and consolation, not only to individuals but to the life of the nation. Americans have lived with a profound sense of themselves and of their national identity, of-

46. Kwame Bediako, *Christianity in Africa: The Renewal of Non-Western Religion* (Maryknoll: Orbis, 1996); John Parratt, *Reinventing Christianity: African Theology Today* (Grand Rapids: Eerdmans; Trenton, NJ: African World Press, 1995).

47. Felix Wilfred, *The Sling of Utopia* (New Delhi: ISPCK, 2005); see the chapters "Struggles of Suppressed Identities" (pp. 23-45) and "Minorities in an Age of Globalisation" (pp. 46-76).

48. Kwame Anthony Appiah, *The Ethics of Identity* (Princeton: Princeton University Press, 2005).

49. The term "integral mission" (Spanish: *mission integral*), forged by the Latin American Theological Fraternity (FTL), a theological movement since the 1970s.

50. Rodney Petersen, "Church and University: The Threefold Ministry and the Offices of Christ," in *The Contentious Triangle: Church, State and University. A Festschrift in Honor of Professor George Huntston Williams,* ed. Rodney L. Peterson and Calvin Pater (Kirksville, MO: Truman State University, 1999), pp. 359-81; see Alister E. McGrath, *Theology: The Basics* (Oxford: Blackwell, 2004): the work of Christ "summarized under three offices or ministries (the *munus triplex Christi*): prophet, priest, and king . . ." (p. 67).

ten put as it was by historian Sydney Mead that the United States is "a nation with the soul of a church." However, now as evangelicalism moves through the twenty-first century it is challenged by the very forms of Christian faith it has helped to nurture around the world to live by the faith it has espoused.

The health and well-being of evangelicalism requires a dialogue with the state and with the nature of patriotism. Religious meaning is easily co-opted by the state when the state becomes the only socially unifying force in the life of the nation. The implications of this for the separation of church and state and a misplaced civil religion are significant, particularly given the emergence of the National Security State following 1947 and the rise of American militarism concurrent with the evolution of evangelicalism. By taking the challenge of the state seriously, and by taking the challenge of ecumenism seriously, evangelicals can help to promote the freedom of expression and vibrancy of the prophetic office for the well-being of all other institutions in society. This question draws us to assess theologically the very roots which have nurtured a movement of global significance.

How evangelicalism responds to these two challenges — challenges of ecclesiology and of political allegiance — will be worked out in relation to an agenda for mission in the twenty-first century.

An Evangelical Agenda for Mission

What might that agenda be? There have been many different paradigms and ways for doing mission through the history of Christianity. Mission has taken on specific strategies with defined objectives in relation to different models of history, but always with the end in view of forming disciples of Christ.[51] This is the case for each of the great periods of mission and preaching: the early expansion of the church, the preaching of reform by late medieval mendicants and new urban orders, Hussite, Protestant, and Catholic re-formations, periods of mission and revival in the same groups and among the Orthodox. And mission today requires a sense of history. It requires confidence that God through Christ is destroying the powers of oppression, alienation,

51. See, e.g., mission histories by David Bosch, Hans Küng, and Stephen Bevans and Roger Schroeder.

sickness, and death (1 Cor. 15:22-28), that strength is given the church to do God's mission (Rom. 5:3-5), and that the end in view is good (Revelation 21).[52]

A strategy for holistic mission begins with theological self-understanding. The development of such a strategy is the intent of the work of Darrell Guder and others around the idea of a missional church. Guder's thesis is that Christian mission in regions like the United States or Europe "is fraught with theological ambiguity." This ambiguity grows out of the unique histories of these regions and also out of challenges to whether mission is conceived of as method or theology, as constitutive of several tasks to be undertaken by the church or as shaping the church's core identity. For Guder, the tragedies of conflict, genocide, and holocaust through the twentieth century have deepened the theological question of the nature of valid mission even as they have brought its necessity universally to our consciousness and created the need for a missional ecclesiology. Such an ecclesiology has educational implications as the entire church is caught up in the liberating news of the gospel.[53]

The contexts for mission are shaped by contemporary demographic realities — youth alienation, populations under stress, the needs of the poor and marginalized, racial and ethnic hatred and discrimination. The challenge before the churches is to deal with an agenda that involves all peoples in the proclamation of the good news of Jesus Christ, that forgiveness and reconciliation beyond our polarities is possible. It finds specific focus in the pressing issues of our day. These issues can be organized around the following four concerns: the need for human flourishing, the demands of reconciliation in specific settings, an affirmation of religious freedom in the context of a dialogue among religions, and the necessity of freedom from fear.

A vision of human flourishing is defined by the Millennium Devel-

52. I believe this is the intent of Mark 13. On a diversity of perspective, see Robert G. Clouse, Robert N. Hosack, and Richard V. Pierard, eds., *The New Millennium Manual: A Once and Future Guide* (Grand Rapids: Baker Books, 1999); cf. Geiko Müller-Fahrenholz, *America's Battle for God: A European Christian Looks at Civil Religion* (Grand Rapids: Eerdmans, 2006); Barbara Rossing, *The Rapture Exposed: The Message of Hope in the Book of Revelation* (Boulder: Westview Press, 2005); for history of interpretation, Rodney Petersen, *Preaching in the Last Days* (New York: Oxford University Press, 1993).

53. Elizabeth Conde-Frazier and Robert W. Pazmiño, "Antioch Revisited: Educational Implications," in *The Antioch Agenda*.

opment Goals (MDGs). Defined by the United Nations, they form a template for action. The lens of Christian reflection offers missional perspective: the goal of eliminating extreme poverty and hunger draws us to consider how all are made in the image of God; that of reducing child mortality calls us to reflect on the incarnation, that the embodiment of Christian hope came into the world as a child; promoting gender equality draws us to reflect on the mystery of unity and diversity — that of gender, ethnicity, and race; the goal of achieving universal primary education reminds us that education, schools and universities, have been the gift of the church to global cultures; improving maternal health reminds us that the health of the mother is key to the health of the community; the work of combating HIV/AIDS, malaria, and other diseases drives us to ask whether calamity/suffering is payback for sin; the task of ensuring environmental sustainability calls us to stewardship; and developing networks for development raises the question of those with whom we are willing to associate, to issues of "exclusion and embrace."[54] Mission in the twenty-first century fosters human flourishing.

Mission in the twenty-first century is also about reconciliation. A vision for reconciliation is defined by the four challenges raised up by the Decade to Overcome Violence (DOV) and its International Ecumenical Peace Convocation — Peace in the Community, Peace in the Marketplace, Peace among Peoples, and Peace with the Earth. Reconciliation, accompanied by forgiveness, grounded in a restorative justice — these all are central to Christian spirituality and open the gates forward to the repair of the world *(tikkun olam)*. Robert Schreiter, CPPS, calls attention to the vertical, horizontal, and cosmic aspects of reconciliation which can be organized around the DOV's four thematic challenges.[55] In work for the Conference on World Mission and Evangelism of the World Council of Churches (Athens, 2005), he outlines six aspects of reconciliation and healing: truth, memory, repentance, justice, forgiveness, and

54. Sabina Alkire, *What Can One Person Do? Faith to Heal a Broken World* (New York: Church Publishing, 2005). Economist and Anglican priest Sabina Alkire calls us to craft mission goals that begin with prayer and then move through stages of study, financial giving, connecting with the impoverished, ritual, advocacy, and politics so as to be the *Ambassadors of Hope* (Robert Seiple) that we are called to be. The phrase *"exclusion and embrace"* is from the book of that title by Miroslav Volf.

55. Robert Schreiter, *Reconciliation: Mission and Ministry in a Changing Social Order* (New York and Cambridge: BTI/Orbis, 1992). Schreiter has gone on to develop his ideas in different settings and articles.

love.[56] Reconciliation begins in particular settings and reaches out to cosmic dimensions. If there is a role for reconciliation in the political realm, it finds its deepest grounding in theological reflection on God's work in Jesus Christ.[57] This is where cycles of revenge and release are first encountered within a movement toward health and wholeness.[58] Reconciliation involves, to use the words of Samuel Escobar, "Transforming Service."[59] It is the "liturgy after the liturgy," to adopt the expression of Orthodox theologian Ion Bria.[60]

Third, Christian mission assumes and promotes religious freedom.[61] There is a growing sense across the globe that rights and obligations arise from the people as embodied in the Universal Declaration of Human Rights set forth by the United Nations (1948). This was given further significance for religious consciousness and liberties in the UN's Declaration on the Elimination of All Forms of Intolerance and of Discrimination Based on Religion or Belief (November 25, 1981). The social reality of people migrating around the world, contemporary technology, and media — as well as an increasing tendency to standardize

56. Jacques Matthey and the Ecumenical Formation Team, "Mission as Ministry of Reconciliation," Preparatory Paper No. 1, Conference on World Mission and Evangelism, Athens, May 2005; cf. John Paul Lederach, *The Journey Toward Reconciliation* (Scottdale, PA: Herald Press, 1999).

57. Desmond Tutu, *No Future without Forgiveness* (New York: Doubleday, 2000); and with attention to the overtly political, see Martha Minow, *Breaking Cycles of Hatred: Memory, Law, and Repair* (Princeton: Princeton University Press, 2002); also, Olga Botcharova, "Implementation of Track Two Diplomacy: Developing a Model of Forgiveness," in *Forgiveness and Reconciliation: Religion, Public Policy and Conflict Transformation,* ed. Raymond Helmick and Rodney Petersen (Philadelphia: Templeton Press, 2002), pp. 279-304; Christopher D. Marshall, *Beyond Retribution: A New Testament Vision for Justice, Crime, and Punishment* (Grand Rapids: Eerdmans, 2001), pp. 251-80.

58. Literature on forgiveness is now legion. One might begin with Robert D. Enright and Joanna North, eds., *Exploring Forgiveness* (Madison: University of Wisconsin Press, 1998); Michael Henderson, *Forgiveness: Breaking the Chain of Hate* (Wilsonville, OR: Book Partners, 1999). A theology of forgiveness has been written by L. Gregory Jones, *Embodying Forgiveness: A Theological Analysis* (Grand Rapids: Eerdmans, 1995); cf. Paul Ricoeur, *Memory, History, Forgetting* (Chicago: University of Chicago Press, 2004); and Vladimir Jankelevitch, *Forgiveness* (Chicago: University of Chicago Press, 2005).

59. Samuel Escobar, *The New Global Mission: The Gospel from Everywhere to Everyone* (Downers Grove, IL: InterVarsity Press, 2003), pp. 142-54.

60. Ion Bria, *The Liturgy After the Liturgy: Mission and Witness from an Orthodox Perspective* (Geneva: WCC, 1996).

61. Brian Grim and Roger Finke, *The Price of Freedom Denied: Religious Persecution and Conflict in the Twenty-First Century* (Cambridge: Cambridge University Press, 2010).

national citizenship — have all promoted a sense of global citizenship. With this has come an increasing understanding of the necessity for a dialogue among religions[62] in the context of the freedom of religion.[63] Religious citizenship takes shape around issues of identity, lifestyle, specific needs, and networks.[64] Just as Christianity played a role in globalization through the democracy of salvation, fostering global religious freedom in the context of a dialogue among religions must also be affirmed as a mission goal so as to promote the authenticity of religious choice and commitment.

A fourth goal for mission in the twenty-first century is to promote freedom from fear. "Do not fear" is the charge given to Abraham, alike to Joshua, then with resonances through the prophets and from Jesus to the Johannine vision, the Apocalypse: "Be strong and courageous. . . . I will be with you" (Deut. 31:23). The monotheistic faiths tell us that we live in a world of the one God, upon whose goodness we can totally rely.[65] At another time and place Franklin Delano Roosevelt offered a vision of a world founded upon four essential freedoms: the freedom of speech, the freedom of religion, the freedom from want, and the freedom from fear.[66] This must also be a dimension of mission in the twenty-first century. The world is not divided between the good and the bad. Rather, as put so well by Alexander Solzhenitsyn in his Harvard Address, it runs through the heart of every person.[67] The victory cry of the Lamb who was slain is that "He will wipe away every tear from their

62. Hans Küng has long argued for the importance of a dialogue of respect among the religions; see the Parliament of the World's Religions, *Global Ethic: The Declaration of the Parliament of the World's Religions* (New York: Continuum, 1994).

63. On religious citizenship, see Bart van Steenbergen, "The Condition of Citizenship," in *The Condition of Citizenship,* ed. Bart van Steenbergen (London: Sage Publications, 1994), pp. 1-9, esp. p. 2.

64. On "lifestyle politics," see Anthony Giddens, *The Consequences of Modernity* (Stanford: Stanford University Press, 1991). On the "politics of identity" and related matters, see Jonathan Sacks, "Judaism and Politics in the Modern World," in *The Desecularization of the World: Resurgent Religion and World Politics,* ed. Peter Berger (Grand Rapids: Eerdmans, 1999), pp. 51-63.

65. Raymond Helmick, SJ, *Living Catholic Faith in a Contentious Age* (New York: Continuum, 2010), pp. 101ff.

66. Franklin D. Roosevelt, "Four Freedoms," Address to Congress, January 6, 1941 (Congressional Record, 1941, Vol. 87, Pt. I).

67. Alexander Solzhenitsyn, "A World Split Apart," Address given at Harvard Class Day Afternoon Exercises, Thursday, June 8, 1978; accessed on the web, August 2010, at http://www.columbia.edu/cu/augustine/arch/solzhenitsyn/harvard1978.html.

eyes. There will be no more death or mourning or crying or pain, for the old order of things has passed away" (Rev. 21:4).

Evangelical identity has been defined by its sense of mission in the past. This identity, grounded in the work of the cross, shaped by an epistemology given form by the Christian Scriptures, with a shared experience of grace that works itself out in mission and in a shared vision of the spiritual renewal of church and culture, can provide the underlying superstructure for the daunting challenges confronting this generation. How evangelicalism shapes its ecclesiology in relation to the ecumenical movement and its public policy with respect to political identity will shape the next generation of evangelicals and of what it means to be evangelical.

Found Faithful:
Standing Fast in Faith in the
Advanced Modern Era

Os Guinness

A FEW YEARS AGO I was asked to address the CEO Forum in Shanghai. The proceedings were fascinating, and at the end of the day, the dean of the Business School asked me this question: "What am I missing? We in China are fascinated with the Christian roots of the Western past, for the sake of China's future." (We had been discussing the so-called "gifts" of the Christian faith to Western life and civilization, such as philanthropy, the gentling of the European peoples, the rise of modern science, capitalism, democracy, the reform movements, and so on.) "We in China are fascinated with the Christian roots of the Western past, for the sake of China's future," he said. *"But you in the West are cutting off your roots.* What am I missing?"

As followers of Jesus, we are responsible to serve God's purpose only in our own generation, but what a time in which to be responsible. Like St. Augustine living at the transition between the end of the Classical age and the beginning of the Dark ages, we stand on the verge of a post-Christian West and a post-Western Christian church, with immense but unknown significance for both the church and the world.

The identity, unity, and dominance of the West have all been called into question. The American republic is going through its own series of crises, many of which call into question the character of the republic as the founders established it. Problems in the European church are plain for all to see, but troubling signs of Christian decline are now visible in the United States too. And we evangelicals, who once were the renewing and reforming movement within the church, have today become profoundly worldly and in need of renewing ourselves. This is the challenging setting we face.

But what does it mean to be "evangelical"? The term "post-evangelical" that became vogue in certain circles was silly, confused, and led nowhere. But in my travels around this country, I meet many who are renouncing their identity as evangelicals. Often embarrassed, sometimes frustrated and angry, they have lost confidence in both the term and the movement because of the political and cultural baggage that weighs it down. In contrast, I stand here unashamed to call myself an evangelical, because I define the term theologically rather than politically or culturally — one who defines my faith and my life according to the good news of Jesus Christ. Needless to say, that definition requires elaboration, just as Jesus' opening announcement of the good news of the kingdom was elaborated over the three years of his ministry, but it means that the definition is true to Jesus, as well as one that is decisive, positive, and foundational.

When asked to summarize the challenge facing the church today, I often answer that it can be stated in three words: *integrity, credibility, civility*. First and foremost, we face a challenge of integrity, in terms of whether we are faithfully living out the good news of God's kingdom in the way Jesus called us to. Second, we face a challenge of credibility, because the educated elites of our day, shaped by the Enlightenment, see us all, in Richard Dawkins's term, as "faith-heads." It is time for every follower of Jesus to love God with all our minds, and to show that we think in believing, and that we believe in thinking. Third, we face a challenge of civility, in terms of how we respond to one the world's greatest issues: how we live with the deepest differences of others. Do we really defend truth with love? Do we truly love our enemies, and do good to those who wrong us? Or do we respond in kind, and join so much of the culture-warring ugliness of our day?

But let me go beyond these three words, and set out seven major challenges that we face as followers of Jesus, and that we certainly face as evangelicals. All of them are germane to the renewal of our mission as evangelicals.

Challenge One: We Must Face Up to the Grand Cultural Transformations of Our Age

Change and choice are at the heart of the modern world, and so also are the hyped and inflated claims surrounding them. We should therefore be healthily skeptical of many claimed "watersheds" and "turning points" that are really insignificant. But some changes truly carry immense transformations within them. Consider three:

First: Globalization and the Shift from the Industrial Era to the Information Era

Many economists, and the *Economist* magazine itself, use the term "globalization" to refer to the spread of market capitalism, but that does not get to the heart of the matter. Capitalism is one of the major forces that use globalization, but globalization itself is the result of the revolution in information technology. For the first time in human history, thanks to such inventions as the computer, we have expanded our social interconnectedness to a genuinely global level.

There are obviously many earlier impulses toward globalization, including trade, imperialism, and the missionary spread of world religions. Equally, there are important precedents for our current phase of globalization, including the invention of the wheel, the alphabet, and the sailing ship. But there are aspects of this present wave that are unique — for instance, the capacity for instant, worldwide communication, which has the effect of the compression, acceleration, and intensification of life in the global era. We have yet to chart and grasp the full ramifications of this revolution, but what we can trace already indicates profound transformations in areas that are foundational to human experience and understanding — for example, the impact on our human identity, on our sense of time and place, on the speed at which we think and live, on the family and our relationships, on work, on politics, on nationhood, on religion, on evil, and so on.

Unquestionably, the next generation will be the "crunch generation," which will have to make critical decisions about these issues that will shape the future of the earth and the prospects for humanity. This is a crucial and most extraordinary period of human development, and we need to grapple with the implications for the gospel and the church that go far beyond any of our understandings today.

Second: The Shift from a "Singular Modernity" to "Multiple Modernities"

For 600 years, whichever empire or superpower was the lead society in the West was the superpower in the world. It might have been Portugal, Spain, France, Holland, Britain, or more recently the United States, but whichever was number one had only to look over its shoulder to see the potential rival coming up behind it. That is no longer so, for one of the consequences of globalization is that we have shifted from this "singular modernity" to "multiple modernities" — there are different ways of being modern.

Different regions of the world, with their own histories and their own cultures, can understand, interpret, and adapt to modernity in their own ways. There is certainly an "American modernity" and a "European modernity," but there is also an "Asian modernity," and within Asia a "Korean modernity," and a "Japanese modernity," and a "Chinese modernity," and so on. Perhaps the second Iraq war was the last gasp of our Western conceit as to how freedom would spread, and the last gasp of the delusion that "globalization equals Westernization, equals Americanization." We need to come to terms with this fact with both realism and humility.

Third: The Shift in Spiritual Gravity from the West to the Global South

We all know the story and the main contours of this shift, so well described by Philip Jenkins, Mark Noll, and others. I personally am hugely encouraged by it as I was born in China in the province that is epicenter of the growth of the church that is said to be the fastest expansion of the Christian church in 2,000 years. And as an Anglican, I gladly recognize that, were it not for our courageous and faithful brothers and sisters from Africa, Anglican orthodoxy would be in even deeper trouble today because of the extreme apostasy of the American Episcopal Church. A major reason for the Western crisis stems from an irony. The Christian faith was the single, strongest factor in the rise of the modern world, but the church has fallen captive to the modern world it helped to create.

Many Christians, however, miss the sting in the tail of this account. The churches in the global South are truly exploding, but most of the global South is pre-modern. They have yet to face what Peter Berger calls "the fiery brook" of modernity, in which we were so badly burned. This means that much of what we have to share with our sisters and brothers in the global South is a confession and a caution: "Don't do what we did."

On a recent visit to China, I was told of the slowing of church growth, partly because of the challenges raised as Christians joined the mass migration from the rural areas to the exploding cities. Even the faith that was stalwart and courageous enough to stand against vicious Communist persecution began to founder when faced with the challenges of modern city life.

Challenge Two: We Must Be Prepared for a "War of Spirits"

Immanuel Kant famously predicted that the outcome of the spreading sun of the Enlightenment would be a cosmopolitan world and an age of "perpetual peace." Yet a century later in *Ecce Homo,* his last book before he went mad, Friedrich Nietzsche gave an opposing vision. Almost echoing Jesus, he warned that the world was about to see a "war of spirits" the like of which had never been seen. Clearly, Nietzsche was far closer to the reality of where we are today than Kant, and the "war of spirits" can be seen at three levels.

First, the "War of Spirits" in the Public Square

Much of public life in the modern world is a three-cornered contest of ideas. In one corner are the "old faiths" that have helped make the modern world: Judaism and the Christian faith. In another corner are the varieties of secularist faiths, such the humanists, the anti-humanists, the strident New Atheists, and the like. And in the third corner are the resurgent religions from the rest of the world, supremely Islam. It is no exaggeration to say that in today's world you can find almost every religion and ideology ever known, either present physically or available virtually. The saying is only a little exaggerated: "Everyone is now everywhere."

As this happens, the outcome is more than a colorful diversity of little private stories that forms the happy illusion of multiculturalism. We now have increasing tensions between entire worldviews and ways of life that are living cheek by jowl, elbow to elbow, with other entire worldviews and ways of life *in the same societies.* The question of how we live with our deep differences has become a profound world question. Though abstract sounding in comparison with problems such as terrorism, HIV-AIDS, or nuclear proliferation, it is an issue in itself and an issue that underlies many other issues.

The effects are evident in many of the public squares of the world. And now we are beginning to see a very rudimentary beginning of a "global public square." As incidents such as the Danish cartoon controversy and the furor over the pope's speech at Regensburg show, even when we are not speaking to the world, we can be heard by the world, and the world can react to all that we say. Unless this issue is resolved, the forty odd years of culture-warring in America will pale in comparison to what is coming in the next generation. In Europe, the discrimination against evangelicals and Roman Catholics who take their faith seriously and take it into public life is already apparent. Tarred by association with state churches in the past or ideological movements such as the Christian right today, evangelicals are now seen as a threat *in Europe* to liberty and divisive to the public order.

Second, the "War of Spirits" within the Denominations

Earlier mention of the disastrous conflicts within the Anglican churches tells the story by itself, but the problem is not limited to Anglicans. For a generation, it has been noted that those who are orthodox in one denomination are closer to the orthodox in other denominations than they are to the extreme liberals and revisionists in their own. The resulting conflicts have been as damaging as they are tragically necessary.

A few years ago, I had dinner with a Roman Catholic cardinal. It was a memorable evening, with most of the conversation centered on a shared concern for religious liberty. Then, just as we were about to stand up, he said to me, "Tell me about the crisis in the Episcopal church."

In our family, that is what we call a "soup question," not a "dessert question." So to head him off, I said somewhat lightly, "The crisis is terrible, but you have had your Borgia popes."

The cardinal at once grew serious. "You're right," he said. "There has probably never been a more evil leader of the church than Alexander VI. But for all their corruption, not one of the Borgia popes ever denied a single article of the Apostles' Creed — and some of the Episcopal bishops deny almost all of them, and still stay on as Christian leaders."

There was no need to say more, except to pray and plead for God's mercy — and to do all we can to challenge those in other denominations who are rushing heedlessly down the same suicidal path.

Third, the "War of Spirits" in Individual Believers

A troubling trend has become apparent in many recent polls: a steep rise in the number of evangelicals who no longer believe that Jesus is "the way, the truth, and the life." What Jesus stated flatly, and what both first-century Christians in Rome and twentieth-century Christians in China would have died rather than deny, many American Christians now neglect routinely and casually. Recent opinion surveys show, for instance, that evangelicals now range across a vast spectrum from fundamentalists to relativists. The former are often highly partisan and deeply intolerant of differences, whereas the latter no longer believe what was once considered constitutive of the faith itself.

In short, the acid of relativism has corroded dangerously deep and the "war of spirits" is now deep in American Christian hearts, and at a level that will never be touched by culture-warring and political action. If ever prayer and spiritually powerful persuasion were needed, it is now. But Christian apologetics is increasingly being pressed into service as arguments for "we/they" culture-warring, and prayer has become a casualty of the secularized "world without windows" that encloses American religion too.

Perhaps the greatest contrast between the early church and the modern Western church is the absence of spiritual power. Equally, a huge contrast between the world in which I came to faith fifty years ago and the world of today is the general disappearance of prayer in the average evangelical church. Needless to say, neither change helps us to engage in warfare that is in the unseen world as much as the seen.

Challenge Three: Beware the Escalation of Extremism

Did you see the famous photo of the protester who came to a town hall meeting in New Hampshire with a clearly visible gun and a placard with the words, "It is time to water the tree of liberty"? The full quotation is from Thomas Jefferson, and has long been used by White Supremacists and survivalists as a coded call for assassination. It was blazoned on Timothy McVeigh's T-shirt when he bombed the government building in Oklahoma City.

Alexis de Tocqueville saw the New England Town Hall meetings as the seedbed of political liberty and democracy. But what the world saw in the recent health care debates was a dangerous rise in American bitterness, polarization, and extremism. Karl von Clausewitz's classic, *On War,* is often quoted for his comment that "war is the continuation of policy by other means." What is even more important is his insistence that war always reinforces extremism. When a nation or a group of people attacks someone else in war, they attack all-out with a desire to win. The defender then defends all-out, with an equal desire not to be defeated. The result is that the two opponents are locked in all-out combat, and the outcome is a dramatic escalation of extremism.

We should remember that America has recently been fighting wars on three fronts: Iraq, Afghanistan, and the domestic culture wars. Not surprisingly, extremism has mounted steadily and now characterizes American life in many places, including its deeply divided capital. Sadly, far too many Christians have rushed into the fray, and ended up doing what they believed was the Lord's work, but in the world's way.

For a generation, Christians and conservatives have been lamenting the loss of truth in postmodernism, but their culture-warring employs a "whatever it takes" attitude that is Machiavellian and Nietzschean to the core. Who cares about the truth of an allegation? Who checks a cited source if a charge is juicy? Who cares about the baseness of a direct mail appeal to fear and hatred? Who minds about "truthfulness" and "false witness" if a scissors-and-paste editing job can make an opponent say the opposite of what he really said? Power and effectiveness are what count. "Have no fear" and "Love your enemies," the Bible teaches. But if fear motivates and hate moves people to vote or act, so be it.

Not long ago, I talked to a Christian leader and challenged him about his deeply sub-Christian commentary on the recent election debate. As I was talking, he suddenly burst out: "Forget that Christian crap." He caught himself quickly and apologized, but his instincts clearly revealed themselves as far more political than Christian.

Anthropologist Rene Girard has pointed out that, if left unchecked, such extremism all too easily climaxes in an orgy of violence, and then descends on the head of some innocent scapegoat. We should pray that we will see no more assassinations in this land, and pray that we will see no more Christian vigilantes taking the law into their own hands and bringing shame to Christ and his church by their violence. The world watches to see whether we are followers of the way of Jesus or of an ideology. Let us then call our fellow-evangelicals to break with the moral ugliness of much of the current conservative extremes, to stand back from all ideological movements, and to follow the way of him who called us to love our enemies and do good to those who hate us. Let us defuse the extremism, even if — as Jesus did — we have to take the hate and hurt into ourselves.

Challenge Four: We Must Stand Fast and Prevail against the Distortions of Faith in the Modern World

It is a simple but stark truth that modernity has done more damage to the Christian faith than all the persecutors in history, from Nero and Diocletian down to Mao Zedong, Idi Amin, and Saddam Hussein. You can state the overall conclusion simply: the modern world makes evangelism easier but discipleship harder. Evangelism is easier because in our consumer society, as Peter Berger says, everyone is "conversion prone." In a world of change and choice, everyone is looking for the "latest, greatest, new-new thing." We are all "hoppers and shoppers" now. We are all "channel surfers," not only with TV programs but experiences and relationships of all sorts. Evangelism as salesmanship is therefore easy today. But discipleship — Nietzsche's "long obedience in the same direction" — is a far more arduous task. Consider one major shift reinforced by the modern world.

The Shift from Integration to Fragmentation

A striking feature of all three of the great Abrahamic faiths is that they require the integration of faith and the whole of life. For Jews, it is to be under the Torah; for Muslims, under the Qur'an; and for Christians, under the Lordship of Jesus. Yet under the conditions of the modern world, this requirement is often abandoned, if unwittingly.

The point is graphically clear in the story of Sayyid Qu'tb, the Muslim Brotherhood writer whose radical critique of Western decadence is canonical for Islamists, such as Osama bin Laden. He describes how he actually re-discovered Islam in America, and partly through what he saw of the unfaithfulness and weakness of the Christian church. Far from integrated, the churches he saw were suffering from what he called "grotesque schizophrenia" — and this in the 1940s when white picket fence America was still innocent and intact. Later, historian Theodore Roszak charged that such faith was privately engaging, though publicly irrelevant.

When I worked with Francis Schaeffer at L'Abri, we lived in the tiny Swiss village of Huemoz. There were only two hundred people, and you could walk around it in fifteen minutes. In such a world, the integration of home, work, and church was relatively simple because they were all both close and interdependent.

But the modern urban world is characterized by "differentiation," whereby all sorts of diverse spheres are thrown up in different areas, each with its own way of seeing things and doing things. Many of these different worlds are distant from each other, and more importantly, they are quite different in the way they operate. Little wonder that connecting the dots between all those worlds is a far more arduous task, and one that many people do not even try. So they end up wearing different hats in different places, and developing different souls.

To be sure, some religions such as the New Age require no integration. They are protean and adaptable to different spheres, and lose nothing if they are not integrated everywhere. Not so with our Christian faith. As John R. Mott repeated famously, "If Jesus Christ is not Lord of all, he is not Lord at all." The Christian faith is integrated, or it is not itself.

Challenge Five: We Must Recognize the Oddities of Communication in the Great Age of Communications

The Christian faith is the communicating faith par excellence, and Christians are great communicators, almost by definition. Communication is also at the heart of the global era. As a result, communications have never been as powerful, as accessible, and as cheap as today. So it is not surprising that some Christians have fallen for the illusion that communication is easy, and that "we will win the world by the day after tomorrow afternoon," as one teenager said to me. But in fact, there are oddities in modern communication that actually make it harder, not easier. Take two examples:

Modern Communication Is Harder because of Inattention

The rarest commodity in America today is not gold, but attention. Everyone is speaking (or emailing, texting, politicking, selling, protesting, blogging, and tweeting), and hardly anyone is listening. Needless to say, listening in the Bible is not just physical hearing, but personal and moral heeding, or giving focused attention. So who has a moment to listen? If ever there was a time when we needed the power of the Holy Spirit to say things in a fresh, simple way in order to be heard above the noise, it is today.

Modern Communication Is Harder because of Inflation

There are many kinds of inflation, but the nub of them all is that when more and more is available, less and less is valuable. Most people automatically think of inflation as an economic problem, but there are relatively easy solutions for that. America's problem lies far deeper. It is suffering an inflation of ideas and sources. For a nation founded by intention and by ideas, and for Christians for whom the Word of God is decisive, this type of inflation is deadly because all words have become "words, words, words."

An obvious source of this inflation is advertising. I remember several trips to the Soviet Union when I was growing up. You instinctively knew propaganda when you heard it, and its falsity would grate on Western ears. American advertising hit me in the same way when I first came here in 1968. Who on earth could believe such a barrage of false claims, non-sequiturs, irrationalities, semi-lies, full lies, and the way important things were used to give a leg up to less important products? What does it say about 1776 that Chevrolet is now an "American Revolution"? What would Mr. Jefferson think of Cadillac's promise to fulfill

"Life, Liberty, and the Pursuit"? When Americans in general and Christians in particular cheapen their words by the hour, the effect on witnessing is lethal. Even the gospel sounds like another jingle, or one more sales pitch.

Another source of inflation is ghost writing. I am sure you remember George W. Bush's infamous "sixteen words" — about uranium in Niger in the State of the Union address. They were wrong, and there was as a huge debate in Washington as to who put the words in. Was it the State Department? The Defense Department? The CIA? The NSC? The White House speech writer? As far as I know, no one in all the debate asked whether the president put them in. Today's speeches are routinely written by others.

To be sure, the president of the United States is busier than most of us, and there are good reasons why someone should write his speeches for him. But there is also a price. The less the author's participation, the less the responsibility, and the greater the audience's mistrust and cynicism. However skilled the speechwriter, a modern presidential speech will never rival the Gettysburg Address because there is no Abraham Lincoln behind it. When Senator Bob Dole was asked whether he read a certain book by a fellow congressman, he replied, "No, and I'm not going to read it until I know who wrote it." What he did know for sure was that the person whose name was on the cover had not written the book.

All this is far more serious when it comes to books, speeches, and sermons by Christians. How many of today's "bestselling Christian authors" actually write the books with their names on the cover? One expose of ghostwriting, which was quietly shunted aside by Christian publishers, was to have been titled *Haunted Houses*. Worse still, we now have pastors fired each year for downloading sermons from eminent preachers such as Rick Warren and Tim Keller, and then preaching them word for word as if they were their own, including Warren's illustrations from Orange County and Keller's from New York. When men of God bring the Word of God to the people of God, but have not prayed or wrestled with the Scriptures for themselves, they make a mockery of "Thus says the Lord."

If ever the simple words of the gospel are to be fresh and authoritative in America again, it will not be through some brilliant new technique or gee-whiz media link-up, but through a naked dependence on the Word and the Spirit alone.

Challenge Six: We Must Make Sure Our People Have the Needed Tools to Engage the World Well

Every age is close to God, and every age has its own blessings and temptations. But it is doubtful whether the church in any previous age has faced a world as powerful, as pressurizing, and as pervasive as the advanced modern world in the global era. How then are we to carry out our ongoing Christian tasks of discerning, assessing, and engaging? Each of these core tasks has been made immeasurably more difficult in the global era, because of its speed, scope, and simultaneity — or if you like, its acceleration, compression, and intensification. There are three essential tools needed by followers of Jesus in today's world.

First and foremost, we need deep biblical convictions.
That goes without saying, most would say, but therein lies the problem. What "goes without saying" often goes unsaid, and is then forgotten. That neglect is surely a major reason for the mounting biblical illiteracy among many Christians, though there are other reasons too.

Second, we need a sure grasp of the history of ideas.
Nietzsche rightly stressed the importance of the genealogy of morals and ideas. To judge a claim solely by its source is to commit the genetic fallacy, but to ignore its source and its development is naïve. Many an idea betrays its peril in its pedigree. A clear example of such naïveté is the attitude of many in the emergent movement toward postmodernism. Anyone tracing the story of postmodernism from Nietzsche to Martin Heidegger, to Michel Foucault and Jacques Derrida, to their American disciples, should be on the alert at once. But vigilance is hardly the hallmark of the more extreme emergents.

Fully and rightly critical of modernism, many emergent Christians are uncritical of postmodernism. Both schools of thought should be critiqued, of course, but there is a simple reason why postmodernism has recently been a greater danger: it is today's danger rather than yesterday's.

Third, we need a skillful use of the sociology of knowledge.
This last term sounds strange and forbidding, but the idea is actually simpler and more practical than the history of ideas, so what matters is to get the idea, and drop the term. This point is all the more urgent in

"worldview thinking" is inadequate!

light of the recent vogue for "worldview thinking" in evangelical circles. This new emphasis is welcome and admirable, but it is also inadequate because it concentrates on ideas at the expense of institutions and culture in general.

The two approaches are of course complementary, not contradictory. The history of ideas traces ideas from thinkers, to their thoughts, and then to the influence of their thoughts on ordinary life — "how ideas wash down in the rain," as Francis Schaeffer used to say. But the sociology of knowledge does the opposite. It starts with the social context of our lives, and traces how it has an influence on our thinking.

Take an example that is very obvious if you think about it, though most people don't — our modern view of time that we call "fast life" or "24/7 living." We live in a culture of instant immediacy, and talk easily of "business at the speed of light," or "war at warp speed," and so on. But where does this highly distinctive modern fast-life come from? Which philosophers should we credit for this extraordinary new state of affairs?

The fact is that modern fast-life does not come from any philosopher at all. It comes from the invention of the clock, industrialized in the nineteenth century and now digitized. To be sure, there are thinkers such as Frederick Taylor who had a huge impact through his time and management studies, but only through using the clock. Africans are much closer to the mark when they say, "All Westerners have watches. Africans have time."

Another example is the way cell phones shape our sense of presence. We humans have always had the capacity to be somewhere and somewhere else at the same time — in our daydreaming, for example. But with the humble BlackBerry, many people today are with people physically, but simply "not there." I once spoke on the topic at a large Christian congress, which was followed by Holy Communion. I was staggered to see that six bishops in my row were texting during the presentation of the bread and wine. At what should be the deepest "I/Thou" moment of worship of Christian worship, they were "not there."

These two tools, the history of ideas and sociology, are complementary, and they are both crucial. Put differently, it is important to come to grips with a comprehensive understanding of worldliness that includes both ideas and all the things that make up the settings of our lives — television as well as Nietzsche, and BlackBerrys no less than postmodernism. The church ignores the humbler ones of these pairs at its peril, for in many ways it has the more powerful impact today.

OS GUINNESS

Challenge Seven: We Must Pray and Work
for a Renewal of Evangelicalism

Many of you will have read and studied "An Evangelical Manifesto," which was published in May 2008. It set out three major concerns that are vital for our present theme of the renewal of evangelical mission.

First, it is time for a re-affirmation of evangelical identity.

We have a crying need to reaffirm the identity and distinctiveness of what it means to be evangelical in the face of all the confusions and distortions that surround the term today. The idea for the declaration came when, in the space of a single fortnight, I met twelve people giving up on the evangelical commitment and the movement, all of them for non-theological reasons. Hearing of their understandable disgust with the political and cultural baggage that now weighs down evangelicalism, I told them that if that was what "evangelical" was, I would have left long ago, for the movement itself is all too often shallow, noisy, and worldly.

To be evangelical, however, is not a matter of politics or culture, but of theology. Evangelicals are those who define themselves and their faith by the "good news" of the kingdom announced by Jesus. Not only is this decisively different from defining evangelicalism politically and culturally, it stands in decisive judgment over against all such other ways of defining it.

Some theologians fear that so simple a definition will end up alongside the earlier liberal pieties about "the fatherhood of God and the brotherhood of man," or current simplistic maxims about "Jesus plus nothing." But these are wrong precisely because they did not define themselves fully and decisively by the good news of Jesus. Better examples of those who followed the profound logic of the "good news" of Jesus in all its dimensions are the soaring profundity of St. John's view of Jesus as Logos and St. Paul's glorying in the cosmic Christ in whom all the universe coheres.

And dare it be said in these ecumenical times? Such a definition of "evangelical" trumps the defining principles of other traditions in the church. However much we admire the Orthodox commitment to right worship and right belief, and the Catholic insistence on the universality of the church, neither defining principle is as early, as foundational, and as decisive as "evangelical." A living robust faith in Jesus the Christ

104

looks to the blazing core of the announcement of his Good News from which all other theological beliefs, including the importance of new birth and the authority of the Scriptures, must follow. In this sense, the Reformation was an "evangelical reformation," and we are "the evangelical people," the people of the good news.

Put differently, Jesus did not come merely announcing a list of essential doctrines that would define his followers. He came to introduce us to himself and his Father, to set out his way of life, and to commission us as his disciples in the world. All of which, needless to say, entails an understanding of, and commitment to, profound and essential doctrines, such as the place of grace in God's acceptance of us and the supreme authority of the Scriptures in our lives as in the life of Jesus himself. But it is a mistake to start by defining the good news of Jesus as a creed, or to say that evangelicals are those who believe a particular list of doctrines.

If this definition is true and fruitful, the present confusions surrounding the term "evangelical" offer us a rare opportunity to reaffirm what is the heart of the gospel itself and the defining principles of those of us who call ourselves evangelicals. Regardless of academic categories, journalistic labels, and popular stereotypes, we evangelicals are not to be defined politically or culturally. We are the people of the good news of Jesus.

Second, it is time for a renewal of evangelical life.

By its very nature, this reaffirmation of evangelical identity also carries an imperative toward reformation, for whatever falls short of the standards of all that is the good news of Jesus must be judged and reformed. Herein lies the Reformation principle of *semper reformanda* and the ongoing process of reform that must not cease until our Lord returns.

One of the newer colleges in Oxford is named after Thomas Linacre, who was Henry VIII's doctor, the founder of the Royal College of Surgeons, and a friend of Erasmus and Sir Thomas More. Prior to the Reformation, only the clergy had access to the Bible, and there is a famous account of the time when a priest gave Linacre a copy of the four Gospels. Knowing Greek, he read them quickly, and handed them back with the comment, "Either these are not the Gospels or we are not Christians."

Not long afterward, Martin Luther, troubled by the same disparity, hammered his 95 theses to the door in Wittenberg and the Reformation was underway. Is there any doubt that the Western church is in a similar "Babylonian captivity" today, and that we are in need of a similar Reformation and another Great Awakening? If we look at ourselves — and I truly include myself — we must surely ask: Is there something wrong with the gospel, or is there something wrong with us when our witness is often so weak and ineffectual today?

Third, it is time for a repositioning of evangelicals in public life.
The present moment also cries for a repositioning of evangelicals in public life. For myself, I thank God for the decline of the Christian right, though I regret both the reasons why and the consequences that will surely follow. For most of the twentieth century, evangelicals played little part in public life because their faith was privatized. In a word, it lacked integration. The wake-up year for evangelicals was 1973 (which witnessed Watergate, *Roe v. Wade,* and the OPEC oil crisis). But many evangelicals then swung from a privatized to a politicized faith, as the mid-1970s saw the rise of the religious right, and in 1979, the beginning of Moral Majority, followed by the election of Ronald Reagan.

The strategies of the religious right have clearly failed, and the reason is clear. On the one hand, its leaders trusted political action to do what politics can never do, forgetting that politics is "downstream" from many of the real sources of the problems, such as the universities and Hollywood. They would have done well to remember Richard Neuhaus's timely maxim: "The first thing to say about politics is that politics is not the first thing."

On the other hand, the religious right often pursued their policies, to use the nineteenth-century parlance, by "doing the Lord's work in the world's way." For example, as mentioned above, when Christians deal with their enemies in any way except the way Jesus called us to, they mimic the way of the world and tarnish the name of Christ.

The alternative to the faulty extremes of being *privatized* and *politicized* is to be *prophetic* in the precise biblical sense of living and speaking "according to the word of the Lord." (This phrase is much repeated in the Old Testament, though overlooked in comparison with the more famous "Thus say the Lord." See, for example, 2 Kings.) I do not suggest that we use the word "prophetic" in public, for at a time when many an angry tirade is described as "prophetic," the word has lost its definition and been devalued.

Two aspects of the Old Testament use are pertinent today. First, we must follow the prophetic example in our lives. Whenever Israel departed from the way of the Lord, those who remained faithful insisted on still living in accord with the covenant with God. The tragedy of evangelicals today is that we are simultaneously complaining about the anti-Christian drift of secular culture while all the while living in ways that are little different.

Second, we must follow the prophetic example in our speaking. Strikingly, the prophets called the people back to God by actually pushing them out. "If the Lord is God, follow him; but if Baal, follow him," Elijah thundered famously, pushing his hearers toward the logic of their settled choice (1 Kings 18:21). Similarly, Samuel warned Israel by laying bare the consequences of their loyalties. If they chose a king like the nations around them, when God should have been their king, they would reap the consequences of their choice (1 Samuel 8). In the person of King Saul and most of the later desultory kings of the Davidic dynasty, they received their just deserts just as Samuel had warned.

I believe we need more of a prophetic stance in the world today. It is not up to us to turn our culture around, or to turn this country back to God, but we can highlight our generation's choices and their consequences. Choices always have consequences, and Americans must be challenged to face the logic of their choices and the responsibility of their consequences. Woe to us if we do not live faithfully, speak out clearly, and warn our contemporaries with candor and compassion.

Found Faithful

When I was doing my graduate studies at Oxford, I used to walk or cycle every day past the cobblestone cross on Broad Street that marks the spot where Nicholas Ridley, Hugh Latimer, and Thomas Cranmer were burned at the stake during the Reformation. There was a little question going around Christians studying in Oxford in my time, "Would someone or other mount the stake?" In other words, would they remain faithful to Christ through their studies, or would they succumb to the pressures of the arrogance, disdain, or outright opposition of an elite university?

I have always been deeply challenged by the words of our Lord in Luke 18:8, "When the Son of Man comes, will He find faith on the earth?" Having grown up in China, where I was a witness to the beginning of the horrendous persecutions of the Chinese church under Mao Zedong, I used to think Jesus was referring to the results of a terrible worldwide persecution.

It is equally possible, and after a lifetime of thought I believe it is even more likely, that Jesus is referring to something far closer to our Western position. We face no real persecution here, though opposition and discrimination are mounting discernibly. But we may well reach a stage where millions and millions of people still identify themselves as "Christians," but are unrecognizable by the standards to which Jesus called the followers of his Way.

Are we evangelicals — who in our very identity claim to be "the people of the good news" — are we as faithful and prophetic as we are called to be by our Lord? Am I? Surely, it is no secret that we evangelicals, always so passionate about renewal and reformation, are the ones who need renewing and reforming today — so that freed from our cultural captivity, we can go out with a robust and thoughtful faith, and engage this crazy, wonderful, and challenging modern world without losing our soul.

This is no time for Luddites, or for nostalgic romantics. Our golden age is always ahead, not behind. We are called to embrace the times in which we live, and to wrestle with them. Then perhaps, it can be said of us as it was said by St. Paul of King David in Acts 13:36: "David, after he had served the purpose of God in his own generation, fell asleep." No less than that is our calling, our responsibility, our privilege — and our challenge as we face the task of renewing our evangelical mission.

PART TWO

Renewing the Evangelical Mission

The Return to Catechesis:
Lessons from the Great Tradition

J. I. PACKER WITH GARY A. PARRETT

IN THE EARLY, HEADY DAYS of the ecumenical movement, before the
Second World War, William Temple, archbishop of Canterbury, declared on one occasion: "I believe in one holy catholic and apostolic
church, and sincerely regret that it does not at present exist." In saying
this Temple was not, of course, proposing a provocative new thesis in
ecclesiology; he was, rather, using paradoxical rhetoric to issue a wake-
up call, phrasing things startlingly in order to raise consciousness
about the unhappiness of the divisions within the visible church and
ram home the need to do something about them. What I have to say in
this essay has a parallel purpose, which I could express by affirming: "I
believe in the return to catechesis, and sincerely regret that as yet there
is hardly any sign of it." Positively, you see, I believe that the evangelical
mission of generating mainstream renewal within the church and evangelistic outreach through it is impossible to fulfill and sustain without
embracing all-age catechizing as a permanent feature of the church's
life. And negatively, I believe that David Wells's soberly expressed fears
regarding the future of evangelical churches are all too likely to be fulfilled if this addition to present practice does not take place. So there
you have it. What you will now hear from me is advocacy from the heart,
a genuine *cri du coeur* (cry of the heart) for a renewed grasp of what the
Reformers meant by reformation and a plea for constructive change of
our ways with regard to teaching in the church.

The Nature of Catechesis

The place and practice of catechesis, then, is my theme; but what exactly is that? The simple answer is that catechesis is the integrated, orderly — you could say, systematic — teaching of the truths that Christians do and must live by, coupled with instruction on the way to live by them. Catechesis is the practically oriented imparting of the doctrine and ethics of discipleship, along with such apologetic wisdom as will keep the substance and application of this teaching from being distorted, obscured, or undervalued. So catechesis, or catechizing, to use the more familiar term, is a pastoral discipline with fundamental theological, moral, anthropological, pneumatological, ecclesiological, defensive, and devotional ramifications. Rooted in the realities of the gospel revelation of the divine economy of saving grace for sinners in and through Jesus Christ, catechesis is Bible-based in method, Christocentric in perspective, declarative in style, and doxological in thrust. Its purpose is to lead those whom we will henceforth call catechumens to realize and respond to the greatness and goodness of their God. ("Catechumens" means "persons under instruction"; the word comes from the present passive participle of *katecheo,* a standard New Testament word for "instruct.") Educational evangelism and nurture — that is, didactic discipling to Christ and the Father through the Holy Spirit — is thus what catechesis is about.

The warrant for catechesis is quite simply the fact that Christian belief and behavior, being strange and alien to fallen human nature, have both to be *learned.* In the heyday of Western liberal Protestantism, in which the fall of man was discounted as a sick fancy, the tendency was to treat Christianity as in essence humankind's natural religion, needing only to be purged of bad habits and attitudes imposed upon it by corrupt cultural forces from outside. It was the culture that needed changing; bring in Western-type general education, good housing, full employment, and the abolition of poverty, and natural religion would express itself naturally, running in channels of unalloyed neighbor-love and so realizing the kingdom of God on earth. Christianity, it was sometimes said, is the religion of all good men, and all men are good at heart. Against the backcloth of the morally horrendous twentieth century, the naïveté of this simplistic optimism is clear, and it is now largely a thing of the past; but it has left behind it scorched earth in the church, in the sense of a general assumption that catechesis belonged to the past and has no place in the present. The fact that Christianity has to be learned must itself now be learned all over again, first and foremost, I think, by those who call themselves evangelicals.

Catechesis has had two great periods: the patristic and the Reformational. A glance at each will help our discussion along.

Patristic Catechesis

The apostles established churches in cities, where cults already abounded, and soon it became standard practice for each congregation to maintain some form of ongoing catechetical instruction for adult inquirers. The syllabus soon became stable, being the inter-church "rule of faith" *(regula fidei),* the essence of our Apostles' Creed, and the course length was fixed also — ordinarily, three years, leading up to an Eastertide baptism. Countering Jewish anti-Christianity and Gnostic and other heresies came to be included in the syllabus, and in Alexandria, under Clement and Origen, the catechetical school became in effect a Christian arts university, engaging with secular philosophies as well as with deviant alternatives to apostolic faith. But later, as entire communities became nominally Christian, and Jewish opposition subsided and Gnostic groups ran out of steam, the adult catechumenate shrank to vanishing point, and catechizing for practical purposes ceased. Lay ignorance of the faith during the Dark and the Middle Ages was melancholy legacy of this decline.

Reformational Catechesis

From one standpoint, the Reformation was a revival of Christian education and of a vision of the church as always a learning community, so that every Christian would be a lifelong learner in his or her walk with God. Unsurprisingly, therefore, the Reformation saw an immediate new emphasis on catechizing. Children and young people were to be catechized to prepare them for adult communicant discipleship and church involvement, and the renewing of adult catechesis was targeted too. Luther and Calvin both declared that without catechizing the church could not survive, and both wrote catechisms fairly early in their ministry, seeing this as a priority task. Luther composed his Small Catechism and his Large Catechism for children and for adults respectively; Calvin produced three catechisms for general use. In England, a children's catechism to be taught in church each Lord's Day was included in both the 1549 and 1552 versions of Cranmer's Book of Common Prayer, and this was later complemented by Alexander Nowell's *Large Catechism* of 1570, which covered the whole Christian faith at adult level in dialogue form. On the continent, the Heidelberg Catechism was put together as a tool for all-age instruction. Most Reformation catechisms were built around some or all of the five following realities of discipleship: the baptismal covenant, the Creed, the Ten Commandments, the Lord's Prayer, and the the Lord's Supper, so as to inculcate a comprehensive commitment of belief, behavior, and communion with God both in personal prayer and at the Holy Table with the church.

All-age catechizing was a big thing with the English Puritans, who saw themselves as called to complete the Reformation in this respect as in others. The Westminster Shorter and Larger Catechisms of 1647 bear witness to this full-scale discipling purpose, as did the immediate and widespread embrace of Richard Baxter's model, spelled out in his *Reformed Pastor* (1656), for catechizing whole families year by year: a practice that was unhappily squelched after only six years through the ejections of 1662. Throughout the Puritan period many pastors produced catechisms of their own for use among their own people and Christian discipling, it would seem, proceeded apace.

But 1662 began a retreat throughout England from all things Puritan, and though the catechizing of children to prepare them for confirmation and communicant status continued, it became more and more a formality and less and less a significant stage in nurture until in the twentieth century the older Anglican churches effectively mothballed the Prayer Book Catechism, substituting anything or nothing as individual clergy saw fit. Today's lay ignorance of the faith and unawareness of the need to learn it in Anglican circles is the sad fruit of this downhill process, and it is a mindset matched, by and large, in most mainline churches of the Old West, as I call it — the British Isles, North America, and Australasia. Some small evangelical bodies still keep serious catechesis going, but the vast majority would seem to know and care nothing about it.

Restoring Catechesis

So is it really the case that deliverance of the evangelical churches from the ongoing doctrinal downgrade, and the recovery of health and strength for our future mission, depends on a renewing of catechesis among us? As I have already indicated, I think so. Granted, we have in recent years become familiar with many modes of devotional and liturgical renewal; we have seen something of a renewal of expository preaching and of small-group fellowship for biblical discussion and prayer; we have seen evangelicals regain eminence in academic theology, philosophy, missiology, and worldview studies; do we also now need a renewal of catechesis in our church life, and of enthusiasm for learning ever more of God in our personal lives, if we are to fulfill our mission in the world at this time? Yes; for anti-Christian pressure in North American culture is still building up, and a realistic reconnaissance seems to me to tell us that it will continue to do so. Let me spell this out as I see it.

The culture that surrounds us, social, intellectual, educational, literary, musical, aesthetic, domestic, recreational, and in all other departments of community life, is now consciously post-Christian and again and again anti-Christian. The Christian worldview and value-system has virtually disappeared from school and university, and from home life too; also from the worlds of human imagination and art, community programs and relationships, self-understanding and reflection on life's purposes. The triumphs of technology have effectively redefined the cosmos for us in materialistic and natural-forces terms, and we who adhere to historic Christianity are seen as throwbacks and shellbacks, marginal eccentrics at best, quite irrelevant to mainstream global cultural development. Logically, all paths of thought lead to some form of relativism and ultimate skepticism, for there are no agreed first principles anymore. Pluralism has come to stay. Such is the supposedly progressive Western world, and it looks to be only a matter of time until this current Western mindset spreads its tentacles and (to change the metaphor) becomes a global infection.

This is where David Wells's massive Jeremiadic survey of sub- and ex-Christian North America can teach us necessary realism. Wells shows us consistently that the heart of our cultural headache is that the word "God" has been emptied of its Christian content, so that instead of signifying the awesome Creator-Governor-Judge of the Bible, the God who is "infinite, eternal, and unchangeable, in his being, wisdom, power, holiness, justice, goodness and truth," as answer 4 of the Westminster Shorter Catechism puts it, the word now stands in a loose way for whatever version we embrace of what we may call the ineffable transcendent — the kind of reality which a lady had in mind two generations ago when she said to an English bishop: "But surely, Bishop, we all believe in a sort of a something." Wells's series of diagnostic reports can well be read as an extended commentary on this memorable dictum.

So it appears that re-establishing catechesis as a permanent ingredient in local church life will require of us a sustained swimming against the cultural stream, and an uphill battle all the way. We have to challenge a debased view of revelation, which substitutes inner inklings for the Bible's disclosure of transcultural saving truth centering on a divine Savior. We have to challenge a diseased view of Christianity as an ethical ethos whose transcendent values, however conceived, are subjectively derived and not related to any specific creedal content. And we have to challenge a debased view of the moral and spiritual education of persons, which votes self-realization from within, with teachers acting as midwives rather than mentors. So it will be uphill all the way, starting no doubt from the comfort-controlled and entertainment-oriented expectations of so many evangelical congregations today.

The Catechetical Syllabus

Catechesis is the communicating of Christian fundamentals of doctrine and ethics for personal spiritual response. Different people in our churches answer the question, "What are the fundamentals?" in different ways, so at this point I need to sketch out my own bird's-eye view of the basics. Let me say explicitly that this comes from coherent, canonical interpretation of the canonical Scriptures, via the patristic creeds, the Thirty-nine Articles, the Westminster Standards, and the Christian theological tradition. Let me also say explicitly that what I dream of is ongoing catechesis in the local church through an ongoing series of courses, short or long, and at different levels, but all analyzing, illuminating, vindicating, and applying items contained in the following archetypal sequence of themes which together, so I submit, constitute basic Christianity. Notice, please, that I present each of these themes with a practical, relational slant, for this in fact is the true catechetical (as it is

116

also, of course, the biblical) perspective. Only as this perspective is responsibly maintained in actual life does authentic discipleship advance.

- *The Authority of Scripture* — The canonical Bible is our true, trustworthy, God-given, and God-interpreted source of knowledge about God in relation to his world and ourselves as part of it. Regular preaching and teaching of the Bible is central to the worship and health of the churches, and constant reading of and meditation on the Bible is necessary for personal spiritual growth in the devoted and doxological life to which we are called.
- *The Sovereignty of God,* in creation, providence, and grace, undergirding the subjective reality of our own free and responsible decisions, guaranteeing the ultimate moral rationality of all that happens, and ensuring that all things always work together for long-term good to lovers of God.
- *The Truth of the Trinity,* the tripersonal, perichoretic reality of God's being, whereby the three persons, bonded together in unbroken love, make themselves known and cooperate as a team to save us sinners.
- *The Holiness of God's Law* — Crystallized negatively for God's people in the Decalogue, and summarized positively in Jesus' two great commandments of love, God's moral standards are absolute for everyone everywhere at all times. Evangelically, these standards are the measuring-rod of our guilt, for which Christ on the cross endured our penalty; morally, they are embodied in the Christlikeness to which we forgiven sinners are now called. The moral perfection of God's character, his recoil from sin in all its forms, and his inflexible retribution for it, either vicariously at the cross or personally through final judgment, are central facets of the divine holiness.
- *The Sinfulness of Sin* — Sin is total egocentric perversity of heart, leading to total inability to respond to God from the heart, and total unacceptability in God's sight by reason of the sins into which our sinful hearts lead us constantly, and which under ordinary circumstances we love.
- *The Centrality of Jesus Christ* — Jesus is God incarnate, appointed our Mediator and penal substitute, our prophet (instructor), priest (sin-bearer, by self-sacrifice), and king (that is, Lord), crucified, risen, reigning, returning; Savior, Master, and Friend to all who turn to him; our Companion through life, both here and eternally

117

hereafter. He is the pledge and embodiment of divine love, and the focus of faith, repentance, and discipleship.

- *The Graciousness of Salvation* — Salvation is God's gift of a new status (reconciliation, justification, adoption) and a new state (regeneration and sanctification with bodily resurrection and perfection to come); all of which is bestowed by Christ through the Holy Spirit, embraced by faith and repentance, and expressed in a life of worship, prayer, thanksgiving, and purposeful obedient service.

- *The Power of the Holy Spirit* — Through the Spirit, who indwells believers, faith, repentance, "good works," Christian assurance, Christian hoping, and Christian love become realities; Christians undergo character transformation, being changed from one degree of glory (Christlikeness) to another, with occasional touches (healings, strengthenings) on our bodies too; spiritual battles with indwelling sin, temptation, and Satanic forces are successfully fought; and gifts for the service of Christ and of others for Christ's sake are bestowed, discovered, and put to use.

- *The Circuitry of Communion* — Through the means of grace (Scripture, prayer, worship and the Lord's Supper, and the various interchanges of Christian fellowship), Christ and the Father come to us in a personal awareness of their presence, and the Holy Spirit, who empowers the whole process, spurs us to respond in devotion and doxology, with faith, love, hope, service, and disciplined practice of the presence of God.

- *The Truth about the Church* — The church is an international society of believers who congregate in local units to worship and work for God. It is the people of God, the body of Christ, and the fellowship animated by the Holy Spirit, and is one with Christ in the communion of his risen life to everyone who believes. Being the church — that is, doing the things the church does — means praise and prayer, preaching and teaching, celebrating the sacraments, practicing discipleship and discipline corporately, spreading the faith worldwide, warring against all forms of evil and unbelief, founding congregations, Christianizing communities, vindicating Christian truth in the wider arena of debate, and opposing public sin and all that dehumanizes.

- *The Promised Hope* — God's comprehensive purpose, as the New Testament announces it, is a total re-make and reintegration of the entire created universe in and under Christ. Within this purpose lies a promise to complete our personal salvation by bodily resurrection of us with the demonic energy of sin finally eliminated from our hearts. This twofold act of grace will lead into a judgment in which God will assess the quality of our discipleship while on earth and reward faithfulness. Endless love and joy with Christ and Christians in the new world will follow. This hope now sustains Christians in eager and enterprising perseverance as servants of God while they await the fulfillment of these promises.

- *The Glory of God* — This phrase signifies both the praiseworthiness of God, shown to us through his self-manifestation, that is, the display of his attributes and perfections in action in creation, providence, and grace, and also the praise of God, given to him in response as we learn to honor him by word and deed in the way that we shall be doing forever hereafter. God's glory in both these senses has always been his will and goal in all his dealings with his rational creatures; the two-way street of love in a good marriage reflects it; and though some will finally reject God's love and hence themselves be rejected, the revelation of God's justice in this will itself evoke praise rather than reduce it. As the supremacy of Christ is focal in God's self-revelation, so the praise of Christ must be central in our doxology.

There are many ways in which expository, apologetic, and hortatory courses, of varying scope and length, can be constructed from the material outlined above, which itself can be formulated in several different ways, and such courses should surely be made available as teachers' resources right now. Yet competent instructors should always be free within the frame of this syllabus to develop presentations that most fully crystallize and express their own vision of the greatness of God's love in Christ, which is what the whole story, from start to finish, is really about. Thus will be generated within them most effectively the infectious enthusiasm to honor God by celebrating this story which as communicators they need. The credibility of catechizing will be undermined straight away if it appears that the catechist is not personally thrilled and excited by this truly amazing plan of God, for moods are catching, and no mood short of adoration befits commerce with truths like these. Always, the catechetical presentation must be *God-centered*, God appearing as the subject and ourselves as, so to speak, the predicate throughout; it must be *practical*, pointing up the response that God requires to

119

each truth taught; and it must be, as was said before, *doxological,* showing how in each action God reveals his praiseworthiness and calls for a direct exercise of praise as well as a formal acknowledgment in orthodoxy. The renewed blossoming of evangelical catechesis for which I plead must have this threefold quality, or it will end up in Paul's noisy-gong and clanging-cymbal category, not really any use at all.

Catechetical Methods

Catechizing has been done, historically in several ways. In the Reformation period, for instance, what we may call the schoolroom method, of which Luther was pioneer, was the usual norm. The catechisms themselves were structured, more or less directly, around four fundamental formulations, three drawn directly from Scripture and one distilled out of much hard work vindicating and interpreting Scripture. The latter was the so-called Apostles' Creed, the former were the Decalogue, the Lord's Prayer, and the gospel sacraments which Christ instituted. The verbal form was question and answer: answers to questions were first memorized, then repeated under *viva voce* questioning, and then the catechist exhorted the catechumen to live by the truths learned. In his *Reformed Pastor,* Baxter tells how he constantly used this method in catechizing whole families (children first, adults after). The 1662 ejections, however, dealt an effective death-blow to family catechizing, which had caught on widely among the Puritans during the six years since Baxter's book was published; the Church of England turned its back on all things Puritan; the post-toleration nonconformist denominations, Baptist, Congregationalist, Presbyterian, and Quaker, never took up all-age catechesis in any form, and by the end of the seventeenth century adult catechesis had simply petered out in England and Wales. (Scotland seems to have done a little better.) Nowadays, non-Anglican evangelicals everywhere, and some Anglicans with them, ordinarily link an instruction hour with the Sunday morning service, but it is not catechesis that fills those times, and Anglicans as a body, while ignorant of what Free Churchmen seek and gain in these teaching sessions, seem sure that after confirmation they themselves need no further instruction in the faith than their Sunday sermons will give them.

The routine of asking-for-memorized-answers-to-preset-questions as one's method of teaching is today regarded by most as a barren burden from the past, mechanical, superficial, and stupefying. (In fact, memorizing has a much deeper educational value than is usually recognized, but we cannot go into that here.) We need to be clear, then, that though rote memorizing, thus negatively estimated, is what comes to most people's minds when they hear catechizing mentioned, it is no necessary part of catechetical method. On the contrary, the method of early church catechesis was, it seems, a didactic presentation further elucidated by discussion; something similar to, though perhaps more austere than, the way of some modern courses introducing Christianity — *Alpha,* for instance, a runaway global success story, and *Christianity Explored,* to name just two.[1] Courses like these are really first steps in re-inventing and re-establishing adult catechesis within the frame of ongoing church life, and should be appreciated and capitalized on accordingly.

There are two basic points to be made about Christian catechetical method. The first is that it is in fact a pastoral and discipling mode of *education* — of teaching and learning, that is, and of personal formation through both. To bracket learning with teaching here is not superfluous, for in the churches it is not always appreciated that teaching is a mode of communicative action that has to be defined, not by its intention, but by its effect. Only when (a) the learners have the subject matter clear in their minds and lodged in their memories, so as to be accessible to them for the future; and only when (b) they can discern its inner connections and coherence, and see its implications for a larger conceptual synthesis, and thus show that they have got the hang of its systematic structure, and only when (c) they can make appropriate application of their knowledge and insight to new facts in the same field of reality — only then may it fairly be claimed that teaching has taken place. Otherwise, such a claim would be invalid, no matter how many words had been spoken with teaching intent. As you are only a leader if you have followers, so you are only a teacher if people learn from you in these three ways.

A time-honored tag among schoolteachers is, "no *im*pression without *ex*pression," and this is as true when the gospel and the Christian scheme, or any part of it, is being taught to persons of any age as it is of

---

1. *Alpha* comes from Holy Trinity Church, Brompton, London, UK. *Christianity Explored* comes from All Souls' Church, Langham Place, London, UK, and is marketed by Authentic Media, Milton Keynes, UK.

teaching anything else to anyone else. Expression takes at least three forms: one, imaginative objectification of what has been presented (a child's picture, an adult's declaration); two, working out logically its implications and applications; three, positioning oneself by personal commitment to act on the truth taught by forming habits of thought and behavior that reflect it. Genuine response to the gospel message, whether the latter is spelled out in full or is for the moment focused in a Christ-centered abbreviation (such as, "Believe in the Lord Jesus, and you will be saved," Acts 16:31), involves all three forms of expression. Catechizing is thus in reality discipling on its intellectual side, and so the catechist, in addition to being master of what must be taught, needs to understand that the catechetical job is not done until those at the receiving end can and do, in however simple a way, actively express in word and life the faith that has been shared with them.

The second basic point, following on from this, is that catechizing is a spiritual discipline for both catechist and catechumen — not only a *personal* discipline for each of them, but also a *partnership* discipline, one that can only be properly practiced when both parties are properly committed to what is happening. In recent years personal spiritual disciplines have been well studied,[2] but partnership disciplines — the corporate disciplines of married life, for instance, or of congregational membership and worship, or of this present discipline of catechesis — need more focusing in today's terms than they have yet received. What needs to be said here is that the discipline of learning the faith is needed to complement the discipline of teaching it, whether one-on-one or in a group, and the parties need to be committed to each other in the shared task of spiritual advance together. The more explicit everyone can be about this, the better.

The Catechist

In Paul's pastoral letters to his juniors, Timothy and Titus, a recurring emphasis, like a constantly tolling bell, is the directive to teach. "Com-

---

2. See particularly Richard Foster, *Celebration of Discipline* (San Francisco: Harper & Row, 1978); Dallas Willard, *The Spirit of the Disciplines* (San Francisco: Harper & Row, 1988); R. Kent Hughes, *Disciplines of a Godly Man* (Wheaton: Crossway, 1991); Donald S. Whitney, *Spiritual Disciplines for the Christian Life* (Colorado Springs: NavPress, 1991).

mand and *teach* these things. . . . devote yourself to the public reading of Scripture, to exhortation, to *teaching.* . . . Keep a close watch on yourself and on the *teaching*" (1 Tim. 4:11, 13, 16). "*Teach* and urge these things . . . the *teaching* that accords with godliness" (6:2-3). "What you have heard from me . . . entrust to faithful men who will be able to *teach* others also" (2 Tim. 2:2). "The Lord's servant must be able to *teach*" (2:24). "*Teach* what accords with sound doctrine" (Tit. 2:1). Paul identifies himself as a *teacher* (2 Tim. 1:11), and describes his own ministry as *teaching* (Col. 1:28). As, for him, the ability to teach was a spiritual gift (Rom. 12:7; 1 Cor. 12:28; Eph. 4:11), so the task and ministry of teaching was for him a spiritual discipline, ongoing within the church. When Paul calls on his addressees to accept his teaching authority, he speaks both as an apostle and as a catechist, viewing his pastoral teaching as one aspect of a partnership discipline whereby, through responsive learning, his addressees — his lifelong catechumens, as we may properly call them — will ripen in faith and godliness, so that he and they will inherit glory together.

A great deal, then, depends on the character of catechists and the example they set. Paul was the pioneer here too, requiring those he discipled to be "imitators of me, as I am of Christ" (1 Cor. 11:1; cf. 4:16-17; Phil. 3:17; 4:9; 1 Thess. 1:6; 2 Thess. 3:19). And today's catechist, like Paul, needs to be a convincing, winsome example of living by the Holy Spirit in the power of the truth being taught, and in a way that consistently reflects the example of Christ. Catechizing, as we have seen, is for what we may call continuous conversion; it seeks to shape us into faithful worshipers of God in Jesus Christ, devoted and disciplined followers of our Lord, self-denying servants of God in his church, clear-headed travelers through this often hostile world, and passionate outreachers to those benighted, misguided, and lost. And it is vital that catechists themselves be good role-models of all this.

Who are the catechists? Not every catechist will be a church pastor, but every pastor must be a catechist, and a healthy church needs to have one or more catechists on the ministry team in addition, so that the demands of all-age catechetical instruction may be adequately met.

Meeting those demands will inescapably involve adjustments, additions, and replacements involving church programs as they stand at present, and to plan this out will be demanding; but my observation, such as it is, tells me that this will be gain rather than loss. Let me put this point pictorially. When you play darts or take part in archery or rifle shooting contests, the goal is always to hit the bull's-eye of the target. Hitting the target somewhere is meritorious in a way that not hitting it at all would not be, but yet hitting the bull's-eye and nothing less remains the goal, and I am suggesting that the programs in evangelical churches, by and large, are not quite doing that, however close to doing it they come. I rejoice that in evangelical churches generally the Bible is established as the center of attention through expository preaching, congregational Bible schools, thematic biblical explorations in large or small groups, direct group Bible study, and other Bible-focused church events; let me say explicitly, I want to see all churches passionate about digging into the Bible in this way, and where the passion has already taken hold I do not want to see it damped down, or treated as of secondary rather than primary importance. I want, rather, to see it enriched, and I believe that the didactic, devotional, disciple-making, doxological catechesis that I am arguing for will have that effect. For there is a reciprocal relation between good theology and good Bible study; each helps the other forward. Good theology enables us to see more of what is set before us in Scripture, and to see it more distinctly, while good Bible study helps us discern what should and should not be said in our theology. For true wisdom, theology and Bible-work must walk hand in hand.

Preliminary Conclusion

I round off by pulling the threads of the foregoing discussion together in the following four statements:

1. Ongoing catechetical discipling of all age groups in our churches, evangelical churches as much as any, is urgently needed today, and will be needed for the foreseeable future.
2. Joining a congregation should involve an explicit commitment to accept catechetical discipling.
3. Ongoing catechesis should always be planned into the pattern of ongoing programs in local congregations.
4. As surveys of the professedly evangelical West, such as that of David Wells, make evident, there is really no hope of a fruitful evangelical future unless these changes are made.

A Concluding Postscript (Gary A. Parrett)

It has been my pleasure to engage in a recent book project[3] on the recovery of catechesis with Dr. Packer, my former professor and long-time theological mentor. In the essay above, Dr. Packer has crystallized many of the arguments we set forth in that book. In these words of response, I wish to add my "amen" to his remarks, and to offer some further principles and practices for catechetical renewal in contemporary congregations. As an organizing device for the points I wish to make, I employ a mini-acrostic, using the letters A through J. Further, I present the various points using what Dr. Packer often calls "apt alliteration." I was not surprised to learn that he and I are both very fond of using such devices, for these have a long history in the practices of catechesis — partly as helps toward recollection and retention. What is more, there is clear biblical precedent for such tools, especially in the Old Testament writings. Acrostics are found in several places, most notably in the Book of Lamentations and in several of the psalms, including Psalm 119. Alliteration and similar devices are also apparent in the Hebrew Scriptures, including a phenomenon to which scholars have applied the happy handle of "polysemous pivotal parallelism"[4] — an alliterative treasure in its own right!

Here, then, are my suggestions:

Accessibility for All

The ministry of catechesis proceeds from the conviction that the faith which was once for all delivered to the saints (Jude 3) must be accessible for all God's people, not only for an educationally elite few. This means that even profound points of theology should (and can) be taught in ways that average believers can — by the aid of sound pedagogical practices and with the promised help of the Holy Spirit — understand at some level. This conviction may call for attitude adjust-

3. The book that we have produced together is *Grounded in the Gospel: Building Believers the Old-Fashioned Way* (Grand Rapids: Baker Books, 2010). The book is dedicated: "To David Wells, who diagnoses so well the malaise for which catechesis is the prescription."

4. See, for example, Bryon Curtis, "Hosea 6:7 and Covenant Breaking like/at Adam," in *The Law Is Not of Faith,* ed. Bryan Estelle, J. V. Fesko, and David VanDrunen (Phillipsburg, NJ: P&R Publishing, 2009), p. 205.

ments on the part of both theologically educated church leaders and the lay members of our churches.

Those leaders who have been formally trained in Scripture and theology must acknowledge their duty to teach all the flock and must be willing to engage in the hard work that such duty requires. They must recognize the inherent limits of what we might call "trickle down theology" (the notion that if scholars write theology for one another's sakes, it will eventually have its influence on the rest of God's people). They must learn from the examples of great catechist-theologians who have gone before us, from Augustine to Luther to Calvin to Owen and Baxter and Spurgeon. And I would very happily add another name to this august list — that of Dr. Packer himself, who has labored so faithfully and so effectively in this spirit.

The members of our congregations may also need to adjust their own attitudes in light of this conviction. They dare not content themselves with bumper sticker-sized or t-shirt sized theology. It is incumbent upon them to learn and embrace and obey this faith. This calls for hard work on their parts, too. When the Apostle Paul wrote his letter to the Romans, it was not "the theologians in Rome" or "the scholars in Rome" whom he addressed, but "the saints in Rome." The same point, of course, can be made about nearly all the New Testament letters. The church today surely needs to freshly commit itself to substantive teaching and learning of the gospel and its implications for all that we believe and do, and to do so in ways that are appropriate for all believers — regardless of age level or educational background.

Baptismal Beginnings

Our second point is that a prudent place to first focus our catechetical efforts is in helping people prepare for baptism. We might think of catechesis in several stages. There is what might be called a pro-catechesis or proto-catechesis for those the ancients might have called "inquirers" (and whom contemporaries might call "seekers"). Such a phase could spill over into an open-ended period during which the "inquirer" becomes a "catechumen," placing himself or herself under the instruction of the church by regularly attending services of worship and other opportunities for growth. This stage could take on a wide variety of forms in terms of both content and process.

Next, a phase of formal catechesis should be offered to those wishing to become baptized members of the community. It is this phase which, we are suggesting, is often a missed catechetical opportunity in contemporary evangelical churches. Too frequently, people are baptized without adequate instruction about the faith, about the Body, and about the Triune Name into which they are being baptized. Many church leaders seem to believe that mere profession of faith in Jesus Christ is all we should ask for or expect before bringing one to the waters of baptism.

Biblical support for baptizing professing believers quickly is usually based upon the fact that in the Book of Acts we read of many being baptized almost immediately after professing faith in Christ. But in almost every one of those cases (a possible exception being the Philippian jailor), those being baptized were either observant Jews or God-fearing Gentiles who already had significant exposure to the teachings of the Hebrew Scriptures. Clearly this is not the case for many or most who come to faith in Christ in our settings today. In many cases, the worldviews of contemporary baptismal candidates are deeply and profoundly at odds with biblical teaching. Such worldviews must be challenged and, at the same time, the faith of the Bible must be presented through careful catechetical instruction. Otherwise, those being baptized may have only the most superficial idea of what they are doing, and of what is being done to them as they are baptized.

Preparing candidates for baptism is a marvelous opportunity to provide several weeks or even months of instruction in the gospel and its implications for doctrine and life. We neglect this to the detriment of both those being baptized and the church communities into which they are being baptized. Once a properly catechetical baptismal beginning is attended to, we can then carry on with attention to life-long learning. There are further stages of catechesis to consider, including instruction to help the newly baptized more fully and faithfully find their places in the church, and ongoing instruction for all the faithful toward growth "in grace and in the knowledge of our Lord Jesus Christ" (2 Pet. 3:18).

Contextualization and Confrontation

The faith that was once for all delivered to the saints must be presented in ways that are culturally congruent for the catechumens. Like Jesus, we seize upon language, forms, and situations that are part of the lived realities of our learners as we teach the truths and values of the king-dom. Likewise Paul — for the sake of the gospel — was willing "to be-come all things to all people that by all possible means I might save some" (1 Cor. 9:22).

But to call for cultural congruence in our catechizing is not to sug-gest that we are always to affirm the culture. To the contrary, there will be many times when we must confront, challenge, and even condemn ele-ments within the cultures where we live and minister. Again, Jesus and Paul both model such things for us.[5] The false isms, worthless idols, and evil practices evident in our cultures are to be confronted with a clear presentation of Christ who is the Truth, the Life, and the Way (Col. 1:28; John 14:6). This sort of confrontation has been a feature of catechesis from the beginning. It echoes Jesus' approach in the Sermon on the Mount: "You have heard that it was said, but I say to you. . . ." In the same way, sound catechesis requires that we teach the unchanging faith in ways which speak prophetically to our own times and settings.

Diversity of Domains

Next, faithful and effective catechesis also requires a comprehensive-ness of concern. Educators have long identified three primary domains for effective teaching — the cognitive, the affective, and the behavioral. To put it simply, we must teach in such ways as to engage heads, hearts, and hands. In the best of the historic catechetical practices, these things have been kept in view. Teaching for cognitive apprehension of theology, for example, is not to be seen as the sole or primary aim of catechesis. Rather, as Jesus instructed his followers to do, we are to be "teaching them to obey" all that Jesus has commanded (Matt. 28:19). To thus impact the lifestyles of people, we will necessarily engage their minds and hearts as well. All this points out the obvious need to vary our venues for catechesis. Formal settings may serve us well for impart-ing theological truth. But to fully engage hearts and hands, we will also need to utilize non-formal and informal opportunities for experiencing the gospel together.

This comprehensiveness of concern is evident also in the historic

5. See, for example, Jesus' cleansings of the temple in John 2 and Mark 11, and Paul's condemnation of the idolatrous feasts in Corinth in 1 Corinthians 10.

content of catechesis, which has focused attention on three historic summaries of the faith — the Creed, the Lord's Prayer, and the Decalogue. The Creed is a sort of primer in theology, and takes particular aim at our intellects. The Lord's Prayer is a primer in communion with God, and so aims at our affections. The Decalogue is a primer in both worship and ethics and aims at our actions and behaviors. All these areas of the spiritual life to which these ancient formulas point us call for attention at every stage of catechesis. To drop the ball in any one of these areas is really to mishandle the catechetical task entirely.

Emphasis on Essentials

Another element of healthy and health-giving catechesis is an emphasis on the essentials of the faith rather than on secondary or non-essential doctrines and concerns.

We would not diminish the importance of understanding and pointing out the differences that exist between our various communions — Baptist, Presbyterian, Methodist, Pentecostal, and so on. But sound catechesis takes pains to point out that these distinctions are on matters of lesser import than those things that unite us. There are many theological and ethical commitments, for example, that evangelical Protestants share in common with each other across denominational lines. There are also many matters that most evangelical Christians share in common with Eastern Orthodox and Roman Catholic Christians. In our teaching, it really is important that we note these things, and that we help learners understand how to discern the relative weightiness of our various doctrines.

In this spirit, we would suggest that our catechesis should regularly identify at least four levels of distinction, which we label as:

- Christian Consensus — "that which has been believed everywhere, always, and by all."[6]
- Evangelical Essentials — that which Protestants have affirmed together from the Reformation onward.[7]

---

6. A saying attributed to St. Vincent of Laurens.

7. One helpful way to identify these points is to utilize the Reformation *"solas,"* though such an approach is not without its challenges in the current evangelical climate.

- Denominational Distinctives — those matters on which evangelical Protestants have disagreed with one another even as they share in common the points above.
- Congregational Commitments — those points of particular burden or calling unique to each of our own congregations.

Focus on Families and Children

We must and do advocate and champion a return to a rigorous catechesis for adults. But wisdom compels us to focus also on families and children as we craft our catechetical strategies. The fact is that because we too often have fallen short in this regard, we must expend a great deal of time and energy on remedial work. If church leaders worked more faithfully and diligently with children and with their parents, we would not likely find ourselves so often having to scramble to make up for lost time. And, in fact, there is a good deal of evidence to suggest that in order to deeply impress the things of God upon hearts and minds, we must begin with the very young.

In Old Testament passages like Deuteronomy 6 and 11 and Psalm 78, parents and other adults in the faith community were required to diligently teach their children both what God had done for them and what he required of them. The New Testament wholly affirms this approach (see, for example, Eph. 6:4 and 2 Tim. 3:15). In neither Testament would it be conceivable that parents should raise their children in a sort of spiritual neutral. No indeed! Covenant children are always and unashamedly to be raised in the fear and instruction of the Lord.

Grounding and Growing in the Gospel

In our book, Dr. Packer and I suggest that catechesis is the church's ministry of grounding and growing God's people in the gospel and its implications for doctrine, devotion, duty, and delight. From this definition, I would presently make the following few points:

Point 1 — Catechesis is the ministry of the whole church. There are gifted and appointed leaders who must champion this vital ministry. But *all* mature believers have a part to play in helping to shape the faith-life of younger believers in their community. It is partly due to the fact that our churches have often neglected such commitments that parachurch organizations have arisen to help take up the slack. But catechesis occurs best and has the most staying power when it occurs within the context of healthy, multi-generational congregations.

Point 2 — Catechesis is a multi-dimensional ministry, touching upon issues of doctrine, devotion, and duty, and all done with a view toward delighting in the Lord. We addressed such concerns above, under the heading "Diversity of Domains."

Point 3 — Catechesis assumes a healthy progress in one's faith development. We are to be "rooted and built up in him" (Col. 2:6). Thus catechesis aims at both grounding and growing believers in the gospel. We touched upon these ideas above, under the heading "Baptismal Beginnings."

Point 4 — The only proper content and ethos for catechesis is the glorious gospel of the blessed God. Catechesis is fundamentally a proclaiming of and pointing to Christ crucified for our sins and gloriously risen from the dead. With this gospel before us, we consider the implications of Christ's death and resurrection for all our doctrine and all our living, so that in all ways we would be more rightly aligned with the truth of the gospel (see 1 Tim. 1:10-11; Tit. 2:1; Gal. 2:14). Staying gospel-centered in our catechizing will keep the whole enterprise from lapsing into a programmatic, mechanical, and/or legalistic human scheme.

A Healthy and Holy, Sometimes Happy, Often Hurtful, Always Hopeful Hymnody

As we noted earlier, we cannot leave catechesis to only formal educational structures and settings. One of the more powerful venues for catechesis — and one that is both biblical and historically affirmed to be vital — is that of congregational worship. Few if any things are more potently formative than when the Body gathers itself in the name of Jesus Christ to worship the Triune God.

Historical catechists have long recognized the power of hymnody as a catechetical tool within the context of gathered worship. From St. Ambrose to Martin Luther to Isaac Watts and the Wesleys, hymns have

131

been used intentionally not only to deepen the believers' communion with God but also to deepen their understanding of God's character, of his saving work in Christ, and of his present will for our lives.

Such an approach to our singing has clear biblical models (as in the Psalms) and mandates (as in Col. 3:16 and Eph. 5:18f.). We should choose our songs very carefully, then, with concern for biblical fidelity and gospel-centricity.[8]

Integrity in the Instructors

For catechesis to be faithful and effective, it is also critical that those who are in the role of catechists — pastors, parents, disciplers of all ages — must be people of integrity. This is of course biblically mandated. We see this in Paul's "Follow my example as I follow the example of Christ" (1 Cor. 11:1; see also Phil. 4:9; 2 Tim. 2:2). We see it most clearly in the ministry of Jesus, who fully incarnated the Way, the Truth, and the Life of God. We see it also in the examples of Old Testament figures such as Samuel (1 Sam. 12:1-5, 23) and Ezra (Ezra 7:10). It is also pedagogically realistic, for the fact is that people learn more from what they see in our lives than from what they hear from our mouths. We should heed Richard Baxter's words in this regard: "Take heed to yourselves . . . lest you unsay with your lives, what you say with your tongues; and be the greatest hinderers of the success of your own labours."[9]

Joy in the Journey to Jesus

With this, our final lettered point, I offer two final thoughts. First, the ministry of catechesis should be done with an aim to knowing Jesus Christ more deeply and intimately. It is, in other words, all about our "journey to Jesus," as Robert Webber expressed it in his own book on the subject.[10] We must always fix our eyes on Jesus as we run the race

8. At the conference in honor of David Wells, we sang together a catechetical hymn that I had written in David's honor. It is a celebration of the Reformation *solas* and is reproduced as an appendix to this volume.

9. Richard Baxter, *The Reformed Pastor* (Carlisle, PA: The Banner of Truth Trust, 1974), p. 63.

10. See Robert Webber, *Journey to Jesus: The Worship, Evangelism and Nurture Mission of the Church* (Nashville: Abingdon Press, 2001).

before us (Heb. 12:2). Catechists must not forget this, either for their own sakes or for those alongside whom they have been called to run. Together with our catechumens, we must "keep our eyes on the prize as we catechize."[11]

The second thought is simply that such a journey ought to be a joyous and life-giving one. By God's grace it will be. If we would champion catechesis in our congregations but come to find ourselves participating in just another joy-less, life-less program, we will surely have gone seriously off course somewhere along the way. To avoid such a missing of our mark, we should regularly take inventory of ourselves and of all our catechetical endeavors, and the entire process must be bathed in prayer and conducted always in grace.

11. This playful line from our book aims to make a serious point.

The Church after Evangelicalism

MICHAEL S. HORTON

IT IS NOT DIFFICULT to make the case that evangelicalism (generally speaking) exhibits a low doctrine of the church. Emerging out of the churches of the Reformation as well as the Anabaptist heritage, pietism — especially in the United States and Britain — evangelicalism was defined by a series of "awakenings" and a subsequent history of revivals. Often, these movements were celebrated as extraordinary works of the Spirit in contrast with the ordinary ministry of the church and they spawned a vast network of parachurch ministries.

It is possible today for a professing believer to go from the nursery to children's church to the youth group to campus ministries to groups for singles, then young marrieds, all the way to "empty nesters" and "golden oldies," without ever having actually joined a church, or at least without having been immersed in the cross-generational and cross-cultural communion of saints that is generated through the public ministry of Word, sacrament, and discipline. Is it then any wonder that so many evangelical young people abandon the church by their sophomore year in college, especially when they have routinely heard the distinction between "becoming a Christian" and "joining a church"?

Sometimes it is even the church itself that creates a panoply of "ministries" that unintentionally convey the impression that this is where the real growth occurs and that the public gathering of the saints for the Word, the sacraments, fellowship, and the prayers is secondary. And given the evidence that there has been no real growth in the number of new professions of faith — in fact, decline — it seems hardly efficient even in practical terms to move Christians from the churches of their youth to megachurches with the appeal to anonymity. In short, evangelicalism has a pronounced tendency toward losing the reached in the name of reaching the lost. It is not simply that evangelicals tend to embrace a "low ecclesiology." It is that the evangelical movement, held together largely by a common attachment to revivals and the parachurch societies that emerge from them, is a practical subversion of particular churches of any ecclesiological stripe. In *The Courage to Be Protestant,* David Wells observes that parachurch ministries are increasingly replacing the church itself.[1] Focusing on the essentials, conservative ministers within established denominations often downplayed their confessional distinctives in order to cooperate in a common evangelical vision for mission.

Furthermore, a critical attitude toward visible ecclesiastical structures was occasioned by the perceived hostility of mainline Protestantism toward the fundamentals of the Christian faith. The post–World War II renaissance (usually called neo-evangelicalism) was led mainly by mainline Protestants who were increasingly marginalized within their own denominations and the second half of the century witnessed a wide-scale flight to conservative evangelical congregations. The "Jesus Movement" in the 1970s fused fundamentalism with the charismatic movement, offering an alternative to the ecclesiastical establishment analogous to that generation's more general suspicions of organizations, institutions, and bureaucracies. Doubtless, there are many factors behind the lack of interest in ecclesiology (including sociological factors) that cannot be rehearsed in any depth in this essay.

There are hopeful signs of renewed interest in ecclesiology among evangelicals in recent years.[2] However, in spite of rewarding engage-

---

1. David F. Wells, *The Courage to Be Protestant: Truth-lovers, Markers, and Emergents in the Postmodern World* (Grand Rapids: Eerdmans, 2008), pp. 10-12, 209-25.

2. Setting the standard in this respect is Miroslav Volf's *After Our Likeness: The Church as the Image of the Trinity* (Grand Rapids: Eerdmans, 1997). Stanley Grenz and Amos Yong have pointed up the need for a more robust ecclesiology in evangelical and Pentecostal circles. More recently, see Brad Harper and Paul Louis Metzger, *Exploring Ecclesiology: An Evangelical and Ecumenical Introduction* (Grand Rapids: Brazos, 2009). The emergent movement has also sparked renewed interest in ecclesiological questions. See for example Jim Belcher, *Deep Church: A Third Way Beyond Emerging and Traditional* (Downers Grove, IL: InterVarsity, 2009).

ment with Roman Catholic, Eastern Orthodox, Anabaptist, Free Church, and Pentecostal views, evangelicals have generally shown little interest in the seminal ecclesiological insights of Reformation traditions. Evangelicalism is not neutral with respect to ecclesiology. Although the movement's leaders often explain the lack of ecclesiological emphasis as a way of focusing on the truths that unite us, the movement's working assumptions seem chiefly to be indebted to Anabaptist, pietist, and revivalistic traditions. Often, this means that churches of the Reformation that would otherwise share an evangelical faith must either opt out of participation in the evangelical movement or must accept the working assumptions of a quite different ecclesiological paradigm. At least since the Second Great Awakening, the Reformation and its confessional distinctives have played a less discernable role than pietist and revivalistic emphases. In fact, at the end of his U.S. tour, Dietrich Bonhoeffer could summarize his observations concerning American religion generally as "Protestantism without the Reformation."

In this essay I compare and contrast evangelical and Reformed approaches to ecclesiology. Recognizing the danger in generalizations, I focus on broad trajectories in an effort to locate different theological paradigms that, while not offering exhaustive explanation, may go some distance toward understanding the strengths and weaknesses of evangelical ecclesiologies. I offer these remarks in the hope of sparking further conversation for the church's life today, not simply to defend my own tradition.

Ecclesiology is a significant part of the Lutheran and Reformed traditions. Anglican theologian Paul Avis has observed, "Reformation theology is largely dominated by two questions: 'How can I obtain a gracious God?' and 'Where can I find the true Church?' The two questions are inseparably related. . . ."[3] According to the churches of the Reformation, the true church is found "wherever the Word is rightly preached and the sacraments are properly administered." In the remainder of this essay, I want to highlight, from a Reformed perspective, three chief assumptions of evangelical approaches to the church that should be made more explicit in our conversations. Obviously, these are generalizations, but I do think that there are enough family resemblances to identify a working evangelical ecclesiology.

3. Paul D. L. Avis, *The Church in the Theology of the Reformers* (Atlanta: John Knox, 1981), p. 1.

God's Covenant versus Our Contract

The churches of the Reformation maintain that the church is *creatura verbi,* the creature of the Word.[4] Just as "faith comes from hearing the word of Christ" (Rom. 10:17), the church is created out of the darkness and chaos of this passing evil age through the living and active speech of the Triune God. The Father speaks this new creation into being, in the Son, and by the Spirit. The context created by this speech is a covenant.

Eschatology and ecclesiology converge at this point. As I have argued in-depth elsewhere, Reformed interpretations of the kingdom of God embrace the paradox of the "already" and "not-yet" that seems so evident in the New Testament. Given the fall of humankind in Adam, history would have remained closed — a vicious cycle of violence, sin, death, and condemnation — had God not opened it up by proclaiming the gospel. From the woman will come a seed who will crush the serpent's head, lifting the curse (Gen. 3:16). It is this heavenly Word, coming to sinners from outside of themselves, that breaks up the present evil age and creates a community of hearers.

In the upper room (John 14-16), Jesus prepared his disciples for his departure. After he ascends, he will send the Spirit who will bring understanding of everything that he had spoken during his ministry. Christ's ascension, reported at the end of Luke and at the beginning of Acts, and referred to repeatedly in the Epistles, marks a real absence of Jesus in the flesh. He is truly gone. Yet this departure marks his royal entrance into the heavenly temple as the faithful High Priest and conquering King. From there, he reigns through the Word of his apostles and the Spirit whom he and the Father have sent. Where his Word and Spirit are present, Jesus Christ himself is present as well. Yet we await his bodily return at the end of the age.

So this is the paradox. Jesus' departure opens up a fissure in history. It is not allowed to go its own way, but is drawn into his own history of descent, resurrection, ascent, and return in the flesh. In this precarious crevice (to borrow a phrase from Douglas Farrow), the new covenant

4. There is a fine summary of this position in "Lutheran-R.C. Dialogue," *Growth in Agreement II: Reports and Agreed Statements of Ecumenical Conversations on a World Level, 1982-1998,* ed. Jeffrey Gros, FSC, Harding Meyer, and William G. Rusch (Geneva: World Council of Churches; Grand Rapids: Eerdmans, 2000), pp. 802-3. For the Lutheran–Roman Catholic dialogue on this point, see pp. 495-98.

community is born and flourishes against all odds.[5] Like a patch of grass on the cliff of a sea rock, it is battered and blown, but this serves merely to scatter the seeds with verdant life.

The Reformers spoke of the Word of God pre-eminently as the eternal Son, but also as both a *written canon* or rule of faith and life and as a *sacramental Word* — that is, a means of grace, primarily as preaching.[6] In the vision of the valley of dry bones in Ezekiel 37, God tells the prophet to preach to the dry bones and they come together with the breath of life. Especially in our Western culture, words merely refer to reality. They describe certain states of affairs. However, in the biblical worldview, God's Word creates reality and new states of affairs. Just as the Triune God spoke the world into existence (from the Father, in the Son, by the Spirit), the same God speaks salvation — the new creation — into existence here and now. Even the sacraments of baptism and the Supper are Word-events in the sense that they ratify the saving activity of God in the covenant assembly.

The preaching of the Word of God *is* the Word of God, not just a discourse on biblical subjects. In preaching and sacrament, Christ is present in the power of his Spirit, raising those who are spiritually dead and constantly breathing his life into his people. The weekly gathering of the covenant people is God's service to sinners, divine theater in which the church — threatened on all sides from within and without — flourishes and expands to the ends of the earth.

Covenant: The Triune God Creates the Church through the Means of Grace

Thus, the church is a covenant community that comes into being and is sustained in its growth by the action of the Triune God, rooted in God's gracious election. Believers receive Christ and all of his benefits through the gift of faith, but this response does not create the church. Rather, it is the Spirit's working through the ministry of Word and sacrament that creates faith itself. Therefore, the church's existence is ob-

5. This is a repeated metaphor in one of the most helpful treatments of eschatology and ecclesiology I have come across: Douglas Farrow, *Ascension and Ecclesia* (Edinburgh: T&T Clark, 1999).

6. B. A. Gerrish, *Grace and Gratitude: The Eucharistic Theology of John Calvin* (Minneapolis: Augsburg Fortress, 1993), pp. 84-85.

jective, in spite of the ambiguity of its inherent holiness and faithfulness. The church exists wherever *God* is at work. And because God has pledged his saving activity to these creaturely means, there will be faith and it will bear the fruit of good works.

The Spirit applies Christ's redeeming work through the preaching of the gospel and ratifies the gracious promise through baptism and the Lord's Supper. In this conception, the covenant community (or visible church) in both Testaments is *constituted* by the decision and action of the Triune God, not by the decision and action of human beings — whether individuals or a magisterium. It is with faith in the sovereign grace of the triune God that professing Christians embrace the covenant promises not only for themselves but for their children. It is not our contract with God, but God's covenant with us and our children that gives rise to a church.

The covenant community (the visible church) is wider than the company of the elect (the invisible church). Put more eschatologically, the invisible church is the church as it will be fully revealed only on the last day. As in the Old Testament, the visible church or covenant community is at present a "mixed body": "Not all who are descended from Israel belong to Israel" (Rom. 9:6). There are weeds sown among the wheat (Matt. 13:36-43). In short, the visible church is the field in which the Father is at work, in the Son, and by his Spirit, producing a harvest for the end of the age. It is not simply the sum total of regenerate believers deciding and acting in concert, but the heavenly embassy on earth, where Christ is building his kingdom.

The pattern in Acts is consistent with the Old Testament administration of the covenant of grace. Just as Abraham believes and is circumcised, and is then commanded to circumcise his sons as heirs of the promise, Peter declares in his Pentecost sermon, "The promise is for you and for your children and for all who are far off, as many as the Lord our God calls to himself" (Acts 2:39). Cut to the quick by Peter's sermon, many believe and are baptized, and bring their whole household under the covenant promises through baptism (Acts 16:14-15, 31; 1 Cor. 1:16). The children of believers are holy, set apart by God's promise (1 Cor. 7:14), although some will reject their birthright (Heb. 12:16; cf. 6:1-9). Responding to God's promise, parents — and indeed the whole church — vow to raise these children in the covenant. There is the expectation that their children will come to profess faith publicly before the elders and this will be ratified by their being welcomed to the Lord's Table.

Therefore, although it may in some cases begin with a definable experience, conversion is understood primarily as gradual and lifelong growth in repentance and faith through the ordinary means of grace. The inner working of the Spirit is mysterious and varied, but the outward means are always the same, ordained by Christ as the public mark of his abiding and active presence in the world by his Spirit. God's sovereign work is not bound to the outward means of the covenant's administration, but he has pledged to work through them as he pleases. In this view, it is God who makes the church visible in this world and it is his external work that is visible, not his secret operations. The believer's confession of faith is the *fruit* of the Spirit's ministry through the church, rather than the *source* of ecclesial existence.

These covenantal presuppositions generate particular ways of articulating our belief in the church as "one, holy, catholic, and apostolic." To take just catholicity as an example, Reformed ecclesiology emphasizes the point that God not only chose us for himself but chose our brothers and sisters for us as well. We have failed in all sorts of ways to practice this truth in our history, but it remains a potent force for transforming concrete church life. Our modern culture catechizes us in the opposite faith. It claims to be generically catholic (global), but it is deeply sectarian and anti-social. It teaches us through the most pervasive words and sacraments of our daily routines that we are the sovereign choosers. By carving up humankind into niche demographics based on personal choice, this false catholicity feeds both our narcissism and our sense of loneliness. Yet when we enter God's house, we discover an entirely different order where the powers of the age to come are at work even in this present evil age. We are all here together not because we share the same demographic niche, generational profile, or special interests, but because we have been chosen, redeemed, and called into one body by one Spirit. We share "one Lord, one faith, one baptism" (Eph. 4:5). We may not have the same playlist on our iPods or share the same political views, but we eat of one loaf in the Lord's Supper (1 Cor. 10:17). Through these outward means the Spirit binds us together in the deepest inner unity. The church is catholic because Christ "redeemed for God people from every tribe, kindred, tongue, people, and nation" (Rev. 5:9) and our location "in Christ" is more decisive than the sectarian allegiances of ethnicity, gender, socio-economic status, politics, and consumer preferences (Gal. 3:28).

As I look around in the public gathering each Lord's Day, and see many whom I would not ordinarily know, much less choose, for my circle of friends, I catch a glimpse of the everlasting *shalom* that awaits us. We cannot summon this "one, holy, catholic, and apostolic church" into being. We cannot work toward it. It is not a human project. Like the gospel itself, this ecclesial reality can only be received as a gift, through the means that God has promised to use to create it.

Contract: Believers Create the Church by Personal Decision

Against the absorption of personal faith in Christ to the faith of the church, the Reformation emphasized that each of us must repent and believe the gospel. However, as Anabaptist scholars observe, justification was not a concern of the radical reformers for whom the central doctrine was obedient discipleship and the imitation of Christ.[7] Rather than means of grace, baptism and the Lord's Supper were seen as the believer's act of commitment. Some even questioned the validity of these covenantal ordinances and later movements, such as the Society of Friends (Quakers), abandoned them in favor of fellowship and spiritual conversation, each according to his or her "inner light." If Rome virtually eliminates the need for personal decision and identifies the Body of Christ univocally with a particular organization in history, radical Protestants have tended to place the emphasis on personal choice and a voluntary society over against the visible church.

Under the conditions of modernity, everyone has to choose his or her religion and this is salutary for anyone who maintains the importance of personal faith. However, the autonomy of the self has argued for more than this: namely, the recognition that faith is *only* a matter of

---

7. In his excellent volume, *A Contemporary Anabaptist Theology: Biblical, Historical, Constructive* (Downers Grove, IL: InterVarsity, 2004), contemporary Anabaptist theologian Thomas Finger observes, "Robert Friedmann found 'A forensic view of grace, in which the sinner is . . . undeservedly justified . . . simply unacceptable' to Anabaptists. A more nuanced scholar like Arnold Snyder can assert that historic Anabaptists 'never talked about being "justified by faith"'" (p. 109). Finger believes that Anabaptist soteriological emphases (especially on divinization) can bring greater unity especially between marginalized Protestant groups (Pentecostals and Quakers) and Orthodox and Roman Catholic theologies of salvation (p. 110). Finger observes that recent Anabaptist reflection is no more marked in its interest in this topic than its antecedents, with discipleship ("following Jesus") and the inner transformation of the believer as central (pp. 132-33).

personal choice. To the extent that certain forms of Protestantism have given theological sanction to this emphasis, they have not only survived but thrived. If conversion is a matter of "signing up" for salvation, then the church will be conceived as a market niche or a club. Dietrich Bonhoeffer poignantly observed, "What is the point of admitting infants into an association?" he asks. "No chess player, no matter how passionate, would enroll a small child in a chess club. . . . Only a community [*Gemeinschaft*], not a society [*Gesellschaft*], is able to carry children. Infant baptism within an association is an internal contradiction."[8] By the way, Bonhoeffer's main point was to remind paedobaptist churches in Germany of the obligation that they were neglecting.

Although the emergent church movement offers bracing critiques of the megachurch model, is it really a radically new paradigm or is it an updating of the revivalistic paradigm? Stanley Grenz observes, "The post-Reformation discussion of the *vera ecclesia* formed the historical context for the emergence of the covenant idea as the focal understanding of the nature of the church."[9] With its insistence on the marks of the church, "the Reformers shifted the focus to Word and Sacrament," but the Anabaptists and Baptists "took yet a further step," advocating an independent ecclesiology. "This view asserts that the true church is essentially people standing in voluntary covenant with God."[10] Of course, this principle of personal decision excludes the practice of infant baptism, Grenz argues. "As a result, in the order of salvation the believer — and not the church — stands first in priority."[11] "Because the coming together of believers in mutual covenant constitutes the church, it is the covenant community of individuals," although it has a history as well.[12] Although the language of "covenant" is used, notice the crucial difference: it refers to the mutual covenanting of consenting adults, not first of all to the mutual covenanting of the persons of the Trinity and the priority of God's promise.

8. Dietrich Bonhoeffer, *Sanctorum Communio: A Theological Study of the Sociology of the Church,* Dietrich Bonhoeffer Works, Volume 1, ed. Joachim von Soosten; English edition ed. Clifford J. Green; trans. Reinhard Krauss and Nancy Lukens (Minneapolis: Fortress Press, 1998), pp. 254, 257.

9. Stanley Grenz, *Theology for the Community of God* (Nashville: Broadman & Holman, 1997), p. 609.

10. Grenz, *Theology,* pp. 610-11.

11. Grenz, *Theology,* pp. 610-11.

12. Grenz, *Theology,* p. 614.

It was especially in the Second Great Awakening that the centrality of human decision and effort became especially dominant. As Roger Olson observes, the nineteenth-century evangelist Charles Finney was closer to Pelagianism than Arminianism.[13] Rejecting the doctrines of original sin, substitutionary atonement, justification through faith, and the miraculous character of the new birth,[14] the evangelist insisted that salvation was due entirely to human decision and effort. Consequently, the new birth is as dependent on predictable laws of cause-and-effect efficiency as any other natural process. Although Finney's cause-and-effect view shares superficial similarities with the Roman Catholic concept of *ex opere operato* sacramental efficacy, there are two crucial differences: (1) he claimed this efficacy for his new measures rather than for the sacraments that Christ ordained and (2) he denied that their efficacy depended even ultimately on God's grace.

The connection between soteriology and ecclesiology is clear enough in Finney's own thinking. Just as the new birth lies entirely in the hands of the individual, through whatever "excitements" are likely to "induce repentance," the church is conceived primarily as a society of moral reformers. In a letter on revival, Finney issued the following: "Now the great business of the church is to reform the world — to put away every kind of sin. The church of Christ was originally organized to be a body of reformers . . . to reform individuals, communities, and governments." If the churches will not follow, they will simply have to be left behind, Finney contended.[15]

Remarkably, Finney seems to have been fully convinced that Scripture provided clear commands for social reform while remaining virtu-

13. Roger Olson, *Arminian Theology* (Downers Grove, IL: InterVarsity, 2005), p. 28 (including footnote 20). Furthermore, I have been amazed that Arminian friends like Methodist theologian Thomas Oden have defended core evangelical (i.e., Reformation) teachings like justification even while some conservative Protestants seem to be losing their interest in the doctrine. Clearly, the theological divide in our day is less denominational than it is theological.

14. Charles G. Finney, *Systematic Theology* (reprinted, Minneapolis: Bethany, 1976), pp. 31, 46, 57, 206, 209, 236, 320-22.

15. Charles Finney, *Lectures on Revival,* 2nd ed. (New York, 1835), pp. 184-204. "Law, rewards, and punishments — these things and such as these are the very heart and soul of moral suasion. . . . My brethren, if ecclesiastical bodies, colleges, and seminaries will only go forward — who will not bid them God speed? But if they will not go forward — if we hear nothing from them but complaint, denunciation, and rebuke in respect to almost every branch of reform, what can be done?"

ally silent on the ministry of the church. Eventually, the new measures instituted in the protracted meeting (or revival) were adopted as regular features in many regular church services. The chancel, with its prominent pulpit, font, and table, was often replaced with a stage, a choir, and, of course, the very mobile preachers, unchained — literally and often metaphorically — from the text they were expounding. It was no longer clear to many at least what role that the ordinary preaching of the Word, teaching, administration of the sacraments, discipline, and diaconal care fit in and increasingly the burden for outreach, fellowship, and mercy ministries shifted to parachurch agencies.

Given this orientation, it is not surprising that "means of grace" do not seem as relevant as practical methods of attaining our own personal and social transformation, church growth, and daily problem-solving. *If salvation is not a miracle, then the church is not a miracle. If salvation can be orchestrated through clever methods calculated for pragmatic success in terms of numbers, then church growth is a purely natural phenomenon based on the same methods as any other business.* Finney defined his "new measures" as "inducements sufficient to convert sinners with."[16]

At least Jonathan Edwards had taught that a revival was "a surprising work of God," an extraordinary blessing of God's ordinary means of grace. However, Finney insisted, "A revival is not a miracle." In fact, "There is nothing in religion beyond the ordinary powers of nature. It consists in the right exercise of the powers of nature. It is just that, and nothing else. . . . It is a purely philosophical result of the right use of the constituted means — as much so as any other effect produced by the application of means."[17] "God Has Established No Particular Measures" is a chapter subheading in Finney's *Systematic Theology.* "A re-

---

16. Ironically, Finney held to an *ex opere operato* view of his own new measures that he would never allow to baptism and the Supper. As for Pelagian charge, Finney's *Systematic Theology* (Minneapolis: Bethany, 1976) explicitly denies original sin and insists that the power of regeneration lies in the sinner's own hands, rejects any substitutionary notion of Christ's atonement in favor of the moral influence and moral government theories, and regards the doctrine of justification by an alien righteousness as "impossible and absurd." In fact, Roger Olson, in his defense of Arminianism, sees Finney's theology as well beyond the Arminian pale (*Arminian Theology* [Downers Grove, IL: InterVarsity, 2006], p. 27). Thus, it is all the more remarkable that Finney occupies such a distinguished place among evangelicals, as the tribute to him in the Billy Graham Center (Wheaton, IL) illustrates. It is little wonder that American religion struck Bonhoeffer as "Protestantism without the Reformation."

17. Charles G. Finney, *Revivals of Religion* (Old Tappan, NJ: Revell, n.d.), pp. 4-5.

vival will decline and cease," he warned, "unless Christians are frequently re-converted."[18] A revival could be planned, staged, and managed. The Great Commission just said, "Go," says Finney. "*It did not prescribe any forms.* It did not admit any. . . . And [the disciples'] object was to make known the gospel in the *most effectual way . . .* so as to obtain attention and secure obedience of the greatest number possible. No person can find any *form* of doing this laid down in the Bible."[19] This may seem like an odd interpretation, since the substance of the Great Commission is to preach, baptize, and teach.

Writing against the "new measures," a contemporary Reformed pastor and theologian, John Williamson Nevin, pointed out the contrast between "the system of the bench" (precursor to the altar call) and what he called "the system of the catechism": "The old Presbyterian faith, into which I was born, was based throughout on the idea of covenant family religion, church membership by God's holy act in baptism, and following this a regular catechetical training of the young, with direct reference to their coming to the Lord's table. In one word, all proceeded on the theory of sacramental, educational religion." Nevin relates his own involvement in a revival as a young man, where he was expected to disown his covenantal heritage as nothing more than dead formalism. These two systems, Nevin concluded, "involve at the bottom two different theories of religion."[20]

Like the revivals of Finney and his successors, the "new measures" of the church growth movement have been treated by many as science, like the law of gravity. Those who fail to adopt these new models of ministry will be left behind in the spiritual marketplace.

IN 2007, WILLOW CREEK COMMUNITY CHURCH released its findings from a study of its members. Surprised by the revelation that the most committed members described their Christian life as "stalled" or in decline, the leadership nevertheless concluded that it was not because the ministry itself was failing to deepen believers in faith and worship, even though that was the verdict of responders. Rather, the leadership drew the conclusion that as believers grow in their faith, they need the

18. Finney, *Revivals,* p. 321.

19. Quoted in Michael Pasquarello III, *Christian Preaching: A Trinitarian Theology of Proclamation* (Grand Rapids: Baker Academic, 2007), p. 24.

20. John Williamson Nevin, *The Anxious Bench* (London: Taylor & Francis, 1987), pp. 2-5.

church and its programs less. They concluded that the sheep must become "self-feeders" who are able to carry out their workout program without the aid of the church. Ironically, the analogy of church-as-parent was employed to suggest that when believers reach maturity they find the church less important.[21] Where Calvin (following Cyprian) referred to the church as the "mother of the faithful" who carries her children throughout their whole life, this study compared the church to a personal coach at the gym who creates personalized work-out plans and leaves the long-term success in the hands of the customer.[22]

Taken to its extreme, contractual thinking easily leads to the view expressed by George Barna, an evangelical pioneer of church marketing: "Think of your church not as a religious meeting place, but as a service agency — an entity that exists to satisfy people's needs."[23] Not surprisingly, Barna has recently suggested that the institutional church is no longer relevant and should be replaced by informal gatherings for fellowship and Internet communities. In fact, he has introduced a new demographic: the "Revolutionaries," the "millions of believers" who "have moved beyond the established church and chosen to be the church instead."[24] The Revolutionaries have found that in order to pursue an authentic faith they had to abandon the church.[25] Intimate worship, says Barna, does "not require a 'worship service,'" just a personal commitment to the Bible, prayer, and discipleship.[26] Where Luke reports that the church gathered regularly "for the apostles' teaching, the fellowship, the breaking of the bread, and the prayers" (Acts 2:42-47), Barna suggests that preaching is simply "faith-based conversation" and the means of grace are no more than whatever it takes for "intentional spiritual growth," "love," "resource investment," and "spiritual friendships."[27]

Whereas a covenantal approach begins with God's Word and forms a communion of saints, in Barna's paradigm everything begins with the individual's personal decision, strengthened by more personal disci-

21. Greg Hawkins, *Reveal: Where Are You* (Barrington, IL: Willow Creek Resources, 2007).

22. Hawkins, *Reveal.*

23. George Barna, *Marketing the Church* (Colorado Springs: NavPress, 1988), p. 37.

24. George Barna, *Revolution: Finding Vibrant Faith beyond the Walls of the Sanctuary* (Carol Stream, IL: Tyndale House Publishers, 2005), back cover copy.

25. Barna, *Revolution,* p. 17.

26. Barna, *Revolution,* p. 22.

27. Barna, *Revolution,* pp. 24-25.

plines, and ends with the abandonment of the visible church. God's ordained means of grace are replaced with whatever is calculated to facilitate our own means of commitment. "Scripture teaches us that
devoting your life to loving God with all your heart, mind, strength, and
soul is what honors Him. Being part of a local church may facilitate
that. Or it might not."[28] As the embodied communion of the saints is
replaced by the Internet "explorer," the phrase "invisible church" takes
on a new and ominous meaning. Yet it is part of a long history in which
the public gathering of the covenant community for the means of grace
was made subordinate to conventicles or "holy clubs." In the name of
reaching the unchurched, evangelicalism increasingly tends to un-
church the churched.

LIKE FINNEY, GEORGE BARNA asserts that the Bible offers "almost no
restrictions on structures and methods" for the church.[29] Indeed, for
Barna, the visible church itself is of human rather than divine origin.
Nature abhors a vacuum and where Barna imagines that the Bible prescribes no particular structures or methods, the invisible hand of the
market fills the void. Barna recognizes that the shift from the institutional church to "alternative faith communities" is largely due to market forces to which he frankly insists we must conform.[30] The foretaste
of heavenly catholicity surrenders to this powers of this present age in
Barna's vision.[31] "So if you are a Revolutionary," Barna concludes, "it is

28. Barna, *Revolution,* p. 37.
29. Barna, *Revolution,* p. 175.
30. Barna, *Revolution,* pp. 62-63. Following "the 'niching' of America" on the part of
global marketing in the effort to "command greater loyalty (and profits)," we now have
"churches designed for different generations, those offering divergent styles of worship
music, congregations that emphasize ministries of interest to specialized populations,
and so forth. The church landscape now offers these boutique churches alongside the
something-for-everybody megachurches. In the religious marketplace, the churches that
have suffered most are those who stuck with the one-size-fits-all approach, typically proving that one-size-fits-nobody."
31. Perhaps Barna's emphases are the logical outworking of a more general trend
that drew much of its strength from the pioneering missiology of Donald McGavran. See
his *Understanding Church Growth,* ed. and rev. C. Peter Wagner (Grand Rapids: Eerdmans,
1970). Here he especially introduced the model of "homogeneous church growth" (pp.
163-75). C. Peter Wagner defends McGavran's approach in *Our Kind of People: The Ethical
Dimensions of Church Growth in America* (Atlanta: John Knox, 1979). However, some Reformed theologians in South Africa responded in the 1970s and 1980s that this principle

because you have sensed and responded to God's calling to be such an imitator of Christ. It is not a church's responsibility to make you into this mold.... The choice to become a Revolutionary — and it is a choice — is a covenant you make with God alone."[32] Though he employs the word "covenant," his assumptions are more suggestive of a contract: a consumer's decision to accept certain terms in exchange for certain goods and services.

More recently, Barna and Frank Viola co-authored *Pagan Christianity: Exploring the Roots of Our Church Practices.* As the title and subtitle suggest, this sweeping indictment dismisses public worship (including the sermon) along with "pastoral office" (p. 136), and the Lord's Supper is rejected as "a strange pagan-like rite" (p. 197). [In an earlier book, Viola insists that what we really need are "electric" events: "informal gatherings permeated with an atmosphere of freedom, spontaneity and joy," ". . . open and participatory meetings" with "no fixed order of worship" and therefore "impromptu."[33] In this setting, there is no place for "human officiation."[34] Instead, "the Lord Jesus Christ" presides "invisibly" through every-member-ministry.[35] To borrow terminology from Charles

---

was precisely the church's justification for apartheid. Allan Boesak responded, "Manipulation of the word of God to suit culture, prejudices, or ideology is alien to the Reformed tradition" (*Black and Reformed: Apartheid, Liberation and the Calvinist Tradition*, ed. Leonard Sweetman [Maryknoll, NY: Orbis, 1984], p. 87). According to John de Gruchy, Reformed churches were not segregated until the "revivals in the mid-nineteenth century" by holiness preacher Andrew Murray and pietist missionaries. "It was under the dominance of such evangelicalism," says de Gruchy, "rather than the strict Calvinism of Dort, that the Dutch Reformed Church agreed at its Synod of 1857 that congregations could be divided along racial lines." He adds, "Despite the fact that this development went against earlier synodical decisions that segregation in the church was contrary to the Word of God, it was rationalized on grounds of missiology and practical necessity. Missiologically it was argued that people were best evangelized and best worshipped God in their own language and cultural setting, a position reinforced by German Lutheran missiology and somewhat akin to the church-growth philosophy of our own time." *Liberating Reformed Theology: A South African Contribution to an Ecumenical Debate* (Grand Rapids: Eerdmans, 1991), pp. 23-24.

32. De Gruchy, *Liberating Reformed Theology*, p. 70.

33. Frank Viola, *So You Want to Start a House Church? First Century Styled Church Planting for Today* (Jacksonville, FL: Present Testimony Ministry, 2003), p. 88. I am grateful to my colleague, Peter Jones, for pointing out these quotes in his review at Reformation21.

34. Viola, *So You Want to Start a House Church?* p. 234.

35. Viola, *So You Want to Start a House Church?* pp. 234, 246.

Taylor, the revivalistic trajectory celebrates the "disengaged self" of modernity over the "embedded self" of a covenantal consciousness.][36]

Miroslav Volf recognizes the possibility of taking Free Church logic down this contractual path:

> Whether they want to or not, Free Churches often function as "homogeneous units" specializing in the specific needs of specific social classes and cultural circles, and then in mutual competition try to sell their commodity at dumping prices to the religious consumer in the supermarket of life projects; the customer is king and the one best suited to evaluate his or her own religious needs and from whom nothing more is required than a bit of loyalty and as much money as possible. If the Free Churches want to contribute to the salvation of Christendom, they themselves must first be healed.[37]

Volf also points out that the privatization of faith that warps ecclesiology also makes Free Church ecclesiologies more effective in contemporary cultures.[38] Yet he recognizes that when decisions have been privatized, "the transmission of faith" is threatened.[39]

We can see how inextricably linked are soteriology and ecclesiology. If one's relationship to God is determined by personal choice, entering a contract to perform certain regular disciplines in exchange for salvation, then the church exists as a niche market based on personal choice: in Barna's own words, a "service provider." While Reformed and Presbyterian churches are often unfaithful to a covenantal ecclesiology, the dominance of personal choice and pathological church shopping seems entirely consistent with the logic of revivalism. No doubt, this contractual way of thinking is as much a source of evangelicalism's success as it is an indicator of the movement's growing inability to represent an alternative society, a colony of heaven in this passing age.

---

36. For more on this covenantal anthropology, see Michael Horton, *Lord and Servant* (Louisville: WJK, 2005), pp. 91-119.

37. Volf, *After Our Likeness*, p. 18.

38. Volf, *After Our Likeness*, p. 17.

39. Volf, *After Our Likeness*, p. 16.

Outside In vs. Inside Out

Reflecting its roots in radical Protestantism, the revivalistic paradigm exhibits a tendency to regard everything that is visible, external, and formal as a threat to that which is invisible, internal, and spontaneous. If the danger in the medieval church was to reduce the sovereign work of the Spirit to the visible ministry of the church, the reformers challenged the radical Protestants for exhibiting a nearly Gnostic dualism between body and spirit. The reformers called this "enthusiasm," meaning literally, "God-within-ism."

Echoing the medieval mystic Meister Eckhart, Thomas Müntzer contrasted the voice of the Spirit within with the external Word that merely beats the air. Why put so much stock in the ordinary preaching of Scripture, teaching, sacraments, church order, when the Spirit works immediately and inwardly, apart from creaturely means? Why indeed require a learned ministry or continue the ordination of formal officers, hold synods and presbyteries, and imprison the spirit in the body of earthly forms? Comparisons between Müntzer and Finney come pretty easily to me, but my comments on this point will be more general.

The churches of the Reformation were united in their insistence that the saving reign of Christ comes to us from outside of ourselves, whether as individuals or as a group. However, as Calvin especially emphasized, it is the Spirit's role to unite us to Christ here and now, so that the work that he has accomplished for us, outside of us in history, can be received by us personally and inwardly. We will never appreciate sufficiently the role of the Holy Spirit in our ecclesiology unless we reckon with the real absence of Jesus Christ in the flesh. Yet this secret work of the Spirit within us remains inseparable from the Word, as the Spirit inwardly enlightens and convinces us to embrace the gospel. We are transformed inwardly and personally through an external and public Word. By contrast, "enthusiasm" assumes an "inside-out" approach. Salvation is conceived as an inner experience — a personal relationship with Jesus that is direct and private — that may come to public expression.

Over against the "enthusiasts," Lutheran and Reformed confessions insist that whenever the Scriptures are faithfully expounded, God is the primary speaker and the speech is an effectual means of grace even if the minister were an unbeliever. Following Romans 10:17, the Heidelberg Catechism teaches, the gospel that comes to us from outside of ourselves, through the lips of an ambassador, is actually the means through which the Spirit creates faith in our hearts. Or consider the sacraments. It makes literally all of the difference in the world whether baptism and Communion are the believer's expression of an inner experience and commitment or God's official ratification of his promise.

In this perspective, the movement is from the external ministry of Word and sacrament to the inner response of the covenant people. The true church is visible wherever Christ is proclaimed and delivered to sinners, regardless of the spiritual effects that the Spirit generates. Yet precisely because God's Word is "living and active" and the gospel is "the power of God unto salvation . . . ," it produces its intended effects. It is through this external announcement from a herald that the Spirit creates faith in the heart to confess Christ publicly (Rom. 10:5-17). So it moves from the public and external Word to personal and inward conviction and then back out to public confession and works of love.

Christ established a visible church on the earth, not an invisible movement. Ephesians 4 repeats for emphasis the phrase, "it is he [Christ] who gave" the offices of prophet and apostle and now pastors and teachers for the completion of his body. Calvin explains,

> For although God's power is not bound to outward means, he has nonetheless bound us to this ordinary manner of teaching. Fanatics, refusing to hold fast to it, entangle themselves in many deadly snares. Many are led either by pride, dislike, or rivalry to the conviction that they can profit enough from private reading and meditation; hence they despise public assemblies and deem preaching superfluous. But . . . no one escapes the just penalty of this unholy separation without bewitching himself with pestilent errors and foulest delusions.[40]

Miroslav Volf points out that according to Separatist leader John Smyth, those who are "born again . . . should no longer need means of grace," since the persons of the Godhead "are better than all scriptures, or creatures whatsoever."[41] By contrast, Volf notes, the reformers strongly affirmed God's saving activity through creaturely means — even to the point of calling the church the mother of the faithful.[42]

---

40. John Calvin, *Institutes* 4.1.5.
41. Volf, *After Our Likeness,* pp. 161-62.
42. Volf, *After Our Likeness,* p. 162.

Alas, however, John Smyth seems to have had the last — or, at least, the most recent — word on the matter. William McLoughlin reminds us that the effect of pietism in American religious experience (especially culminating in the Second Great Awakening) was to shift the emphasis away from "collective belief, adherence to creedal standards and proper observance of traditional forms, to the emphasis on individual religious experience."[43] If the Enlightenment shifted "the ultimate authority in religion" from the church to "the mind of the individual," pietism and Romanticism located ultimate authority in the *experience* of the individual.[44] All of this suggests that for some time now, evangelicalism has been as much the facilitator as the victim of modern secularism.

Just as the Spirit's inward call is often contrasted with outward means, evangelicalism celebrates the charismatic leader who needs no formal training or external ecclesiastical ordination to confirm a spontaneous, direct, inner call to ministry. Historians may debate whether the Protestant enthusiasm is more of a consequence than a cause of the distinctively American confidence in intuitive individualism over against external authorities and communal instruction, but the connection seems obvious. In *Head and Heart,* Catholic historian Garry Wills observes,

> The camp meeting set the pattern for credentialing Evangelical ministers. They were validated by the crowd's response. Organizational credentialing, doctrinal purity, personal education were useless here — in fact, some educated ministers had to make a pretense of ignorance. The minister was ordained from below, by the converts he made. This was an even more democratic procedure than electoral politics, where a candidate stood for office and spent some time campaigning. This was a spontaneous and instant proclamation that the Spirit accomplished. The do-it-yourself religion called for a make-it-yourself ministry.[45]

43. William McLoughlin, *Revivals, Awakenings, and Reform* (Chicago: University of Chicago Press, 1980), p. 25. I am grateful to Toby Kurth for providing this and the following reference.

44. Ned C. Landsman, *From Colonials to Provincials: American Thought and Culture, 1680-1760* (New York: Twayne Publishers, 1997; Ithaca, NY: Cornell University Press, 2000), p. 66.

45. Garry Wills, *Head and Heart: American Christianities* (New York: The Penguin Press, 2007), p. 294.

Wills repeats Richard Hofstadter's conclusion that "the star system was not born in Hollywood but on the sawdust trail of the revivalists." Where American Transcendentalism was the version of Romanticism that attracted a wide following among Boston intellectuals, Finney's legacy represents "an alternative Romanticism," a popular version of self-reliance and inner experience, "taking up where Transcendentalism left off."[46] Emerson had written, "The height, the deity of man is to be self-sustained, to need no gift, no foreign force" — no external God, with an external Word and sacraments or formal ministry.[47] And revivalism in its own way was popularizing this distinctly American religion on the frontier.

In the light of this history, Wade Clark Roof's findings are hardly surprising when he reports, "The distinction between 'spirit' and 'institution' is of major importance" to spiritual seekers today.[48] "Spirit is the inner, experiential aspect of religion; institution is the outer, established form of religion."[49] He adds, "Direct experience is always more trustworthy, if for no other reason than because of its 'inwardness' and 'withinness' — two qualities that have come to be much appreciated in a highly expressive, narcissistic culture."[50] In fact, Roof comes close to suggesting that evangelicalism works so well in this kind of culture because it helped to create it.

Stanley Grenz defended this inside-out approach. "Although some evangelicals belong to ecclesiological traditions that understand the church as in some sense a dispenser of grace," he observes, "generally we see our congregations foremost as a fellowship of believers."[51] We share our journeys (our "testimony") of personal transformation (p. 33). Therefore, Grenz celebrates the "fundamental shift . . . from a creed-based to a spirituality-based identity" that is more like medieval mysticism than Protestant orthodoxy (pp. 38, 41). "Consequently, spirituality is inward and quietistic" (pp. 41-42), concerned with combating "the lower nature

46. Wills, *Head and Heart*, p. 302.

47. Quoted in Wills, *Head and Heart*, p. 273.

48. Wade Clark Roof, *A Generation of Seekers: The Spiritual Journeys of the Baby Boom Generation* (San Francisco: HarperCollins, 1993), p. 23.

49. Roof, *Generation of Seekers*, p. 30.

50. Roof, *Generation of Seekers*, p. 67.

51. Stanley Grenz, *Revisioning Evangelical Theology: A Fresh Agenda for the 21st Century* (Downers Grove, IL: InterVarsity, 1993), p. 32. Hereafter, page references will be given parenthetically in the text.

and the world" (p. 44), in "a personal commitment that becomes the ultimate focus of the believer's affections" (p. 45). Nowhere in this account does Grenz locate the origin of faith in an external gospel; rather, faith arises from an inner experience. "Because spirituality is *generated from within the individual,* inner motivation is crucial" — more important, in fact, than "grand theological statements" (p. 46; emphasis added).

> The spiritual life is above all the imitation of Christ. . . . In general we eschew religious ritual. Not slavish adherence to rites, but doing what Jesus would do is our concept of true discipleship. Consequently, most evangelicals neither accept the sacramentalism of many mainline churches nor join the Quakers in completely eliminating the sacraments. We practice baptism and the Lord's Supper, but understand the significance of these rites in a guarded manner. (p. 48)

In any case, he says, these rites are practiced as goads to personal experience and out of obedience to divine command (p. 48). "This view marks a radical shift in the relationship of soteriology and ecclesiology, for it exchanges the priority of the church for the priority of the believer" (p. 51).

> "Get on with the task; get your life in order by practicing the aids to growth and see if you do not mature spiritually," we exhort. In fact, if a believer comes to the point where he or she senses that stagnation has set in, evangelical counsel is to redouble one's efforts in the task of exercising the disciplines. "Check up on yourself," the evangelical spiritual counselor admonishes. (p. 52)

The emphasis on the individual believer is evident, he says, in the expectation to "find a ministry" within the local fellowship (p. 55).

All of this is at odds with an emphasis on doctrine and especially, Grenz adds, an emphasis on "a material and a formal principle" — referring to the Reformation slogans, "sola fide" (justification by Christ alone through faith alone) and "sola scriptura" (by Scripture alone) (p. 62). In spite of the fact that the Scriptures declare that "faith comes by hearing and hearing by the word of Christ," Grenz says, "Faith is by nature immediate" (p. 80). Consistent with his emphasis on the priority of inner experience, Grenz urges "a revisioned understanding of the *nature* of the Bible's authority" (p. 88). Our own religious experience today needs to be included in the process of inspiration (p. 122). Accordingly, Grenz believes that this will "chart the way beyond the evangelical tendency to equate in a simple fashion the revelation of God with the Bible — that is, to make a one-to-one correspondence between the words of the Bible and the very Word of God" (p. 130).[52]

When Luther said that "The church is not a pen-house but a mouth-house" he was pointing up the importance of hearing the Word in the public assembly even over the private reading of the Bible which he had translated into the vernacular.[53] Similarly, the Westminster divines confessed that the Spirit blesses "the reading but especially the preaching of the Word" as a "means of grace" precisely because through it the Spirit is "calling us out of ourselves" to cling to Christ.[54] They were asserting that faithful, meditative, and prayerful reading of Scripture in private or family devotions was essential but nevertheless subordinate to the public ministry of the Word in the common life of the church. Just as the Word creates the community, it can only be truly heard, received, and followed in the concrete covenantal exchanges within that community. In the widely held perspective articulated by Grenz, the visibility of the church is identified more with the inner work of the Spirit than with the means of grace. The result is that the church's visibility is subjective rather than objective and individual rather than corporate. The visibility of the church becomes located in spiritual effects rather than the means of grace that God has promised to make effectual.

Marks vs. Mission

Often today, the ordinary ministry of preaching, baptizing, teaching, and sharing in the Lord's Supper is separated from the mission of the

---

52. At stake in this loss of *sola scriptura* (by Scripture alone) are the corollaries: *solo Christo* (by Christ alone), *sola gratia* (by grace alone), *sola fide* (through faith alone), and *soli Deo gloria* (to God alone be glory). These stakes are not too high for Brian McLaren, for example, who scolds Reformed Christians for "their love-affair with the Latin word 'sola.'" Brian McLaren, *A Generous Orthodoxy* (Grand Rapids: Zondervan, 2004), p. 23.

53. Quoted in Stephen H. Webb, *The Divine Voice: Christian Proclamation and a Theology of Sound* (Grand Rapids: Brazos, 2004), p. 143, from Martin Luther, *Church Postil* of 1522.

54. Westminster Shorter Catechism in *The Book of Confessions* (PCUSA General Assembly, 1991), Q. 89.

church in the world. This is frequently posed in the form of a contrast between "going to church" and "being the church." The church is not a place where certain things happen, we are told, but a people who do certain things.

Although it is often considered new and "emerging," this dichotomy belongs to a long history in radical Protestantism, from Thomas Müntzer to representatives as varied as Charles Finney and Harvey Cox. As George Marsden has shown, the Second Great Awakening is in many respects the common source of both Protestant liberalism and fundamentalism.[55] In *The Secular City* (1965), Cox wrote, "The insistence of the Reformers that the church was 'where the word is rightly preached and the sacraments rightly administered' will simply not do today." Rather, he says, "the church appears" wherever "a new inclusive human community emerges" through social action.[56] It is increasingly common today to hear evangelicals shifting their focus from the uniqueness of Christ's incarnation and redeeming work to talk about the church as a community of disciples extending Christ's incarnation and his redeeming work in the world. Evangelicals have long spoken of "living the gospel," as if our lives could be any more than an often ambiguous testimony to it.

According to Dan Kimball, for example, "We can't *go* to church because *we are* the church."[57] From this Kimball draws the familiar contrast between evangelism (mission) and the marks of the church (means of grace). Appealing to Darrell Guder's *The Missional Church*, Kimball thinks that things went wrong at the Reformation.

> The Reformers, in their effort to raise the authority of the Bible and ensure sound doctrine, defined the marks of a true church: a place where the gospel is rightly preached, the sacraments are rightly administered, and church discipline is exercised. However, over time these marks narrowed the definition of the church itself as a "place where" instead of a "people who are" reality. The word church be-

---

55. George M. Marsden, *The Evangelical Mind and the New School Presbyterian Experience: A Case Study of Thought and Theology in Nineteenth Century America* (New Haven: Yale University Press, 1970).

56. Harvey Cox, *The Secular City* (London: SCM Press, 1965), p. 145.

57. Dan Kimball, *The Emerging Church: Vintage Christianity for New Generations* (Grand Rapids: Zondervan, 2003), p. 91.

came defined as "a place where certain things happen," such as preaching and communion.[58]

However, there are at least three problems with this increasingly widespread thesis. *First, it confuses the law and the gospel.* Unless the church is first of all a place where God judges and justifies the guilty, renewing them by his Word and Spirit, it cannot be a people who constitute anything more than another special interest group. Believers are called to do a great many things, but this is the third use of the law, not the gospel. The logic of the apostle in Romans 10 moves seamlessly from the content of the gospel (grace, Christ, and faith) to the means (hearing Christ proclaimed). Yet the oft-quoted line attributed to Francis of Assisi, "Always preach the gospel, and when necessary use words," assumes that we are the good news. Our good works bring glory to God and service to our neighbor. They flow from the gospel and adorn the gospel, but to suggest that they are in any way part of the gospel itself is a fatal confusion.

Second, this view introduces a dilemma between the church's essence and its mission that is not found in the New Testament. There is not first of all a church assembling by its own decision and then certain things that the church does. Rather, the church itself comes into being, is sustained, and grows, through the same Word that it proclaims to the world. Wherever this gospel concerning Christ is proclaimed to sinners, and ratified in the sacraments, a fragile piece of this passing evil age becomes a theater for God's performance and the site of a mysterious intrusion of the powers of the age to come. In that precarious crevice between these two ages, a church is born, grows, and becomes an embassy of Christ's heavenly reign on earth. Christ himself instituted a visible new covenant assembly, delivering not only its message but its public rites and offices.

From the Great Commission and the Book of Acts, we hear of a kingdom that descends from heaven and expands to every nation precisely through the marks of preaching, sacrament, and discipline. There are many things besides these marks that identify a *healthy* church, such as the gifts of hospitality, generosity, administration, and service. However, all of these gifts are given and strengthened through the Word and the sacraments. Hence, a church that lacks *friendliness* is

---

58. Kimball, *Emerging Church,* p. 93.

unhealthy, but a church that lacks the *Word* is *not a church.* And a church that is not missional is not faithfully proclaiming the Word, baptizing, and teaching all that Christ delivered, just as a church that is not faithful in executing these marks is not missional.

We do not need a proliferation of marks (almost all of which shift the focus from God's action to our inner experience and activity), but to fulfill the Great Commission each week, delivering Christ to the sheep already gathered ("to you and your children") and "to those who are far off . . ." (Acts 2:39). Where confessional churches sometimes fail by losing their missional zeal "for all who are far off," revivalism creates a revolving door, as "you and your children" starve under a diet of often unscriptural imperatives abstracted from gospel indicatives.

Third, this view confuses the church-as-gathered with the church-as-scattered. Or, to put it differently, it tends to assimilate the visible church to the invisible church. We do not have to choose between the church as place and as people. Because it is first of all a place where God is at work, it becomes a people who leave the assembly as forgiven, renewed, and strengthened disciples who are prepared to love and serve their neighbors in the world. Of course, the church is not a building, but it *is* a public assembly where the Triune God is the primary actor. We are not the church merely as individuals and our private spiritual disciplines and moral activity are effects of grace, not the means of grace. Therefore, we must *go* to church if we are to *be* the church. The suggestion that we cannot go to church because we are the church invites the obvious question as to why we should participate regularly in church services at all. As George Barna has reminded us, resources for personal spirituality and social action may be found on any number of Internet sites. However, if the public service is the place where the Triune God is the playwright, central character, and casting director in the drama of redemption, then a new society emerges that participates even now in the powers of the age to come. We are not "self-feeders." The church is the creation of the Word, not only initially but throughout its growth in history.

The church gathers to receive God's judgment and forgiveness and, to hear an external Word, to receive it as it is ratified in the sacraments, to indwell it through teaching, fellowship, singing, and the prayers. And then, renewed with God's saving gifts, the church is scattered into the world as salt and light. In relation to God and his gifts, we are passive recipients; in relation to the claim of our neighbors, we are active distributors of God's gifts, in both our witness and service in our daily callings. God works from the outside in, not from the inside out. It is a public faith that creates a personal response, not a personal faith that creates a public response.

Conclusion

In my view, evangelicalism remains an important gathering place or rallying point for Christians from a variety of churches. Yet it is not merely an empty space. It is dominated by ecclesiological assumptions that often work against as well as for the cause of the church to which Christ pledged his undying presence. To the extent that evangelicalism knows its place, as a non-ecclesiastical meeting place for mutual edification and admonition, it remains important. Yet to the extent that it substitutes itself for the church and its parachurch ministries for the ordinary ministry of Word and sacrament, it subverts the intention of its Lord.

In treating the continuing significance of evangelicalism, I have suggested on occasion the analogy of an old village green, framed by various churches.[59] Evangelicalism is not the Big Tent or the cathedral that reduces these churches to chapels, but the place where they spill out from their own churches into mutual fellowship, encouragement, admonition, service, and witness. While avoiding a sectarianism that shuns the green, we should also recognize that it is in those particular churches where our Savior promises to establish and increase his gracious empire.

C. S. Lewis employed a similar analogy, whose intent seems too often ignored:

I hope no reader will suppose that "mere" Christianity is here put forward as an alternative to the creeds of the existing communions — as if a man could adopt it in preference to Congregationalism or Greek Orthodoxy or anything else. It is more like a hall out of which doors open into several rooms. If I can bring anyone into that hall I shall have done what I attempted. But it is in the rooms, not in the hall,

---

59. Michael Horton, "Is Evangelicalism Reformed? Re-evaluating the Marsden-Dayton Debate," *Christian Scholars' Review* 2 (Winter 2001): 3-15.

that there are fires and chairs and meals. The hall is a place to wait in, a place from which to try the various doors, not a place to live in. For that purpose the worst of the rooms (whichever that may be) is, I think, preferable. . . . And above all, you must be asking which door is the true one; not which pleases you best by its paint and panelling.[60]

This essay has not taken up inconsistencies in the history of Reformed churches. A covenantal ecclesiology is as easily subverted by ethnocentricity and mere formalism as by individualism and enthusiasm. We have not lived up to our professed ecclesiological values. Positively, churches in the Reformed tradition have not only contributed to evangelical coalitions over the last three centuries, but have benefited significantly from mutual encouragement and critique.

Nevertheless, the church is not a dead planet. For all of its weeds, it is this field that Christ has purchased with his own life and in which he has planted his wheat that even now is growing into a worldwide harvest. And it is to this real world that we must return for our own life as well as our corporate witness. For all of her failures, the church is the mother of the faithful and only under her care can we flourish as part of that new creation that Christ has inaugurated by his resurrection from the dead. There is life in the real church, however devastated the landscape. There are fertile valleys and rivers. Her pools are not a mirage but are fountains where the dead are raised and the thirsty drink to their heart's content.

60. C. S. Lewis, *Mere Christianity* (New York: Macmillan, 1980), Preface, p. 11.

A Post-Partisan Partisan Ecclesiology

Richard Lints

Our public discourse about diversity runs hot and cold. When the language of diversity provides resources to restrain the abuse of power, we seem to embrace it heartily. We believe the power of the American president is kept in check by the diverse branches of government: Congress and the Courts. A diverse electorate also keeps it in check. We tend to believe that the hegemonic power of one person or group over another is an evil restrained by the accountability of democratic structures. But democracy can also be experienced as anarchic and as expressing its consensus in morally repugnant ways.[1] Most citizens of the late modern world believe that a nation of slave-owners was not virtuous merely because there was a diverse social consensus about slavery at some point in the history of the West. Diversity is not always a virtue if virtue itself is left behind in the cacophony of diverse voices.[2]

Mapping diversity within the church follows analogous lines. Democratic intuitions within congregations can lead to greater accountability of pastoral powers. Clergy abuses as forms of hegemonic power of one person over others are less likely in an ecclesiastical polity where authority is rooted in the private conscience of its members. But

---

1. Joseph Ellis captures well the two opposing sides of democracy in his *American Creation: Triumphs and Tragedies at the Founding of the Republic* (New York: Knopf, 2007).

2. Jeffrey Stout argues that democracy without a constraining tradition(s) will inevitably veer toward moral anarchy and polarization. See his *Democracy and Tradition* (Princeton: Princeton University Press, 2004). Much of what follows takes initial clues from Stout's argument, though the application in this essay is toward a churchly polity rather than a national polity.

ecclesial democracy often runs amok at the other end of the spectrum, viz. when whole communities or congregations are captured by the cultural breezes blowing through them.[3] Groups freed to determine their own destiny may well lack sufficient wisdom to do this wisely. The pressures of conformity in a commercialized world are as deeply felt by congregations as they are by individuals.

Widespread concerns have been articulated in our time about the chaotic conflicts seemingly hardwired into our public consciousness. These conflicts are experienced most acutely in the public political discourse as mediated through the popular media. The deeply partisan nature of politics has produced a certain cynicism in the populace at large about the possibilities of any structural alternatives. Though freedom had been viewed as an abiding virtue of public polities through most of the twentieth century, as the twenty-first century has dawned, there are grave doubts about the ability to keep those freedoms from imploding in endless and bitter partisanship. The yearning for a post-partisan style of public discourse has been embraced not only by those in the muddled middle of our conflicts, but also by political partisans tired of the endless strife and the inability to end the policy paralysis. The sad irony is that the hankering for a post-partisan political culture has resulted in deeper forms of partisanship.[4] Americans appear to want a post-partisan set of politicians with one proviso — that all politicians agree with them. Whether on the left or right, the political will for compromise and reconciliation has been met with a surprising lack of enthusiasm.[5]

Politics is not the key that unlocks all cultural doors, but it is surprisingly reflective of how Americans deal with diversity. When it suits

3. Nathan Hatch's brilliant work, *The Democratization of American Christianity* (New Haven: Yale University Press, 1989), makes this a compelling argument against the backdrop of colonial American religious history.

4. *New York Times* columnist David Brooks ("Getting Obama Right," *New York Times*, OpEd, March 12, 2010, accessed at: http://www.nytimes.com/2010/03/12/opinion/12brooks.html?ref=davidbrooks) has chronicled the strikingly different portrayals of President Obama during his first year in office. Brooks pointed at the surprisingly entrenched partisan nature of national political discourse about Obama in the aftermath of the election cycle of 2008 when there was such public outcry for a new "post-partisan Washington D.C."

5. James Davison Hunter draws out this dilemma in sociological terms in his *To Change the World: The Irony, Tragedy, and Possibility of Christianity in the Late Modern World* (New York: Oxford University Press, 2010).

their interests, diversity is an unqualified good. When it impedes their private interests, diversity is considered an unmitigated disaster. Disparate voices that keep opponents at bay may serve the common good. But those same disparate voices can also bring every agenda to a standstill. This is as true in church politics as it is in national politics. Intuitions about politics bleed over into ecclesiology very naturally in the contemporary world.

In what follows I want to lay out a theological framework for thinking about unity and diversity within the church — not simply within congregations but also across denominations and networks of churches. The question of the unity of the body of Christ has become a compelling question in our time because of the fractious nature of our ecclesial discourse.[6] As that discourse has developed, it has been the Protestant conflicts in particular which appear to manifest most clearly the broken state of the church. Anglicans have been notoriously at odds with each other.[7] The mainline Protestant bodies, Presbyterian, Methodist, and Congregational, each have major schisms looming on the horizon.[8] The evangelical denominations, though growing and thriving, have been notoriously uninterested in ecumenical unities across the breadth of Christ's church. This question of unity then, for different reasons, has become the Achilles heel of Protestant churches and Protestant evangelical ecclesiologies in particular.[9] Protestants, unlike their Roman Catholic or Eastern Orthodox counterparts, have too often avoided the theological questions regarding the

---

6. Martin Marty notes, "As theologians in the church, we deal with polarities: the ontological nature of the church and empirical reality, being and choosing, unity and diversity, given and novel. Our culture is all on the side of the empirical, on choosing, on diversity, and the novel. Our increasingly postmodern culture lacks 'meta-narratives.' Without these known and shared sacred stories, we become increasingly fragmented." As cited in Mark Hanson, "The Future of Denominations: Asking Uppercase Questions," *Word & World* 25, no. 1 (Winter 2005): 8.

7. See Ephraim Radner and Philip Turner, *The Fate of Communion: The Agony of Anglicanism and the Future of a Global Church* (Grand Rapids: Eerdmans, 2006).

8. See *Church, Identity, and Change: Theology and Denominational Structures in Unsettled Times,* ed. David Roozen and James Nieman (Grand Rapids: Eerdmans, 2005) for a helpful collection of essays detailing the fracturing nature of the mainline churches.

9. Many of the recent notable evangelical converts to Roman Catholicism cite the issue of schism as one of their primary reasons for returning to Rome. A thoughtful example of this can be found in Francis Beckwith, *Return to Rome: Confessions of an Evangelical Catholic* (Grand Rapids: Brazos Press, 2009).

unity of the church, and have settled (so the sentiment goes) for enduring divisions.[10]

The question of unity, however, is only one half of the ecclesial issue.[11] The question of diversity must be addressed in any adequate account of how churches relate to each other, and how the churches relate
to the Church. In an era that has privileged diversity to an extreme, the
ecclesial reaction has too often been to subsume the fundamental
questions of unity and diversity under the umbrella of unity.[12] The fol-

10. I do not intend to address the related issue of ecumenical relations with Rome or
Constantinople. The working framework of this essay could be extended to that issue, but
the focus here will be on peculiarly Protestant notions of the unity and catholicity of the
church. On the related issue from a free church ecclesiology see Miroslav Volf, *After Our
Likeness: The Church as the Image of the Trinity* (Grand Rapids: Eerdmans, 1997). From the
perspective of a reformed church ecclesiology see Michael S. Horton, *People and Place: A
Covenant Ecclesiology* (Louisville: Westminster/John Knox, 2007).

11. The theological depictions of the unity of the church have historically gravitated
around the relationship of Christ to the church, in particular to the manner in which the
church is viewed as the body of Christ. Augustine's argument that the church exists in
Christ as *totus Christus* inevitably homogenized the church's unity since the church was
nothing less than the very real body of Christ on earth. Protestant discussions of
ecclesiology have most often been uncomfortable with the radical Augustinian equation
of Christ and the church. A helpful summary of this theological unease can be found in
Michael Horton, *People and Place: A Covenant Ecclesiology* (Louisville: Westminster/John
Knox, 2008). See especially chapter 6, "*Totus Christus:* One and Many."

12. Admittedly there are some evangelicals who have gone in the opposite direction,
too strongly affirming all manner of diversity. John Franke writes, "As Christian communities formed in a variety of cultural situations, they established traditions that became
integral to their cultural and communal outlook. These traditions shaped their understanding of the Christian faith, their reading of the Bible, and the particular shape of their
witness to the gospel. This plurality is part of the work of the Spirit in guiding the church
into truth and serves as a defining mark of the Christian tradition." *Manifold Witness: The
Plurality of Truth* (Nashville: Abingdon, 2009), p. 33. Surely evangelical Protestants have
been slow to affirm the plurality of interpretative traditions within Protestantism. In the
last half-century, ecumenical conflicts and conversations with Roman Catholicism have
put evangelicals on the defensive when it comes to defending the unity of the church.
This has sometimes led to an over-spiritualizing of the unity of the church. Franke and
other emergents have rightly called the wider Protestant movement to think theologically
about the plurality of church communities within Protestantism not simply as an obstacle to overcome but also as an expression of the situatedness of all ecclesial bodies. The
danger, however, is equating plurality with the ongoing work of the Spirit. Not all contextual differences are appropriate to the well-being of the church and therefore not all contextual differences ought to be attributed to the work of the Spirit. Contextual distortions
of the gospel are as frequent as contextual appropriations of the gospel. It is the gospel

lowing sketch of diversity in an evangelical ecclesiology is intended to take seriously the present cultural landscape as it inevitably filters the way we interpret the biblical material on unity and diversity.

Thinking wisely about diversity requires in turn thinking in diverse ways about diversity. The models by which we conceptualize our lives together will not fit every situation nor will one map fit all landscapes.[13] Circumstances change and the temptations in one context are different from another. Trying a "one-size-fits-all" template upon the structures of our lives inevitably distorts the places where diversity is appropriate and constructive and flattens out the places where diversity may be dangerous and destructive. The rhetoric of pluralism is a popular mode by which our culture talks about diversity. But the language of pluralism often masks the many different kinds of differences we encounter, and thus also submerges the diversely appropriate ways we might deal with different kinds of diversity.

To some the language of pluralism signals the unmitigated disaster of postmodern democratic culture. To others the language of pluralism protects all that we should cherish in a modern democracy. Oftentimes the heated rhetoric of our public discourse does not allow us to find the virtues of diversity which we might hold in common, the vices of other forms of diversity about which reconciliation is needed, and a host of other forms of diversity about which we will have to learn to deal with wisely.[14]

---

therefore which finally must serve as the criterion for better or worse contextualizations. It is the gospel which is the norm which norms the cultural norms.

13. Richard Mouw writes instructively of different kinds of cultural diversity in his essay, "On Creation's 'Several Parts': Modal Diversity in Dooyeweerd's Social Thought," in *Christian Philosophy at the Close of the Twentieth Century: Assessment and Perspective,* ed. Sander Griffioen and Bert Balk (Kampen: Kok, 1995), pp. 175-83. Mouw is one of the few seeking to problematize the discussion of pluralism not by dismissing it, but rather by recognizing its complexity. I attempt to draw some analogies to the issue of ecclesiology in what follows.

14. The very best account of religious diversity in American history is William R. Hutchison, *Religious Pluralism in America* (New Haven: Yale University Press, 2003). Hutchison deftly describes the diverse ways in which religious diversity has been understood across the ages relative to the common national polity of religious tolerance.

Models of Unity and Diversity

Throughout the biblical witness large constructs illuminate the nature of unity and diversity in the church. The central ones are clearly the analogies of relationships in which God embeds us: Marriage, Trinity, and Community. Prior to analyzing those let me focus on an underlying form of unity and diversity in the Scripture, which often goes unnoticed in discussions about the church. This has to do with the ways in which the story of redemption is narrated across the breadth of the canon.[15] The Scriptures were written across a millennium and a half and serve as an authorized witness to a surprising unity of God's redeeming activity which develops across diverse ages and in diverse contexts. No single literary genre finally captures the richness of this divine redemption, and none are thereby insignificant. The grand historical narratives, the epic poetry, the highly symbolic apocalyptic books, biographically oriented gospels, and personal and didactic epistles — all combine to remind us that redemption is not exhausted by any single genre. The "gospel" can surely be summarized in a variety of forms and embraced with assurance, but our articulation of it ought to strive to retain its robust depth and its surprising simplicity. The many textured treatments of redemption in the Scriptures call us to think about unity and diversity in surprising ways.[16]

The fact that we have such rich diversity of forms in the canon strongly argues that whatever models of unity are embraced, they must be sufficiently complex to account for the surprising diversity in the divine communication of redemption. Wisdom suggests that knowing the difference between gospel and epistle, between apocalyptic literature and historical narrative, is essential to understanding why all these diverse books belong to one canon.[17] The good news of redemption is

15. See Christopher Wright, *The Mission of God: Unlocking the Bible's Grand Narrative* (Downers Grove, IL: InterVarsity Press, 2006).

16. The richness of this unity and diversity is nicely captured in Douglas Stuart and Gordon Fee, *How to Read the Bible Book by Book: A Guided Tour* (Grand Rapids: Zondervan, 2002).

17. See Nicholas Wolterstorff, "The Unity Behind the Canon," in *One Scripture or Many? Canon in Biblical, Theological and Philosophical Perspectives,* ed. Christine Helmer and Christof Landmesser (Oxford: Oxford University Press, 2004), pp. 217-32, for an extended argument for the overarching unity of Scripture as a single work of God that yet is also a multitude of authorial collections.

one story whose plot line is simple (not simplistic) and from another angle it is richly complex (not contradictory). The unity of the canon and the diversity of genres in the canon keep these realities connected in appropriate ways.

By analogy, the church may be thought of as a distinct genre in which the gospel is written and lived out. It is a living text, whose authority derives not from the immediate inspiration of the Holy Spirit but rather from the ongoing providential guidance of the Spirit.[18] The church's identity is simple (in the call to be faithful to the gospel) and richly complex (in the need to contextualize the gospel across many ages and infinitely diverse cultural settings). Its mission is derived from the apostolic mission in proclaiming the risen Christ and faithfully submitting to Christ's Lordship.[19] Its proclamation is articulated in as many diverse languages as there are people groups who speak with distinctive tongues.[20]

The diversity of the church is thus grounded theologically in the progress of redemption narrated across the canon. The church's boundaries must be as wide and deep as the Scriptures, even as the church gives voice to the way in which those Scriptures provide the interpretive boundaries for themselves.[21] The church can bind the conscience no further than the Scriptures do nor should it suppose that the

18. Gabriel Fackre, *The Church: Signs of the Spirit and Signs of the Times* (Grand Rapids: Eerdmans, 2007), carefully connects the enduring work of the Spirit in the mission of the church and the changing contexts in which that work is brought to life.

19. Cf. Edmund Clowney, *The Doctrine of the Church* (Philadelphia: Presbyterian and Reformed, 1969), for a thoughtful traditional defense of the Christological foundation of the church.

20. A representative evangelical statement to this effect can be found in *Explaining the Gospel in Today's World,* ed. the Lausanne Committee for World Evangelization (London: Scripture Union, 1978).

21. Local churches inevitably use two different kinds of stories to understand themselves. They use narratives about their own local history. They also routinely use biblical narratives to describe their identity. This is evident in their sermons and their sacraments most especially. Evangelical churches have also woven these biblical narratives into the glue that binds the small groups of the church together. By means of this local churches express their particularity and their universality. The churches are part of the One Church by means of a common universal (biblical) narrative, even if they are also richly diverse in their own peculiar local narratives. Cf. David Kelsey, "A Theological Curriculum About and Against the Church," in *Beyond Clericalism: The Congregation as a Focus for Theological Education,* ed. Joseph C. Hough and Barbara Wheeler (Atlanta: Scholars Press, 1988), pp. 37-48.

binding occurs outside of God's covenantal communication of salvation by the finished work of Christ in the power of the Spirit.

This would require that we understand the confessional distinctives of the different Protestant traditions not primarily in sociological terms, but in theological ones — as their attempt at reading the Scriptures faithfully. This would permit the different traditions to bump into each other by means of reading the Scriptures together. It would also problematize the drawing of confessional boundaries outside the express boundaries of the Scriptures. When the distinctives of any tradition are interpreted sociologically, then pastoral wisdom would be the primary arbiter in adjudicating the (in)appropriateness of the distinctives in that particular cultural context.[22] So for example the frequency with which the Lord's Supper is practiced may be interpreted as an issue of contextualization (traditional cultures require more traditional practices, more democratic cultures require less ritual and tradition) or as a matter of theology (the connection of Word and Sacrament). The same practice may have different reasons that ground them. How churches bump into each other requires that those diverse grounds be treated appropriately.

Analogies of Marriage and the Trinity

The primary analogy to the unity and diversity of the church in Scripture is that of marriage. It appears in the opening chapters in the Bible. Genesis 1 narrates the creation not of one individual, but of two diverse persons who nonetheless are united by a relationship into "one flesh." They are different but they belong to each other. Male and female are created as beings who offer something the other does not have. They find satisfaction in the intimacy of their union that is richer by virtue of their differences.[23] We might say the primal idea of "person" from the beginning of Scripture is a "being-in-relation." In some important sense, persons find out who they are only in relation to another person

22. On the theological notions of wisdom, see Daniel J. Treier, *Virtue and the Voice of God: Toward Theology as Wisdom* (Grand Rapids: Eerdmans, 2006).

23. Gender differences are notoriously difficult to spell out beyond the obvious physical differences of the sexes. However these differences are understood, the important claim from Genesis 2 still stands, Man and Woman were/are different, and that difference is intended to enrich their union.

who is different from them. The words instituting marriage in Genesis 2 function not merely to cement a social contract between consenting parties, but rather as a deeply theological reflection on their created identity. Marriage is a significant recognition of this unity-in-diversity across the canon.

Scripture presents human persons as "social" in the sense that individuals gain an identity in relation to the wider network of relationships of which they are a part. Joseph was deeply rooted in the family line of his father (Jacob), his grandfather (Isaac), and his great-grandfather (Abraham) because of the enduring nature of the covenant made originally with Abraham. He took clues about his mission and his calling from the unique relationships of his family tree. His identity was formed also in part from the relationship to his brothers, who sold him into slavery. Joseph's time in Egypt left a lasting imprint on his identity. Joseph's social networks were small (e.g., his immediate family), midsize (e.g., tribe and clan), and large (e.g., Egyptian empire as well as the family line of four generations). These social networks were always interpreted in the Scripture relative to the covenant with Abraham. The "sociality" of Joseph's identity amounted to the claim that he was part of a history of covenant relationships that were situated in a peculiar time and place.[24]

That history of covenant relationships with Abraham, Isaac, Jacob, and Joseph served as a foundational history for Israel and were interpreted by the apostles as foundational also for the church.[25] That covenant history frames the social networks in which Christian identity is embedded even today. Israel's patriarchs are part of the story of our past and inform our lives. Hebrews 11 lists a set of figures which are to be emulated by Christians because of their faith and it is the patriarchs in particular that are highlighted as the line from which were "born descendants as many as the stars of heaven and as many as the innumerable grains of sand by the seashore."[26] The New Testament argues that we belong to this line. In Christ, we are now members of this family. This social network is now our social network. It is not our natural family of origin, but it is our theologically adopted family. We are embed-

---

24. Cf. Joyce Baldwin, *The Message of Genesis 12–50: From Abraham to Joseph* (Downers Grove, IL: InterVarsity Press, 1986).

25. Acts 3, Romans 4, Galatians 3, Hebrews 6.

26. Hebrews 11:12.

ded in the story that leads from Abraham to the cross and resurrection of Jesus and which will find its consummation in the new heavens and new earth. The story of this adopted family has become by grace our story line also. But we should not understand that story to entail that we dress like Abraham, or travel by caravan like Abraham, or speak in Abraham's mother tongue. Belonging to the line of Abraham is not the story of adopting a particular cultural expression of that story.

Hebrews 11 argues that there are important differences from Abraham critical to our identity. Abraham believed in an inheritance he could not see. He went to a place "not knowing where he was going." By contrast, our inheritance is now rooted in the finished work of Christ, which has been seen. Our identity is rooted in a story whose plot has progressed beyond the episode narrating the life and times of Abraham.[27] The Abrahamic chapter is part of our narrative but there are other chapters introducing elements into our identity not present in that early chapter with Abraham. The fulfillment of the covenant promises to Abraham has been revealed in Christ and that fulfillment is part of the foundation of our Christian identity.

Our unity and diversity as Christians are rooted in a social network that extends across time. We also confess that they are rooted in another kind of sociality, viz., the peculiar relationship of creature to Creator. If God is, as the Bible surely affirms, in some sense ontologically prior to us, then it is also the case that God is the source of all that we mean by "person." This argues for the distinctive and particular relationship to God as that which most fully captures the identity of personhood. God is tri-personal and we are (dim) mirrors of that. It is appropriate to say, Christianly speaking, that our relationship to God is not only that which gives identity to humans, but also that which constitutes our personhood.[28] Our existing as persons is rooted in our

27. This is not a new insight that emerged in the present era, as is often assumed. Representatively see the older work, Francis Foulkes, *The Acts of God: A Study of the Basis of Typology in the Old Testament* (London: Tyndale, 1940).

28. Personhood is here distinguished from human nature. Personhood is a reference simply to the ways in which identity and self-consciousness go hand in hand. A full theory of human nature would consider all those attributes, which human persons share in common. David Kelsey makes a compelling case that Scripture does not give us a rich account of human nature. It does not have much to say about how embodiment is to be articulated, or how brain waves function, or how human rationality grasps the external world. See his massive two-volume theological anthropology, *Eccentric Existence: A Theo-*

relation-to-God. It is also true to say asymmetrically that God's identity is not rooted in a relation-to-humanity. God's identity is rooted in the triune relationships that exist prior to and apart from creation. The very permanence of God as "three-persons-in-eternal-communion-with-each-other" grounds the independence of God from human person-hood.[29] By contrast, it is the very transitory character of human person-hood that grounds our dependence on the Triune Creator. The central consequence of this is that God enters into personal relationships with us because God is personal and he has created us as persons.[30] Those personal relationships are grounded in God's covenant with Adam, with Abraham, with Moses, with David, and ultimately with Jesus. The covenant framework gives shape to the personal relationship of God to his creatures. In the covenant God speaks in ways that reveal the genuine nature of mercy and justice. God promises blessings and curses to his covenant partners. And in Christ, God fulfills the covenant promises and gives us a glimpse of eternal communion with him.

Lest we become too enamored with the similarities of human personhood and divine personhood, we must remember that in the mystery of the Godhead there are not three individual Gods but one God in three persons. Immediately comes the caution of speaking too fully about the inter-Trinitarian life of the Godhead. Trying to remove the veil behind this great mystery tempts in either of two directions in the search for theological clarity about unity and diversity in human communities. It is possible to privilege the three persons of the Triune God in such a fashion that individual (and communal) diversity always trumps the overarching unity of God. Likewise it is possible to privilege the oneness of God's being in such a fashion that there is no room for diversity of any interesting kind.[31] Keeping the tension in the mystery

---

logical Anthropology (Louisville: Westminster/John Knox, 2009). I am arguing here that Scripture does give us a robust account of personhood and personal identity in theological perspective. See also my "Imaging and Idolatry: The Sociality of Personhood in the Canon," in *Personal Identity in Theological Perspective,* ed. Richard Lints, Michael Horton, and Mark Talbot (Grand Rapids: Eerdmans, 2006).

29. See Colin Gunton, *The Triune Creator* (Grand Rapids: Eerdmans, 1998).

30. It is worth noting here Karl Barth's well-known insistence that the divine plural in Genesis 1:26-27 is a reference to the tri-personal nature of God. See his *Church Dogmatics,* III/1, *The Doctrine of Creation,* ed. G. W. Bromiley and T. F. Torrance (Edinburgh: T&T Clark, 1958), pp. 191-93.

31. Volf writes, "to think in Trinitarian ways means to escape the dichotomy between

of the triunity of God is difficult but important in order to prevent the theological pendulum from swinging too far to one side or the other.[32]

In addition caution is necessary because analogies between the divine and the human are always delicate. There is a great conceptual chasm between the infinite, omniscient, and omnipotent God and finite and limited human agents.[33] There is some analogy between the two because there is some reflection of God in human persons. The book of Genesis is clear that humans, created in the image of God, are "like" God. They are not God but they are like God in some respects. Like all analogies, this analogy breaks down if pressed too far.[34] Knowing the limits to the analogy is key to understanding the analogy in the first place. When the rhetorical question is asked of Job in the whirlwind, "Have you an arm like God, and can you thunder with a voice like his?" (Job 40:9), the analogy moves in two directions, from Job to God and from God to Job. The "arm" of God is a reference by analogy that compares human strength to divine might. The "thunderous voice" is a reference by analogy contrasting the power of divine speech to the impotence of Job. Quite obviously the analogies also break down if pressed too far. God is not an embodied person with arms, nor does Job have vocal cords capable of producing thunder. The conclusion is straightforward. Humans are like God in some respects, and different from God in some respects.

---

universalization and pluralization. If unity and multiplicity are equiprimal in God, then He is the ground of both unity and multiplicity. Since God is the one God, reality does not degenerate into individual scenes like a bad play; yet since the one God is a communion of the divine persons, the world drama does not degenerate into a boring monologue." *After Our Likeness*, p. 193.

32. See Colin Gunton, *The One, the Three and the Many: God, Creation and the Culture of Modernity* (Cambridge: Cambridge University Press, 1993). Gunton argued that Western theology until recently privileged the oneness of God as the means to protect the uniformity of culture. In late modernity the pendulum swung in the opposite direction to underwrite the embrace of pluralism.

33. Cf. *Philosophical and Theological Essays on the Trinity*, ed. Thomas McCall and Michael Rea (New York: Oxford University Press, 2009), for extended discussions of the tensions with Trinitarian analogies of community. The social Trinitarian strategy tends to privilege the relations of the three persons of the Godhead while the Latin Trinitarian strategy tends to privilege the ontic unity of the Godhead.

34. A helpful discussion of the limits of the doctrine of analogy is Laurence Hemming, "*Analogia non Entis sed Entitatis:* The Ontological Consequences of the Doctrine of Analogy," *International Journal of Systematic Theology* 6, no. 2 (April 2004): 118-29.

Affirming that God is a divine community encourages an affirmation that there is a reflection of communal life among humans, but there is also a sense in which it must not undermine important differences between the divine community and human communities.[35] Human communities are not infinite. Human communities are always embodied. Human communities are always gendered. Human communities on this side of the grave are always corrupt to some extent. Recognizing similarities and differences is crucial to understanding both the way in which human communities function to illuminate the being of God in constructive ways and the potential of communities to distort the Creator's imprint.

It must also be said that God experiences diversity differently than we do as humans. There is no fundamental conflict of perspectives in the Godhead. This is grounded in the claim that God is one and in God there is no corruption. If we take seriously the human experience of Jesus, we must nonetheless affirm that there is a mystery in the tension between the desire of Jesus not to suffer on the cross and the desire of Jesus to be faithful to his Father's will regarding the cross. When Jesus prayed to the Father, "Not my will, but your will be done" the gospels revealed that there were different perspectives between God the Father and God the Son at that juncture in redemptive history by virtue of the incarnate experience of the Son.[36] This does not entail a fundamental conflict of perspectives between the two. However the tension is explained, the consequence is that the divine community expresses a unity in diversity in its relationships, as it is known in the pages of Scripture.

An important canonical consequence of being created-in-relationship-to-God is that humans are created to be in community with those who are also created-in-relationship-to-God. They are not created to be anonymous but rather to be in relationship with those who are in relationship to God. The created order manifests a natural interdependence of humans with other humans. Belonging to others is a function of what it means to be human. Personal identity grows from the communities in which persons belong. Each person takes clues that tell them who they are from those around them. They identify

35. Ironically, one of the most influential treatments in the West of the analogy between divine and human communities can be found in the Eastern Orthodox theologian, John Zizioulas, *Being as Communion: Studies in Personhood and the Church* (Crestwood, NY: St. Vladimir's Seminary Press, 1985).

36. Cf. Matthew 26:39, Mark 14:36, and Luke 22:42.

those to whom they belong by means of vocation or location or education — or any other of an almost infinite number of variables.

There has been a comeback of interest in communities in the West in the last generation or so. It has been accompanied by a corresponding suspicion about older notions of "individualism." The pendulum has swung in our public conscience toward notions of personhood rooted in communities and away from Cartesian "solitary minds."[37] Christians ought to celebrate this swinging of the pendulum in part because it opens the door to thinking more clearly about the nature of our unity and diversity as created human communities framed by the Scriptures.[38]

True in each of those dimensions is the echo of other voices heard in a person's words about themselves. Each person carries on an internal conversation with themselves in large measure as a part of the conversation of the wider relevant community of which they are a part. Running through their thoughts and actions are the phrases and perspectives of the voices of many others. These relevant communities inevitably contain important diversities against which each person bumps into. These are differences of belief and behavior about vices and virtues, about wisdom and foolishness, about things that matter and those that don't. Bumping up against these differences is vital to our flourishing as divinely constituted persons.

Our particular concern in this essay is the distinctive form of human communities found in the church. The Scriptures portray the identity of church community in ways that should seem foreign to modern Western ears. The corporate character of Israel's identity as God's people lacks the individual autonomy so prevalent in contemporary democracies. Those who have been reconciled to God in Christ likewise belong to each other in peculiarly premodern ways.[39] In the New Testament relationships were defined by a uniqueness of the family tree to which people belonged, not according to inherited genes, but by virtue

37. The phrase is borrowed from William Barrett, *Death of the Soul: From Descartes to the Computer* (New York: Anchor Books, 1986).

38. There is also cause for suspicions in some of the recent revival of communitarian constructs of human identity that problematize any remnant of individual identity. For these cautions see Miroslav Volf, *Exclusion and Embrace: A Theological Exploration of Identity, Otherness, and Reconciliation* (Nashville: Abingdon Press, 1996).

39. I make this case at greater length in my "To Whom Does the Text Belong? Communities of Interpretation and the Interpretation of Communities," in *The Scripture Project,* ed. D. A. Carson (Grand Rapids: Eerdmans, forthcoming).

of a common theological inheritance. It was the great treasure of the gospel which the people of God in the new covenant inherited and which defined their life together.[40]

Those who have been reconciled to God in Christ belong to each other in a peculiar way. Their relationships are defined by the uniqueness of the family tree they belong to — not according to inherited genes, but by virtue of a common theological inheritance. It is the great treasure of the gospel which they have inherited and which defines their life together. They may wear the same clothes, speak the same language, and live in similar places, but none of those characteristics define their connection to each other. In fact those characteristics are often a hindrance to our life-together as Christians, for they can deceive us into thinking that Christian community is built around similarities of fashion or language or location.[41]

Peter's first authoritative proclamation of the gospel in Jerusalem at Pentecost carried with it indications that the church would not be bounded by social location or ethnicity. Luke records for us that Peter's audience in Jerusalem included "Parthians and Medes and Elamites and residents of Mesopotamia, Judea and Cappadocia, Pontus and Asia, Phrygia and Pamphylia, Egypt and the parts of Libya belonging to Cyrene, and visitors from Rome, both Jews and proselytes, Cretans and Arabians."[42] The miracle at Pentecost lay in part with the proclamation of redemption in multiple languages among persons of many diverse ethnicities.

At a critical time in the life of the young Jerusalem church, the gospel was sent out of Jerusalem because of massive persecution. This was no humanly devised strategy. The gospel went from Jerusalem to Samaria, as Luke records it, because of divine intention. And it was critical that the Samaritans were the first recipients of the gospel outside of Jerusalem.[43] At the time of the Assyrian exile, the capital of the northern

40. See the powerful testimony of the Anglican archbishop of Uganda, Henry Luke Orombi, "What Is Anglicanism," *First Things* 175 (August/September 2007): 23-28. He testifies to the theological inheritance of Ugandan Anglicans that carved out a peace among warring tribes grafted onto the same tree of grace by the gospel of Jesus Christ.

41. Dietrich Bonhoeffer's *Life Together,* trans. John W. Doberstein (New York: Harper & Brothers, 1954), remains the classic text on the countercultural nature of the ecclesial community.

42. Acts 2:9-11.

43. F. F. Bruce, *The Book of Acts* (Grand Rapids: Eerdmans, 1988), argues for the struc-

kingdom was Samaria. In the exile the Samaritans were forcefully min-
gled with Gentiles and became a mixed race as a result. Their religious
habits maintained certain Jewish feasts as well as adopting certain Assyrian practices. Jews generally despised them because of this religious
syncretism. It was no accident that Jesus used this intuitive dislike to
set off an intended contrast in the parable of the Good Samaritan.[44]
The Samaritan woman at the well understood the Jewish dislike of her
fellow countrymen and was stunned that Jesus, a Jew, would speak to
her in public.[45]

Against this backdrop, then, it is all the more striking that the gospel would be preached by Jewish disciples of Jesus in Samaria in the
first major post-Pentecost proclamation of the gospel that Luke records
in Acts 8. This was an absolutely critical event in the life of the early
church as the ethnic and national barriers of the old covenant were broken down. Inclusion in the covenant was no longer for the Jews only.
The Holy Spirit was then coming to all without distinction of race or
covenant location. Outsiders were surprisingly treated as insiders, and
insiders were castigated for their exclusionary actions toward outsiders. The initial experience of the tongues of fire brought on by the Spirit
in Acts 2 and repeated in Acts 8 was the heralding of a new king and
thus of the new kind of kingdom where language and culture would be
centrifugal forces carrying the apostolic message and mission outward.
The strange tongues in the book of Acts initiated the announcement in
everyone's own tongue the inbreaking of a new era in the covenant established originally with Abraham.[46]

The upshot of this biblical paradigm is that certain forms of diversity are present in the life of the church to ensure that the gospel will

---

tural significance of the Samaritan Pentecost in Acts 8 as further fulfillment of the Jerusalem Pentecost in Acts 2.

44. Luke 10:25-39.

45. John 4:1-45.

46. Pentecost became the New Covenant's response to the tower of Babel (Gen. 11:1-
9). Sin brought on judgment at Babel with the confusion of languages. Pentecost does not
dissolve diversity of languages, but rather uses that very diversity as a vehicle by which the
gospel goes outward from Jerusalem and a reminder that cultural boundaries will not
limit the *missio dei*. On the relation between Pentecost and Babel see G. K. Beale, "The Descent of the Eschatological Temple in the Form of the Spirit at Pentecost: Part 1: The
Clearest Evidence," *Tyndale Bulletin* 56 (2005): 76-83, and F. F. Bruce, *The Acts of the Apostles: The Greek Text with Introduction and Commentary* (Grand Rapids: Eerdmans, 1990).

not be confused with any specific cultural form. The gospel is not Anglo or African or Asian or Latino. Rather the gospel situates itself in all of these cultures in such a fashion that each of them will be chastened, even as each of them serve as appropriate conduits through which the gospel is proclaimed.

Broken/Corrupted Forms of Diversity

All the communal forms of unity-in-diversity mentioned above can be corrupted and easily distorted. This is obviously so because of the twin nature of corruptions — they are both individual and systemic, neither easily reducible to the other. Corruptions occur in individuals. As individuals bump into each other, they bring these corruptions to bear. Likewise in the systemic corruptions present in every cultural system, there are plausibility structures embedded which bring inordinate (and often unnoticed) corruptions to bear on the enculturated communities.

Conflicts within marriages can overwhelm the connections that originally bound the couple together. There is no pain that compares to the brokenness experienced in marriages. Intimacy betrayed hurts beyond our wildest imaginations.[47] Words of anger can disrupt our identity most profoundly when they are spoken to those to whom we are most intimately connected. There are also systemic corruptions in marriages passed on from generation to generation. Marital dysfunctions spread like bad odors across generations of children. Habits practiced in one generation can become subconsciously present in the next generation.

It may seem trite to say, but the answer to such dysfunctions is not greater autonomy from one another, but more effective resolve to work through the dysfunctions. The brokenness of our identities, which grows out of the brokenness of our relationships, can only be solved by "putting-ourselves-back-together." We must resist the notion that doing our own thing is the ideal toward which we should strive.

So it is that racial divisions can be corrupted both personally and systemically. The volatility of race relations in American history ought to be a pungent reminder of the potential for a corrupted diversity of

---

47. The biblical theological argument for this central reality is poignantly laid out in Raymond Ortlund, *Whoredom: God's Unfaithful Wife in Biblical Theology* (Grand Rapids: Eerdmans, 1996).

race. Hindsight always seems better able to capture this intuition. Colonial slavery was in most forms quite brutal. A slave was a slave for life and the average slave lasted little more than seven years on the plantation. The black family was destroyed and the social structures of the black community were greatly changed in that era.

Conservatives and liberals alike ought to share sadness over the systemic brokenness of these racial realities in our history. This brokenness is interpreted differently today but it continues to reverberate in unpredictable ways. The present has not simply repeated the past, but the echoes of yesteryear continue on today in subtle and surprising ways.[48] We would be culturally naïve to suppose that America has progressed into such an enlightened stage that it need no longer worry about its own corruptions.

If marriages can be corrupted and race relations have been corrupted, then it comes as no biblical surprise that churches can be corrupted as well. Churches are no less prone to hypocrisy and perversion than other human communities. The flaws of ecclesial communities may be more socially acceptable to the churches themselves but, as an outsider might see more clearly, socially acceptable flaws are no less heinous and corrupting. Self-righteousness may seem more palatable to a religious community, but it is every bit as deadly as unbelief itself.

There is no more perplexing problem a pastor faces than building a depth of community which sustains a healthy balance of unity-in-diversity.[49] What may appear as homogeneity from outside the church's walls is in fact experienced as significant diversity within the lived experience of the congregation. Small theological differences can become virtually insurmountable obstacles to the well-being of a church, when there are no means to keep things in a wider perspective.

Maintaining the well-being of the congregation while promoting an appropriate diversity has proven increasingly difficult in this democ-

48. For a sober and realistic portrayal of race relations in distinctively theological categories see Charles Marsh, *The Beloved Community: How Faith Shapes Social Justice, From the Civil Rights Movement to Today* (New York: Basic Books, 2005), and Charles Marsh and John Perkins, *Welcoming Justice: God's Movement Toward Beloved Community* (Downers Grove, IL: InterVarsity Press, 2009).

49. Cf. Douglas L. Fagerstrom and James W. Carlson, *The Lonely Pew: Creating Community in the Local Church* (Grand Rapids: Baker Book House, 1993), and Lyle D. Vander Broek, *Breaking Barriers: The Possibilities of Christian Community in a Lonely World* (Grand Rapids: Brazos Press, 2002).

ratized era for pastors charged with serving as the focal point of an ecclesial identity. The evangelical tendency has been either to stress the unity of the church around the persona of the pastor (and thereby promote an enforced uniformity) or to stress a laissez faire mode that results in a chaotic democracy of convictions.[50] Likewise the task of interpreting the Scriptures within evangelical churches tends toward these two poles. A uniformity of interpretation can be authorized by appeal to a uniform set of elite biblical interpreters. But so likewise is it possible to promote a chaotic democracy of biblical interpretation wherein everyone is one's own interpreter.[51]

The Logic of the Gospel and the Wisdom and Foolishness of Diversity

The goal of inhabiting a unity-in-diversity in the church is not the sheer self-preservation of the church any more than paying attention to how other churches function is a mere matter of theological courtesy. The gospel itself is implicit in this model of unity-in-diversity. It is the gospel for which the church exists and through which the church is to act. It is the consequence of the gospel that the "dividing walls of hostility" are broken down in Christ.[52] He is our "peace" in whom the many are fit into one body and with whom the many diverse members each are to contribute.[53]

50. J. I. Packer adds that evangelical churches were so persuaded of the corruptness of liberal denominations that they supposed independency was the only way to avoid the corruption. The result was too often not merely independent churches but churches whose independent spirit bred believers independent of each other. See his "On Ecclesiology," in *Ancient and Postmodern Christianity: Paleo-Orthodoxy in the 21st Century,* ed. Christopher Hall and Kenneth Tanner (Downers Grove, IL: InterVarsity Press, 2002), pp. 120-28.

51. See George Marsden, "Everyone One's Own Interpreter? The Bible, Science and Authority in Mid-Nineteenth-Century America," in *The Bible in America,* ed. Mark Noll and Nathan Hatch (Oxford: Oxford University Press, 1982), pp. 79-100.

52. Ephesians 2:14. Lesslie Newbigin writes, "There is no place at which mankind can receive the gift of unity except the mercy-seat which God has provided. We can only be made one at the point where our sins are forgiven and we are therefore enabled to forgive one another." In *Is Christ Divided? A Plea for Christian Unity in a Revolutionary Age* (Grand Rapids: Eerdmans, 1961), p. 9.

53. Cf. Ephesians 2:11-16 and 4:1-16. In chapter 2, Paul writes of the "two becoming one," and in chapter 4, he writes of the body being held together by its many joints.

The manner in which we ought to deal with diversity inside the ecclesial square ought to be squarely rooted in the logic of the gospel. The gospel has a sacred wisdom appropriate for dealing with ecclesial diversity. The reconciling work of the gospel contains impulses that take corruption seriously in the hearts of individuals and the lives of communities. The gospel restrains the temptations toward self-righteousness found in the abuse of authority as well as the independence from all authority. Inside the wisdom of the gospel, the democratic impulse is the restraint upon the self-righteous ethos that too often attends those in authority. Inhabiting the gospel also tempers the uninhibited choosing unleashed by the democratic impulse.

Inside the church, democratic impulses beg for a theological account of individuals and the communities in which they are bound together. Democracy as a theologically interpreted category, rather than merely as a political or economic category, demands a wider narrative. There are no such things as bare democracies. Democracy intuitively distrusts the concentration of power, but pleads for a substantive discussion of the common good. In the church the primary theological common good is the communal orientation to the Living God. There may be a host of other goods which the church protects, but it is the central good of its covenant with the Living God which ought to make it always vigilant against the abuse of human authority and the autonomy of an unfettered human will.

The first ecumenical council in Acts 15 manifested theological checks and balances inherent in the gospel in order that the Gentiles would not be excluded. However one construes the structures of authority in the Jerusalem council, it is clear that theologically informed democratic impulses were operative in the deliberations of the council. There was a deeply partisan commitment to the gospel, which in turn finally generated a generous spirit toward the Gentiles.[54]

Peculiar to the gospel is the embrace of diverse tribes, races, and cultures, all because Christ is our peace who has "broken down the dividing wall of hostility." The gospel is expressed in the church as the reconciliation of estranged parties because they belong to the same Lord. At the heart of the gospel is not the overcoming of diversity, but

---

54. Lesslie Newbigin makes this point most powerfully in his *Foolishness to the Greeks* (Grand Rapids: Eerdmans, 1986).

the reconciling impulse in dealing with "strangers."[55] Reconciliation is the goal because we experience reconciliation with God in and through the gospel. Reconciliation does not obliterate the differences between strangers. God is still God and we are still creatures after reconciliation has been effected by the gospel. As a result of the gospel we learn to interpret those differences in different ways.

The power of the Living Word defines this new reality between strangers in the church. It is the power of the gospel proclaimed in word and deed by which God effects the new status in which strangers are now justified together. They no longer share a common death sentence, but rather share in the inheritance of the new heavens and the new earth. It is the forensic character of the gospel in which the adoption papers take on legally binding status, uniting into one family formerly diverse orphans. The adopted orphans do not cease to be strangers in some sense to each other, though they now belong to a common family. They also bring their own unique strengths and weaknesses into the family.

Post-Partisan Partisanship

How then should we think about the ecclesial divides that still persist in congregations and between denominations? It is no answer to say that we'll simply permit the ecclesial square to continue toward the course of yet greater alienation and arbitrariness, nor naïvely suppose our differences will be overcome by forgetting them. The enduring conflicts in marriages are to be treated in similar fashion for similar reasons. Diverse churches in diverse denominations are to live as faithful witnesses in and with the diverse ecclesial square. We must begin to theologically cultivate the desire to live together in, with and through our differences. The animating vision of the gospel calls persons of diverse traditions to live together in truth and love, learning to talk with each other and slowly altering and deepening their traditions in response to that conversation.[56]

55. Michael Horton, *Covenant and Salvation: Union with Christ* (Louisville: Westminster/John Knox, 2007), makes this same point with regard to Christians being united to Christ. Salvation does not "merge" identities but rather reconciles estranged parties. See especially chapter 9, "Covenant Participation: Meeting a Stranger."

56. Martin Marty uses similar language in articulating a framework for how the

A principled and pluralistic ecclesial square is the only option besides oppression or anarchy available to us today.[57] This is the genius of Protestantism and its greatest danger. It adapted easily to the emergence of modern democracies and was comfortable with the separation of church and state by which the politics of the nation-state were not the guarantor of the church's unity.[58] More nearly, the modern democratic temper has proven to be the guarantor of the church's diversity. Methodists and Presbyterians and Pentecostals all find a home quite naturally across the street from each other in America.

Evangelical churches must engage this ecclesial world of diversity on the terms of the gospel rather than the terms of the conventional wisdom of our culture or the natural conventions of secular versions of democracy. Dealing with our differences will not be settled by appeal to a voting electorate. Rather it will be dealt with by appeal to the gospel mandate that the many members belong to the same body. Dealing with diversity therefore requires humility and wisdom. It requires vigilance against resentment and cynicism.[59] It requires a generosity of spirit and a depth of conviction. It requires us to speak prophetically with the resources of our tradition while recognizing our own vested interests in those traditions.

We must engage and not merely tolerate diversity in the ecclesial

---

world's diverse religions ought to relate. I am not persuaded that similar intuitions are present in all of the world's religions, and therefore arguments about tolerance in the civil square may have to be built on different foundations. See his *When Faiths Collide* (Oxford: Blackwell, 2005).

57. For the analogy to the wider public square see James W. Skillen, *Recharging the American Experiment: Principled Pluralism for Genuine Civic Community* (Grand Rapids: Baker Books, 1994).

58. Paul Avis argues that the Reformation debates about ecclesial polity foreshadowed the diverse ways in which Christian churches came to grips with the onset of constitutional forms of governance. It would be a mistake to suggest, however, that ecclesial forms of democratic polity simply mirrored the secular governance structures. Rather they arose primarily in the theological critique of ecclesial monarchicalism. The consequence was the emergence in the diverse Reformation protests of diverse forms of ecclesial conciliarism. The post-Reformation history of conciliarism, according to Avis, is a somewhat sad history as churches increasingly expressed a fundamental independence from all other ecclesial authorities. See his *Beyond the Reformation: Authority, Primacy and Unity in the Conciliar Tradition* (Edinburgh: T&T Clark, 2006).

59. A penetrating analysis of the idolatry of cynicism is Dick Keyes, *Seeing Through Cynicism: A Reconsideration of the Power of Suspicion* (Downers Grove, IL: InterVarsity Press, 2006).

square.[60] The conflicts of a fractured ecclesial polity lie not with keeping emotional distance from those with whom we have fundamental disagreements. It comes rather in the radically counter-intuitive claim that we show hospitality to those with whom we have deep disagreements.[61] We invite the outsider into the common wisdom of our tradition, recognizing that we share the sacred wisdom of the gospel, even if we articulate it differently.[62] We take their ideas seriously not primarily to overthrow their ideas, but rather with the expectation that wisdom is found in the strangest of places, even among those who disagree with us.[63] This requires that churches not merely be tolerant of each other, but rather that they actively engage one another.

Changing the ethos of our ecclesial identity may well require that we think of the commitment to our tradition less in terms of defeating an enemy and more in terms of showing hospitality to the stranger. Without a home (tradition) there is no place to invite the stranger into. A tradition-less Christian is indeed a person without a home. But a tradition construed as a fortress is a most inhospitable place for strangers as well. Our desire is not merely to have a seat at the ecclesial table, but to prepare the meal at the table, which strangers will find curiously satisfying. It is a call to invite the stranger into our tradition as a radical act of hospitality. If the meal is satisfying to the stranger, it is not because we have prepared the meal but rather that the food itself nourishes the soul. And in turn we may be invited into the stranger's tradition and taste some of its delicacies.

60. Cognizant of the Liberal Protestant tendency toward tolerance as the best means of dealing with diversity, Karl Barth asked, "Was it a deliberate acceptance and initiation of the task when from the 18th century onwards the churches began to adopt the idea of mutual civility and tolerance? There is no need to ignore the advantageous results of that development, yet the serious criticism to which this mode of union is open cannot be ignored. The concept of toleration originates in political and philosophical principles which are not only alien but even opposed to the Gospel." *The Church and the Churches* (Grand Rapids: Eerdmans, 2005, orig. 1936), p. 34.

61. A very perceptive treatment of hospitality as a church-uniting strategy is Elizabeth Newman, *Untamed Hospitality: Welcoming God and Other Strangers* (Grand Rapids: Brazos Press, 2007).

62. This account requires that the "gospel" be further cashed out both concretely and theologically. Different articulations of the gospel must be distinguished from different gospels as the apostle Paul affirms in Galatians 1:6-9.

63. Martin Marty extends this suggestion at great length as a prophetic call to Christian churches to engage global diversity on distinctively Christian terms. See his *When Faiths Collide*.

Democracy tempts us to thinking that there are no enduring traditions while itself not being sustainable without a wider moral tradition to underwrite it. Democracies survive because of a common commitment to civility and to justice. These can be grounded in different ways, but democracy does not survive where substantive moral norms are absent. Democracy in this sense is not opposed to traditions but depends upon them. Likewise democracy encourages a multitude of choices, but without a wider moral framework the culture of choice will eventually implode. Relationships are peculiarly prone to implosion when they survive simply on voluntary choices. Intentionally chosen relationships do not last very long and if they do they endure in very different forms than originally conceived. Marriages that last survive on grounds very different from that which motivated the original attraction. Friendships that endure are not very often chosen, but simply "happen" to us.

Robert Putnam in his influential work, *Bowling Alone,* reminded us that our American penchant for choosing often leaves us feeling alone in life. Our choices cannot be sovereign because we inevitably bump into other people who also have their own choices to make. The mechanisms of democracy might give us a political arena in which we have learned to live with these differences, but that diversity of choices cannot be the ultimate value in the communities that matter more urgently and concretely to us. We must choose in some sense to give up our choices. We must be partisans to a set of moral norms that restrains our own partisan commitments. Post-partisan communities will exist only in so far as persons are partisanly loyal to each other in ways that transcend self-interest.

The church is the community where the "individual-as-chooser" never quite feels at home. Church is a place that infringes upon choices, and eventually everyone feels like an outsider because they have bumped into people who make different choices than they do.[64] Pastors that don't recognize this in-built network of potential frictions

64. Gary Babcock notes a common tragedy in this regard in many evangelical churches when he comments, "The exaggerated theology of the church purely as *congregatio fidelium,* understood as a gathered community of individual believers who have experienced individual conversion, is common in evangelical Protestantism." Church in this sense is the place where "'people's religious needs need to be met,' [but] a brief encounter with reality is in order. Amid the individualism of so much of the contemporary church, people's religious needs are very often *not* met." *The House Where God Lives: Renewing the Doctrine of the Church for Today* (Grand Rapids: Eerdmans, 2009), p. 169.

are ripe for burnout. Parishioners that hope they will eventually find a church where everyone will choose as they do are bound to feel restless in every church they choose. It is counter-intuitive today to suppose that God chooses us rather than we who choose God. But if this is true, then the church does not exist because people choose to join it, but rather because God has chosen to gather his people into communities that belong to him.

Gaining traction on this issue requires that we be much more honest about the emotional cost of loneliness and by contrast the benefits of giving up many of our choices. The gospel is a radical form of hospitality that invites outsiders into a new way of thinking about choices and communities. The gospel is about belonging, not to ourselves, but to the Triune God and because of that belonging to others. If we are honest with our own inveterate loneliness, belonging to others can be very attractive. And if God hard wires us this way, little wonder that we feel relief when we no longer simply belong to ourselves. Impossible communities become possible in the gospel.

Churchly cocoons can often leave us isolated from dissenting voices. But sometimes they enable us to privilege the relationships that matter the most. These are the two sides of democracy. Blessing and Curse. After the Fall, part of our experience is the reminder in creation of how things are "supposed to be" and also the reminder that things are "not the way they are supposed to be." The ease of choices is a terrific blessing. It frees us from the restraints of external powers and the enslavements of stereotypes. A terrific blessing. But the accompanying curse is that these choices often make it difficult to settle down into a well-formed community. There is an eternal restlessness to keep making choices that restrain our loyalties to any and all communities. A terrible curse.

The wisdom of the gospel requires that we "bump into" the differences we have with each other which in turn requires that these differences are made intelligible across our diverse cultural and social locations. Being accountable to others is a difficult labor requiring both humility and confidence. At times it also requires the hard work of reconciliation. And if reconciliation is at the heart of the gospel it ought to be reflected in the ways different gospel communities deal with each other across their divisions.

The unity of the gospel demands that we not separate the church where Christ has not separated it. Neither are we to homogenize the church where Christ has not.[65] The revitalization of the ecumenical movement after Vatican II has put pressure upon the diversity of Protestant churches. Praiseworthy in many respects it has nonetheless unleashed a tendency to downplay theological convictions in order to sustain greater harmonization among conflicted churches. It is inevitable that ecumenical concerns will force the question of boundaries in uncomfortable ways. In some quarters those boundaries are themselves always negotiable in light of the greater goal of unity.[66] That is not a sufficiently redemptive manner of dealing with deep differences. The apostolic foundation upon which the church is laid will not sacrifice theological conviction for the sake of unity, any more than it will permit the use of theological conviction as a club to be swung uncharitably at opponents. Being partisans of the gospel requires us to be post-partisans toward those with whom we have even deep disagreements.

65. In an earlier generation the church growth movement suggested that churches grew most efficiently along class and racial lines. Accordingly churches were not to cross ethnic, race, or class lines. But this is anathema to the New Testament Church.

66. Donald Bloesch rightly chides the "beguiling romanticism" among disenchanted Protestants who suppose that the return to Rome will solve the unity question. He criticizes the claim of Carl Braaten and Robert Jenson that there can be no discipline of pastors and parishes with the Catholic ecclesial structure headed by the pope. Bloesch wisely notes, however, that the "Roman church is not theologically healthy nor missiologically vital. It has not held fast to the gospel of free justification through faith in the living Christ." *The Church: Sacraments, Worship, Ministry and Mission* (Downers Grove, IL: InterVarsity Press, 2002), p. 255. Braaten and Jenson's concrete strategy for unity is laid out in *In One Body: The Princeton Proposal for Christian Unity* (Grand Rapids: Eerdmans, 2003).

PART THREE

Renewing the Theological Mission

Renewal of Evangelical Theology:
The Contribution of David F. Wells

Cornelius Plantinga Jr.

Twenty years ago David Wells, Mark Noll, and I received a grant from the Pew Charitable Trusts to write a trio of books on the decline of evangelical theology and on ways it might rebound. We hoped our books would themselves contribute to some of the rebounding. Prof. Noll wrote a book titled *The Scandal of the Evangelical Mind* and I wrote one titled *Not the Way It's Supposed to Be: A Breviary of Sin*. Our colleague David Wells, for his part, wrote five books. He wrote half a shelf of books — good books, provocative books, books that are at once accessible and also alarmingly learned. I'm speaking of his books titled *No Place for Truth, God in the Wasteland, Losing Our Virtue, Above All Earthly Pow'rs,* and *The Courage to Be Protestant.*

It turns out that David is a man "born to grapple with whole libraries," in Samuel Johnson's apt phrasing. David's books display immense learning in theology, philosophy, psychology, sociology, literature, the history of Wenham, MA, political science, popular culture, the history of obituaries, the history of city planning and architecture, the Church Growth movement, biblical studies, the belief patterns of seminarians in the '90s, the history of *Christianity Today* magazine, homiletics, and the history of American immigration. And those are only the fields I can think of without reviewing all of David's footnotes.

You know, certain metaphysical naturalists are fond of observing that we human beings share 98.4% of our DNA with the chimps. Reading David Wells makes me mighty proud of what he's done with his 1.6%.

Six years into the grant from Pew, David, Mark, and I wrote an article for *Theology Today* on the state of evangelical theology (January

189

1995). In our article we said that for all their dynamism and success at a popular level, modern American evangelicals have largely failed in sustaining serious intellectual life. We have nourished millions of believers in the simple verities of the gospel, but have often abandoned the universities, the arts, and other realms of high culture. Active enterprises like feeding the hungry and living simply, sitting in at abortion clinics and promoting family values, launching coffee break ministries and televangelism projects — these are the sorts of tasks at which evangelicals expend great energy.

But these endeavors are seldom accompanied by first-level intellectual effort. Worse, the lack of solid grounding in classical theology within the churches has contributed to their remarkable slide into worldliness. Evangelicals have become remarkably worldly, we said, accepting without debate, without question — often without notice — the assumptions, practices, and worldview of the larger American culture.

We cited Martin Marty, who has been observing for a couple of decades that few contemporary Christian groups have become more worldly than Christian fundamentalists. If fundamentalists count as a subset of evangelicals, and if certain non-fundamentalist evangelicals get contaminated by such worldliness, not surprisingly one can find in conservative Protestant settings altogether too much by way of what Marty calls "Christian bodybuilding and beauty-queening," rock music "with a Jesus gloss on it," and entrepreneurs "hawking a complete line of Christian celebrity cosmetics and panty-hose" — all this in combination with considerable suspicion of the synoptic problem.

The spectacle is one in which the powers that might maintain integrity against all the corrupting influences of modernity — namely, the serious appropriation of Scripture, the intelligent study of great ecumenical and then Reformational confessions, and the blending of these together with other intellectual sources into vigorous contemporary theology — these powers often get marginalized in evangelicalism today while TV culture, entertainment culture, the cult of self-absorption, and various other anti-intellectualist forces cut their great swaths through the church, mowing down the prophetic protests raised against them. This is, perhaps, the heart of the contemporary evangelical tragedy.

We took as an example of evangelical malaise a confessionally rooted theological seminary. This seminary maintains a fairly classical curriculum. To secure the M.Div. degree students must demonstrate knowledge of Greek and Hebrew plus one modern foreign language. Admission pre-requisites include substantial numbers of courses across the humanities and social sciences, and, in particular, hefty doses of philosophy and literature. The seminary's graduation requirements for the M.Div. degree stipulate substantial numbers of courses in systematic theology, historical theology, philosophical theology, as well as in Old and New Testament — all this besides the courses in church and missions and besides student forays into field work. In short, this seminary prescribes lots of core courses and allows comparatively few electives and almost no lollipops.

For decades students at this seminary accepted requirements like these as proper training for ministry. But beginning in the late '80s, the seminary began to draw students who would listen to a lecture in the doctrine of God, look around curiously during student discussion of it, and then turn to the professor and say seriously, "Look, why do we have to study any of this stuff in order to be ministers?" Further discussion of this student's question would then yield a distressing conclusion, namely, that some evangelical seminary students really believe that they can minister the riches of the faith for years without having to think hard about the doctrine of the Trinity, or the meaning of providence, or the claim that God is both immanent and transcendent. Such students do not object particularly to the *way* a professor teaches the doctrine of God: they object to the whole project of *learning* the doctrine of God. They really see no link between thinking about its topics, on the one hand, and readiness for ministry, on the other. Surely they can think of no reason why any layperson would need a deeply formed view of God.

We wrote this in 1995. David Wells had by then published two of his five books. Perhaps the project of the books could be stated most simply in medical terms: David Wells's five books diagnose the evangelical sickness and prescribe Reformation to cure it. The books, as I said, are deeply learned, and they are also masterfully written. They exhibit solid conceptual architecture and great feel for the English language. Like that of Solzhenitsyn, David Wells's cultural criticism will be read a century from now.

But across the years what has struck me most about David's five books is their desperately deep sense of loss. David Wells's books are a prophet's cry of the heart. He calls out to the church that we have turned our backs on God. We have forgotten God. We have usurped the prerogatives of almighty God and have enthroned the fallen world in his place. We need to repent and then we need to become instruments of the Holy Spirit in reforming the church.

We Evangelicals Have Lost Classical Theology

The need for repentance and reformation is all around us, says Prof. Wells. Our bewildered seminary student is only a symptom of a more general loss of the centrality of God in the church and of a classical theology of God. In a healthy Christian church there will be confession of God, of his nature and acts, of Jesus Christ and his atoning death and resurrection. The church will confess its doctrines, such as God's justification of guilty sinners, faith that attaches to Jesus Christ clothed with his gospel, regeneration, repentance, sanctification, the indwelling Holy Spirit, the church and her sacraments, mighty across the ages, the prospect of the new heaven and earth in which, after centuries of tribal feuds and racial arrogance, after centuries of xenophobia, after we human beings have silted history full with the debris of all our antagonisms — after all that, people from "every nation, from all tribes and people and languages," will see the city of God descending to us and God dwelling with us. God will make all things new.

These truths, placed inside the grand narrative arc of the Bible's story — these truths are the Christian's food and drink, and David Wells says we are losing them. We are losing our deep, nourishing sources of truth and, indeed, our respect for truth itself.

In a healthy Christian church sound doctrine is taught and learned. It then shapes everything — not only preaching and teaching, but also worship, pastoral care, evangelism, even church government (which, you recall, the Reformers went after because they were scandalized by simony and by twelve-year-old bishops). In a healthy Christian church forgiveness of sins is a doctrine that shapes the church's life. If we have been forgiven so much by God, how fitting it would be if we also forgave each other. If we have been forgiven so much, how fitting it would be if our lives would hum with gratitude — one of our most powerful engines of joy.

Time was when sound doctrine plus reflection on it plus the virtues that arise from these things kindled and governed life in the churches. Nowadays, states Prof. Wells, too often classical theology is read only by

theologians and seminarians. People in the churches and their ministers do have a sort of theology, but it has lost its edge. All its sharp
angles are gone. We are reaping some of what the Second Great Awakening sowed — namely its anti-theological, anti-intellectual democratization of the faith. We are reaping some of what the baby boomers
have been sowing as well — people who were coming of age in the '60s,
the Woodstock generation, with its rejection of authority and tradition,
with its love of rock music, and with its rallying cry, "Do your own
thing." We evangelicals are now new liberals, always looking to swap
doctrine for life. We want to talk about how we feel, and about how we
feel about how we feel. We'll give up doctrine if we can get turned on in
church.

In too many churches today, says Prof. Wells, the only theology
around is one in which "God is on easy terms with modernity" and is interested chiefly in church growth and psychological wholeness. Prof.
Wells wants to know what St. Paul would make of our churches — he of
the cosmic Christology, and the rock-ribbed assurance of justification
through faith, and the urgent summons to die and rise with Jesus
Christ, to take out a contract on our worldly selves and then let our new,
image-of-God selves arise in might like Jesus walking out of his tomb.
What would St. Paul make of worship without lament, of pelvic-
thrusting praise teams and beaming ministers on their barstools, swap-
ping stories and jokes with an applauding audience and announcing
"top ten" listings borrowed from Letterman?

According to Prof. Wells St. Paul would not flourish in many of our
churches. After all, where's his easy smile? Why does he want to discipline people? Why is he so dogmatic? Where are the stories in his sermons? And where does he get off implying that the woman singing special music should not do so while lying on top of the church's piano?

Once upon a time we had a doctrine and theology of providence in
the churches — a stout teaching of God's superintendence of history
and of all the events in our lives. In a lovely phrasing, Prof. Wells calls
God's providence "the sacred canopy." But this enormously comforting
doctrine has thinned down to the mere assurance of God's presence in
human life and human tragedy, and Prof. Wells laments the loss. I con-
cur. In the circles in which I live, sometime in the last thirty years ministers quit speaking of God's governance of our lives. After all, how do you
fit throat cancer into it, or sudden crib death? The unspoken assumption has come to be that if we cannot explain what God's reason was for

permitting a tragedy, then there can't have been a reason. There can't have been a reason because if there were one, then we in our infinite wisdom would know it.

Disappearing too is the doctrine of God's holiness. In the Bible, says Prof. Wells, the holiness of God is perhaps his most dominant characteristic. The loving-kindness for which God is eminent is but an expression of his holiness. God is high — in fact, most high. He dwells in realms of glory. He is terrifying in his purity, and the sworn foe of all evil. The Bible tells us that God's holiness in the temple was sometimes so intense that the priests had to back up. God was too hot for them that day. Once upon a time people loved God but they also feared him because he is not domestic, not predictable, not safe at all.

People sometimes speak of meeting God as if it would be like a walk in the garden, or a coffee date with a friend. Meeting God might be like meeting Walter Cronkite. The truth is it might be more like getting electrocuted. Prof. Wells reminds us that, like Isaiah, Luther was *stricken* in the presence of God. Doesn't God shine like a billion stars? Isn't God the one before whom mere human beings have to fall on their faces? Isn't he terrible in his holiness and dramatic in his justice? Isn't God's truth sharper than any two-edged sword? Isn't the desire to meet God a death wish for our sinful selves?

Nowadays, says Prof. Wells, we worship a creamier God. All he does is smile. When we sin, he understands. He has quenched the fires of hell. He has turned all his subjects into chums. He wants not to judge or intimidate. All he wants is cuddle time with his children.

Because we evangelicals no longer think much about the holiness of God — about his absolute moral and spiritual supremacy and purity — we lose the primary sense of our sin, namely that it's an *affront* to God's holiness. God buries our sin in the depths of the sea because he can't stand to look at it. We evangelicals no longer grieve over the fact that we trouble the heart of God with our sin.

Accordingly, our repentance lacks urgency too, and may amount much less to an emergency turn-around and much more to a take-it-or-leave-it Ben Franklin program of self-improvement. There is too little of the prophet Joel in this and too much of the preacher Joel Osteen, who has the recipe for "Your Best Life Now: 7 Steps to Living at Your Full Potential."

When we lose the doctrine of God's holiness in the churches, says Prof. Wells, we also lose the catch-of-the-breath wonder at the high and holy God, the terrible enemy of sin, who also makes his dwelling with those who are "contrite and humble." In sum, says Prof. Wells,

> until we recognize afresh the centrality of God's holiness, until it once again enters into the innermost fibers of evangelical faith, our virtue will lack seriousness, our belief will lack poignancy, our practice will lack moral pungency, our worship will lack joyful seriousness, our preaching will lack the mordancy of grace, and the church will be just one more special interest pleading for a hearing in a world of competing enterprises. (1994, p. 145)

The Worldliness of North American Culture

The brute realities of contemporary life in North America are all around us. Society is organized for commerce, manufacturing, technology, notably information technology. We live on a flat earth, as Thomas Friedman terms it, and Prof. Wells is a master at describing our huge interlocking economies, bureaucracies, education systems, technologies, governments. The mass media envelop us 24/7 with their fast-moving images, headlines, stories, revelations, and polls. (The abbreviation 24/7 has arisen only in the last twenty years or so.) Much of the fast developing media content is meant to be experienced, not reflected upon. As Prof. Wells describes it, flat earth culture is ubiquitous: music, T-shirts, movies, and fast food. It's voice-mail, e-mail, Facebook, and blogs — with the blogs reflecting the fact that even though we live on a flat earth, we are still as tribal as ever, our blogs each commanding their own audience, often in opposition to those of rival blogs.

We've got Twittering and blogging to announce to the world which pair of our lateral incisors has just shredded our dental floss. Our malls are cathedrals to consumerism. We have choices galore, as you can tell when the guy ahead of you at Starbuck's orders a Grande, iced, half-caf, double shot vanilla soy latte with extra foam. We also have corruption galore. Prof. Wells surveys the terrain of abortion, divorce, men who make babies but won't care for them, bribed government officials, and all the rest, and his survey is sobering indeed.

In Prof. Wells's analysis, we North Americans have become our own centers and law-givers. We've lost a lot of our old-fashioned short words like good, bad, right, and wrong. In fact, virtues have given way to mere values, and character to personality. We've lost much of the older sense of public moral character, with its duty, responsibility, and honor. We have lots of laws and lots of freedoms, but no central zone of responsibility, with the result that people now think that anything not illegal is therefore permissible. We no longer value self-denial. It's all self-realization these days, and has been since the '70s at least. Everybody's got an autobiography.

In Prof. Wells's analysis of Our Time, feelings of guilt before God have largely given way to feelings of shame before others. We contemporary Americans writhe not over our sins, but over our profile. We think we are not smart enough, not rich enough, not nearly accomplished or beautiful or mesomorphic enough. Our breasts are too flat and our thighs too thunderous. We are boring, foolish, outstandingly mousy. We belong in good company about as much as a dead cigar belongs in a punchbowl.

Naturally, in a shame-filled culture people try to pump up their profile. Hence the self-esteem industry, the trophies for kids who just show up, all the bumper stickers boasting about family members. (My favorite says "My son was inmate of the month at County Jail.") In one especially eloquent characterization of the drive to find self-identity Prof. Wells tells of all those depleted selves out there who say: "I am my genes; I am my past; I am my sexual orientation; I am my feelings; I am my image; I am my body; I am what I do; I am what I have; I am who I know" (1998, p. 141). All these self-identifications have false and competing anthropologies behind them, and none of them should look very good to a serious Christian.

Worldliness in the Church

Alas, so much North American worldliness has seeped into the evangelical churches. Explicit in David Wells's diagnosis of the evangelical church's loss of classical faith and theology is his conviction that the church is now not only in the world, but also of it. Worldliness has been seeping in since the '70s in North America, and is now pervasive within the evangelical church.

Until the '70s evangelical Christians found common cause in their confession of the great truths of the faith, centrally the doctrine of the authority of Scripture and the doctrine of Jesus Christ's substitutionary atonement on the cross. In the '70s, Prof. Wells notes, we started to lose theological incisiveness, substituting for it a form of civil religion clustering in political causes such as anti-abortion, prayer in the schools, and the like.

According to Prof. Wells's analysis, since the '70s evangelicals have turned more and more away from God and toward the human self as the source of interest and meaning in life. And the self in the center is no longer thought to be a corrupt and sinful self, destined for hell unless a merciful God of grace supernaturally intervenes. Oh no. That human self is so '50s. The new self of the '80s, '90s, and '00s is one whose sin was barely worth talking about. Just as in the rest of society, so in the Christian evangelical churches we lifted up Jesus' tolerance for sinners. Did he not reach out to people he barely knew? Isn't he the one who came into the world not to condemn it, but to save it? Didn't Jesus say to us pointedly, "Do not judge, so that you may not be judged?"

Robert Schuller wasn't standing out there all by himself when he claimed, immodestly enough, that his trumpeting of self-esteem was "a new reformation." There were other indicators. As Prof. Wells states it,

> In 1983 James Hunter discovered that of evangelical books published in that year nine out of ten dealt with matters of the self. In 1989 Lyman Coleman spoke of the assumptions beneath the widely used *Serendipity Bible for Groups,* which he edited. The principal one was that all people were made in the image of God. There was nothing novel about that. However, this old truth was being understood in new ways. Coleman understood it to mean that all people have unlimited potential. (2008, p. 137)

Prof. Wells adds that feeling good about oneself is clearly different from being good. People sometimes feel good about themselves when they humiliate a rival or when they get drunk. In any case, shouldn't evangelicals have noticed that centering the church and its proclamation on the human self is a betrayal of the gospel of grace, which is anathema to all self-help gospels. Self-help gospels, come to think of it, are really cruel gospels, laying the burden of regeneration, as they do, on finite, sinful creatures who then huff and puff away. Self-help gospels ignore that we can be saved only by a God-almighty miracle of regeneration. Pelagianism is a merciless gospel in more than one sense.

Worldliness is in the churches, says Prof. Wells. Churches turn to the self. They also market the gospel like any Silicon Valley startup. So you have the church of Jesus Christ using publicity, entrepreneurship, personalities, novelties, eye-popping spectacles, even comedians — all to attract customers. Like malls, too many evangelical churches — and maybe especially some of the big ones — have become "monuments to consumption." Their audience is sovereign. Only the audience can validate a sermon or a marketing ploy by showing the church whether it appeals to them. The whole church growth movement of the '80s, says Prof. Wells, was explicitly pragmatic. Discern people's felt needs and meet them. It makes no difference whether their felt needs are their real needs. It makes no difference if the people feeling their needs are corrupt people. What you want in church is a constant stream of new customers through the door.

As Prof. Wells puts matters here, "the premise of all marketing is that . . . the customer is always right, and this is precisely what the gospel insists cannot be the case" (1995, p. 82). In fact, the gospel wants us to surrender our sovereign needs to a sovereign God.

Churches turn to the self. They market the gospel. They arrange for zippy worship. Some of them think that "ecclesiastical architecture is, in principle, offensive and that religious symbols, such as crosses should be banned from churches" (2005, p. 282).

Too often, evangelicals these days also turn ministers of the gospel into professional managers whose D.Min. degrees certify them. These ministers read not theology but *Leadership* magazine, which is in the habit of citing not Scripture but psychologists and business managers. Then the ministers preach sermons in which the elder brother of Luke 15 is psychologically bereft, and acts out because of his narcissistic personality disorder. We do not judge him for his self-righteousness. We pity him because his human relational adjustment dynamics are low.

At one time ministers were resident theologians, the congregation's expert on God. Their theology determined their use of all the ministerial tools, such as preaching and pastoral care. In too many evangelical churches today, this older understanding and role have been lost. Now the minister is a manager and a paid people-lover. No dogmatists need apply. What we want is a minister who is vulnerable enough to share his weaknesses while savvy enough to make the church grow.

A large part of David Wells's analysis of the evangelical predicament is that even as the evangelical churches become progressively more worldly, they have also deceived themselves about what is going on. The churches innocently and joyously embrace worldly principles that will corrupt them. They go into Babylonian Captivity singing. A great contribution of David Wells to the renewal of evangelicalism is simply to hold a mirror up to it, to call attention to the worldliness of the world, and how much of this worldliness we evangelicals have been absorbing.

Once upon a time, Puritan ministers strenuously preached the gospel of sovereign grace from their pulpits. Their congregation wanted the gospel to get saved, not to get pleased.

For the last sixteen years David Wells has been a voice crying in the wilderness. As we know, he has had to count the cost. Prophecy is a lonely business, and the prophet is often, at best, ignored and, at worst, reviled as people go right on with whatever gets them juiced. I write to honor David Wells for his courage and tenacity. He has wanted God to reform the church, and he has said so with great passion.

We need reform today. In all of our enthusiasm for common grace, for the signs of God's presence and benevolence in a fallen world, we have lost the sense of antithesis, of the battle between the City of God and the City of this world. We need to recover a sober sense that the darkness hates the light and will try to extinguish it. I'm thinking, for example, of some of the writings of the "new atheists" such as Sam Harris, Daniel Dennent, Richard Dawkins, and to a lesser extent, Christopher Hitchens. In a good deal of their writing we find not mere rejection of revealed religion, but contempt for it, scorn of it, hatred of believers' reverence within it. This is revealing. If we haven't noticed lately, our battle is not against flesh and blood, but against the powers, the authorities, the rulers of popular opinion.

We need reform in the church today. The church needs to die and rise with Jesus Christ, putting off its old self with all its worldly ways, and putting on its new self, which believes firmly and joyously in the gospel of Jesus Christ, incarnate, crucified, resurrected, and ascended. We are not just church customers. We are people of the cross and empty tomb and of all that they mean for a sorry world.

When I read David Wells, I sometimes wonder whether there's much hope for the evangelical church. A straightforward diagnosis of her corruption is by no means pleasant to read. How did we get into such a mess?

But I also remember, right along with Prof. Wells, that the church belongs to Jesus Christ. *Christ* is the head of the church. He has plans for us, and they are full of his sorrow and joy. Christ is always crowned "amidst tears and great laughter." He will prevail.

Our own part requires a recovered faith in the holiness of God, a recovered confidence that God's Word is alive for our time, and a renewed determination to preach Jesus Christ crucified and risen, the head of the church and the Lord of the universe.

WORKS CITED

Noll, Mark, Cornelius Plantinga Jr., and David F. Wells, "Evangelical Theology Today," *Theology Today*. January 1995: 495-507.

Wells, David F., *No Place for Truth; or, Whatever Happened to Evangelical Theology* (Grand Rapids: Eerdmans, 1993).

———, *God in the Wasteland: The Reality of Truth in a World of Fading Dreams* (Grand Rapids: Eerdmans, 1995).

———, *Losing Our Virtue: Why the Church Must Recover Its Moral Vision* (Grand Rapids: Eerdmans, 1998).

———, *Above All Earthly Pow'rs: Christ in a Postmodern World* (Grand Rapids: Eerdmans, 2005).

———, *The Courage to Be Protestant: Truth-lovers, Marketers, and Emergents in the Postmodern World* (Grand Rapids: Eerdmans, 2008).

Interpreting Scripture between the Rock of Biblical Studies and the Hard Place of Systematic Theology: The State of the Evangelical (dis)Union

Kevin J. Vanhoozer

Introduction: Between *Sola Scriptura* and *Sola Cultura*

To be evangelical — a people of the gospel — is to be a people of the book. David Wells's magnum opus, the Courage Quintet, calls evangelicals to build their churches and their theology on the basis of *sola scriptura* rather than *sola cultura*.[1] What does this calling to be biblical mean for the relationship between evangelical exegesis and theology, and for renewing the evangelical mission?

In 1995 Wells co-authored with Mark Noll and Cornelius Plantinga an important article summarizing the findings of their three-year study of ways to reinvigorate evangelical theology.[2] The article pinpointed three problems: a "troubled relation" to Scripture, a neglect of tradition, and a failure to engage the contemporary intellectual milieu. The prescription? A "fresh study of Scripture that proceeds *somewhat independently of the guild of biblical scholarship*,"[3] a harvesting of historical tradition, and an engagement with contemporary intellectual culture.

There is an apparent tension between the call to study Scripture "somewhat independently of . . . biblical scholarship" and Wells's complaint, lodged elsewhere, that evangelicals failed to sustain serious intellectual life. The latter point is true of large swaths of evangelical cul-

---

1. David F. Wells, *The Courage to Be Protestant: Truth-lovers, Marketers, and Emergents in the Postmodern World* (Grand Rapids: Eerdmans, 2008), p. 4.
2. David F. Wells, Cornelius Plantinga Jr., and Mark Noll, "Evangelical Theology Today," *Theology Today* 51 (1995): 495-507.
3. Wells, Plantinga, and Noll, "Evangelical Theology Today," p. 504 (emphasis mine).

ture, but not of evangelical biblical studies. Along with analytic philosophers, biblical scholars now represent the high point of contemporary evangelicalism in the academy. We came, we saw, we conquered. Or did we? Is it possible that even here, in the temple of biblical scholarship, *sola cultura* remains the watchword — not because evangelicals have dumbed down biblical scholarship but because they have adopted the practices of "other nations," as it were, and worshiped foreign gods? We will return to this point below.

Wells's singular contribution as the weeping prophet of contemporary evangelicalism has been to turn the spotlight on the twin endangered species of doctrine and discipleship, and to describe this unfortunate congregational climate change as a consequence of attending to the siren call of *sola cultura* instead of *sola scriptura* (by which he means not Scripture "alone" but Scripture "above" all earthly powers, principalities, and authorities).[4] Being biblical matters: at stake is nothing less than the ministry of the word and the integrity of the church.

Wells knows that sound preaching demands more than technical exegesis or meeting felt needs. It is rather a matter of laying out how *this* world looks in the light of the gospel, of helping congregations "to think God's thoughts after him in *this* world."[5] "What does this Word mean in this world?" ought to be the preacher's constant question and concern.[6] Thus concludes the Wellsian reading, a prologue to my main story.

The State of the Union (and the State of the Question)

Once upon a time there was no "biblical studies" and "systematic theology." We cannot classify Augustine as an exegete as opposed to a theologian or vice versa; the distinction does not apply. The same goes for Thomas Aquinas, Luther, Calvin, Wesley, and many others. Their work displays an integral union of biblical exegesis and theological reflection. Not so their successors. What happened?

First, the ugly ditch dividing history and faith led J. P. Gabler to propose a disciplinary division of labor in his famous 1787 inaugural ad-

4. Wells, *Courage to Be Protestant*, p. 227.
5. Wells, *Courage to Be Protestant*, p. 231.
6. Wells, *Courage to Be Protestant*, p. 232.

dress: biblical theology focuses on the historical ("what it meant"); dogmatic theology on the didactic ("what it means").[7] Second, the Bible became a document of the modern university, where the office of the interpreter was to read it "like any other book."[8] This works very well in the kind of research university established in Berlin in 1810, where critical methods were brought to bear on all subjects in the spirit of inquiry free from authoritative traditions. Biblical theology came to mean the historical investigation into the beliefs of the biblical authors, a purely descriptive enterprise that is safe to pursue in research universities that prize *Wissenschaft* (i.e., scientific knowledge).

The University of Berlin had a Protestant faculty of theology, led by Friedrich Schleiermacher. It operated with a four-part curriculum: the biblical scholar studied the language and historical context of the text, identifying the key religious ideas; dogmatics arranged these ideas into conceptual schemes whose principles could be applied by pastoral theologians; church historians tracked the changes in the church's faith and practice vis-à-vis its dogmas. To put it in terms not of academic fields but of track and field: exegetes run a first descriptive lap around the text and then pass the baton to theologians who run a prescriptive lap around the contemporary context.[9]

Schleiermacher himself observed that academic biblical knowledge is of service to faith only if there is a keen interest in religion, and likened the relation of university to church to the union of body and soul.[10] Fast-forward two centuries: in most universities (and many seminaries) biblical studies and systematic theology now have little or nothing to do with one another. They have not only dropped but lost the baton. Each now represents its own academic specialization, complete with supporting

---

7. See John Sandys-Wunsch and Laurence Eldredge, "J. P. Gabler and the Distinction between Biblical and Dogmatic Theology: Translation, Commentary, and Discussion of His Originality," *Scottish Journal of Theology* 33 (1980): 133-58.

8. Benjamin Jowett, "On the Interpretation of Scripture," in *Essays and Reviews* (1860).

9. See David Kelsey's comment about the intrinsic instability of this arrangement: "The fourfold nature of the curriculum presupposed some sort of grounding in scripture as authority . . . whereas the critical methods, as they gained hegemony, simply ignored the privileged position traditionally claimed for scripture. The rationale and structure of the theological school curriculum suffered a deep self-contradiction" (*To Understand God Truly: What's Theological about a Theological School* [Louisville, KY: Westminster John Knox Press, 1992], pp. 87-88).

10. *Brief Outline of the Study of Theology* (Eugene, OR: Wipf & Stock, 2007), pp. 93-94.

cast of professional societies, journals, jargon, and methods. The honeymoon is over; this couple is not even on speaking terms. For those who care about their ability to serve the church, and their integrity as academic disciplines, the situation has become alarming.

The key dispute concerns the nature of the biblical texts and how they are to be read: are they essentially products of culturally and historically situated religious communities or instruments of God's self-communication? "Biblical scholars increasingly saw themselves as philologists and historians rather than theologians. . . . Unfortunately, theologians and ethicists must sift through the barns of exegetical hay as they search for that rare needle of theological consequence."[11] Some claim that a Christian reading and a scholarly reading of the Bible are mutually exclusive endeavors.[12] At its worst, the current state of disunion resembles the conflict in the Holy Land, where Israel and Palestine have difficulty even acknowledging the other's right to exist.

Mutual Recriminations (and Some Caricatures)

On the Grammatical-Historical Exegetical Industry

The state of the disunion — between biblical studies and systematic theology; between academic disciplines and the life of the church — is becoming common knowledge. People are beginning to talk . . .

Critics of modern biblical studies accuse exegetes of too often producing only thin, non-theological descriptions of biblical texts: "The 'meaning in the original context' approach has made the Old Testament into the Hebrew Bible. To read forward to fulfillment in Christ is the unforgivable sin of modern biblical scholarship."[13] J. K. Riches agrees: "The widespread rejection of theological interpretation in contemporary exegesis is a most extraordinary self-inflicted wound."[14]

---

11. Joel Green, "The Bible, Theology, and Theological Interpretation," http://www.sbl-site.org/publications/article.aspx?articleId=308.

12. Philip Davies, *Whose Bible Is It Anyway?* 2nd ed. (London: T&T Clark, 2004).

13. R. R. Reno, "Recovering the Bible," http://www.firstthings.com/onthesquare/2009/02/recovering-the-bible.

14. Cited in Angus Paddison, *Theological Hermeneutics and 1 Thessalonians* (Cambridge: Cambridge University Press, 2005), p. 9.

Why are they saying such awful things about grammatical-historical exegesis? There are a number of diagnoses:

- exegetes pretend to read from nowhere in particular using an inductive method as if they had no presuppositions.
- exegetes leave faith and tradition at the door, as if biblical scholarship can be pursued like any other neutral, objective science.
- exegetes are historians of religion, not theologians; they report on someone else's speech about God but do not say anything about God themselves.
- exegetes are mired in the past and are unable to address the present and its needs.
- exegetes are mired in the present, unaware of the history of interpretation.[15]
- exegetes are so preoccupied with the world behind the text that they fail adequately to observe the text's properly theological concerns, arguably its main subject matter.[16]

The question is whether biblical studies can ever be more than a species of the genus religious studies (i.e., the history of religion). Put bluntly: can biblical studies ever get beyond descriptions of Israelite and early Christian *religion* in order actually to speak of *God?* The best single piece of evidence as to the state of the union between biblical studies and systematic theology is the commentary. The commentary is the proverbial canary in the mine with regard to hermeneutics: every significant intellectual and social development eventually shows up in the way people read the Bible.[17]

---

15. "[M]odern biblical scholars ignore all interpreters of the Bible except other modern biblical scholars" (R. R. Reno, paraphrasing James L. Kugel, in *First Things* [April 2008]: 13).

16. "[A]n interpretation of Scripture determined to operate wholly without reference to the historic ecclesial context is particularly prone to misapprehend the nature and purpose of its very object of study" (Markus Bockmuehl, *Seeing the Word: Refocusing New Testament Study* [Grand Rapids: Baker, 2006], p. 76).

17. "In recent years, evangelicals have been forced to play catch-up in writing commentaries that supply the advanced philology, text-critical notes, theological implications, socioliterary background, and extrabiblical parallels that have characterized liberal scholarship for decades" (John Glynn, *Commentary and Reference Survey: A Comprehensive Guide to Biblical and Theological Resources,* 9th ed. [Grand Rapids: Kregel Academic & Professional, 2003], p. 43).

The task of the exegete is to explicate or unfold the "world of the text": what the author is saying about something in some way for some purpose. *Exegetical* commentary series focus on words, syntax, and sentences (though many authors also try to do justice to literary forms, broader arguments, and theological message). Modern biblical commentaries typically go to great lengths exploring the world behind the text. For example, the back cover of the *Zondervan Illustrated Bible Backgrounds Commentary* exclaims: "It's like slipping on a set of glasses that lets you read the Bible through the eyes of a first-century reader!" While context is clearly relevant to textual meaning, exaggerating the world "behind" the text risks making biblical texts mere springboards for elucidating the background material rather than vice versa.

Meanwhile, at the other end of the hermeneutical spectrum, some commentaries provide help for the preacher by focusing on the world "in front of" the text. The *NIV Application Commentary* series has for its premise that interpretation should be not a one-way ticket from the twenty-first century to the past but rather a return journey. Commentaries in the series aim to specify what is universal in the human condition, or at least what is analogous between past and present situations of the people of God. The challenge here is to avoid falling into moralism on the one hand or the suggestion that the Bible has primarily utilitarian value on the other.[18]

By and large, evangelical biblical scholars have done well in the academy, if by "doing well" one means mastering the tools of the trade and gaining acceptance in the guild. However, this success has not come without a price, namely, the afore-mentioned disunion between biblical studies and theology as well as the chasm between contemporary biblical scholarship and the church.

The sobering question we must pose to evangelical commentaries is: do they preach? The anecdotal evidence is sobering, as this recent e-mail from one of my doctoral students sadly attests: "Just read Cranfield, Mann and Evans on the cry of dereliction in the Gospel of Mark, and they say virtually nothing! It is so frustrating to be told all this great stuff about biblical theology, and then to turn there and find maybe a paragraph filled with references to parallel statements in ancient works and this and that about a full moon and the darkness cover-

---

18. So D. A. Carson, *New Testament Commentary Survey,* 5th ed. (Grand Rapids: Baker, and Leicester, UK: Inter-Varsity, 2001), p. 24.

ing the earth. . . . New Testament commentators, New Testament commentators, why have you forsaken me?"

Biblical exegetes respond to the above allegations by making at least three points. First, attending to the Bible's "natural history" need not rule out a concern with the supernatural but may be an expression of this concern. Second, sometimes it is only by attending to historical and cultural backgrounds that we can recover the thought-world of the biblical authors. Third, we are so doing theology! Not all of us bow the knee to historical criticism; many of us resist the fragmentation inherent in criticism and seek to synthesize the biblical material, though in ways that respect the Bible's own categories.

The Monstrous Regiment of Systematics

Systematic theologians have their share of critics too: "Systematic theologians for their part have seldom offered any sustained demonstration of their reliance, if any, on the discipline of biblical exegesis."[19] According to G. E. Wright, systematic theologies "lack the colour, the flexibility, the movement of the Bible [and] attempt to freeze into definite, prosaic rationality that which was never intended by the Bible to be so frozen."[20]

Why are they saying such awful things about systematic theology? The following reasons are among the most cited:

- theologians impose confessional frameworks onto the text, encouraging an Athenian captivity of the church.
- theologians are more interested in hermeneutics (how we say what it means) or church tradition (what others have said that it means) than in the language of the Bible or what it says for itself.[21]
- theologians elevate certain themes to such status that they write theologies of hope or play instead of theologies of Hosea and Paul.

19. Murray Rae, "On Reading Scripture Theologically," *Princeton Theological Review* 1 (2008): 14.

20. G. E. Wright, *God Who Acts: Biblical Theology as Recital* (London: SCM Press, 1952), pp. 110-11.

21. I. Howard Marshall reports increasing numbers of graduate students wanting to study "hermeneutics" rather than the New Testament ("Evangelicalism and Biblical Interpretation," in *The Futures of Evangelicalism: Issues and Prospects,* ed. Craig Bartholomew, Robin Parry, and Andrew West [Leicester, UK: Inter-Varsity Press, 2003], p. 101).

- their sweeping generalizations run roughshod over the particularities of the text and their confessional systems wreak interpretive violence.
- theologians are text offenders who commit text abuse.

Systematic theologians have three rebuttals to their critics as well. First, theology is a kind of biblical thinking that focuses more on the subject matter, the broader economy of salvation, than on contextual concerns. Second, if theologians harp on the hermeneutical assumptions that one inevitably brings to exegesis, it is in order to safeguard biblical integrity, not to call it into question. Third, theologians think about contemporary culture and speak in today's terms not to marginalize the Bible, but to render it intelligible.

Loose Confederation or Constitutional Union?

Like America's Founding Fathers, evangelicals have worked a revolution — a Reformation — locating supremacy in Scripture rather than Rome, Constantinople, or Geneva. Will the center hold? We stand at a propitious moment, one that calls for a rethinking, and recovery, of the civil union between biblical studies and systematic theology.

The "Jeffersonian" interpretation of the American Revolution saw it as a liberation movement from corrupt European forms of centralized government: "The core revolutionary principle according to this interpretive tradition is individual liberty."[22] At its most extreme form, however, this becomes a pathological recipe for anarchy. The alternative "Hamiltonian" interpretation saw the Revolution as an incipient national movement, whose core principle is more unifying than individualistic. This, at least, was the thrust of the Federalist Papers, a series of arguments in favor of ratifying the Constitution.

Renewing evangelicalism will involve ratifying (i.e., reaffirming) our commitment to biblical authority. Is this best done in a Jeffersonian or Hamiltonian manner? What does it mean to be biblical? The evangelical mission depends upon its ability to preserve, and to *practice,* the principle of *sola scriptura.*

22. Joseph J. Ellis, *Founding Brothers: The Revolutionary Generation* (New York: Alfred A. Knopf, 2000), p. 14.

Biblical scholars who resist the yoke of systematizing tyranny resemble the Anti-Federalists who fear the dogmatician's tendency too quickly to consolidate the diversity of biblical states into one theological nation. Like the old-style Republicans who fought to defend states' rights, exegetes want to preserve the individual liberty of speech of each biblical author: *texts' rights* — one verse, one voice, one vote. Canonical democracy is, of course, messy. Further, it fails to get us beyond the Articles of Confederation, where "Each state retains its sovereignty, freedom, and independence." Is it possible to make of the many *one?*

The Federalists doubted that a mere Confederation could preserve the Union from either internal or external dangers, which is to say, factions and heresy. In Federalist Paper No. 9 Hamilton describes commonwealths as "wretched nurseries of unceasing discord" — not a bad description of biblical studies in the academy, where one finds the Hebrew Scriptures resisting Christian appropriation, and Jesus set against Paul.

It is tempting to identify all systematic theologians as Monarchists. Dogmaticians at their worse are dogmatic, even Napoleonic: eager to conquer the promised land of the biblical text — canon, nor Canaan — with -isms (e.g., Arminianism; Calvinism; existentialism) that take no prisoners. Like James Madison, I am after a kind of federalism that occupies a "middle ground" between a confederation of sovereign states (all parts, no whole) and a consolidated nation (all whole, no parts). In short: I am after an approach that preserves texts' rights *and* doctrinal union.

We need to get beyond the factionalism that prevents exegetes and theologians from cooperating, beyond what Thomas Jefferson referred to as a "wall of separation" between Federalists and Republicans. In the words of Joel Green: "If we are to engage in a genuinely theological exegesis of Christian Scripture, then both disciplines, biblical studies and systematic theology, must change."[23]

Whom does our current state of disunion hurt most? Who loses out? Academics themselves, in the first instance, but ultimately pastors and their congregations. Why? Because what the disunion disrupts is the preacher's ability to bring the word of God to bear on our world. R. R. Reno says, "Each decade finds new theories of preaching to cover

---

23. Joel B. Green, "Practicing the Gospel in a Post-Critical World: The Promise of Theological Exegesis," *Journal of the Evangelical Theological Society* 47, no. 3 (2004): 387.

the nakedness of seminary training that provides theology without exegesis and exegesis without theology."[24]

For a More Perfect Union . . .

Several recent stirrings offer hope that we can get beyond the status quo. We are positioned at the cutting edge of one of the most exciting developments in biblical scholarship: "the rediscovery of the dialogue with theology about the *subject matter* of the [Old and] New Testaments[s]."[25] The hope is to form a more perfect union that will enable us to exegete with a theological interest in the practical knowledge of God to the glory of God.[26]

Stirrings: New Initiatives on the Bible Front

There are a number of new "federalist" initiatives that we could mention, welcome signs of an interdisciplinary spring thaw. First, there is a series of St. Andrews Conferences on Scripture and Theology that began in 2003 as an attempt to overcome the increasing separation between biblical studies and theology.[27] They offer no methodological quick fixes, only the opportunity for "sustained and patient discussion between scholars from both sides of the disciplinary divide as they together grapple to understand the Scriptures of the Christian Church and their theological implications."[28]

24. Reno, "Series Preface," Brazos Theological Commentary.

25. John Barclay, foreword to Paddison, *Theological Hermeneutics and 1 Thessalonians,* p. xi.

26. For a similar appeal, though addressed more narrowly to the Reformed community, see Michael S. Horton, "What God Hath Joined Together: Westminster and the Uneasy Union of Biblical and Systematic Theology," in *The Pattern of Sound Doctrine: Systematic Theology at the Westminster Seminaries,* ed. David VanDrunen (Phillipsburg, NJ: P&R Publishing, 2004), pp. 43-71.

27. To date there have been three conferences, on the Gospel of John and Christian theology, on the Epistle to the Hebrews and Christian theology, and, in June 2009, on Genesis and Christian theology.

28. Preface to Richard Bauckham, Daniel Driver, Trevor Hart, and Nathan MacDonald, eds., *The Epistle to the Hebrews and Christian Theology* (Grand Rapids: Eerdmans, 2009), p. ix.

Second, there is a new "Christian Theology and the Bible" group in the Society of Biblical Literature.[29] Third, there are new scholarly resources: both a monograph series — "Studies in Theological Interpretation" — and a dictionary.[30] Finally, and perhaps most tellingly, there is a bevy of new commentary series (e.g., Ancient Christian Commentary; Two Horizons; Brazos Theological Commentary), "the ultimate testing ground"[31] for discerning whether we have indeed achieved a more perfect union between biblical studies and systematics.

Ten Theses on the Theological Interpretation of Scripture

According to David Bebbington's definition, "biblicism" is one of the four marks of evangelicalism, along with substitutionary atonement, conversion, and activism. Bebbington's quadrilateral is well known, Vanhoozer's decahedral, a ten-point checklist for fledgling theological interpreters of Scripture, less so. The ten theses are arranged in five pairs: the first term in each pair is properly theological, focusing on some aspect of God's communicative agency; the second draws out its implications for hermeneutics and biblical interpretation.[32]

1. The nature and function of the Bible are insufficiently grasped unless and until we see the Bible as an element in the economy of triune discourse.[33]

29. It also has a blog — http://christiantheologyandbible.wordpress.com — dedicated to exploring the intersection between the two disciplines.

30. Kevin J. Vanhoozer, ed., *Dictionary for Theological Interpretation of the Bible* (Grand Rapids: Baker, 2005).

31. So Steven J. Koskie, "Seeking Comment: The Commentary and the Bible as Christian Scripture," *Journal of Theological Interpretation* 1, no. 2 (2007): 237.

32. For other overviews of the emerging field of theological interpretation of the Bible, see J. Todd Billings, *The Word of God for the People of God: An Entryway to the Theological Interpretation of Scripture* (Grand Rapids: Eerdmans, 2010); Mark Alan Bowald, *Rendering the Word in Theological Hermeneutics: Mapping Divine and Human Agency* (Aldershot, UK: Ashgate, 2007); Stephen Fowl, *Theological Interpretation of Scripture* (Eugene, OR: Cascade Companion, 2009); Joel B. Green, *Seized by Truth: Reading the Bible as Scripture* (Nashville: Abingdon, 2007); Richard Hays, "Reading the Bible with the Eyes of Faith," *Journal of Theological Interpretation* 1, no. 1 (2007): 5-21, esp. pp. 11-15; Daniel J. Treier, *Introducing Theological Interpretation of Scripture: Renewing a Christian Practice* (Grand Rapids: Baker, 2008).

33. See my "Triune Discourse: Theological Reflections on the Claim that God Speaks," in *Trinitarian Theology for the Church: Scripture, Community, Worship,* ed. David Lauber and Daniel J. Treier (Downers Grove, IL: InterVarsity Press, 2009), pp. 25-78.

Those who approach the Bible as Scripture must not abstract it from the Father who ultimately authors it, the Son to whom it witnesses, and the Spirit who inspired and illumines it.

2. An appreciation of the theological nature of the Bible entails a rejection of a methodological atheism that treats the texts as having a "natural history" only.
The Bible is like and unlike other books: like other books, the Bible has authors; unlike other books, its primary author is God. Hence the *analogia lectionis,* or "analogy of reading": the similarity in reading the Bible like other books is marked by an even greater dissimilarity due to its character as the word of God.

3. The message of the Bible is "finally" about the loving power of God for salvation (Rom. 1:16), the definitive or final gospel word of God that comes to brightest light in the word's final form.
The God who authored Scripture sends his Son and Spirit into the dramatic story line. The God who led Israel out of Egypt is the same God who raised Jesus from the dead; the one Exodus anticipates the other.

4. Because God acts in space-time (of Israel, Jesus Christ, and the church), theological interpretation requires thick descriptions that plumb the height and depth of history, not only its length.
An exegetical method is only as rich as its conception of history. Exegetes are not outside the world described by the Bible, looking in; on the contrary, the Bible describes our world, our history. Modern biblical scholarship too often hobbles itself by its purely immanent understanding of history as atomistic and linear. In contrast to this thin conception, theological interpreters insist that to be in history is to participate in the field of God's communicative activity. Grammatical-historical exegesis takes on theological flavor when "historical" implies "a participation in realities known by faith."[34]

5. Theological interpreters view the historical events recounted in Scripture as ingredients in a unified story ordered by an economy of triune providence.
There is no square inch of human history that is extrinsic to the

34. Matthew Levering, *Participatory Biblical Exegesis: A Theology of Biblical Interpretation* (Notre Dame: Notre Dame University Press, 2008), p. 6.

"mission" fields of Son and Spirit. The biblical authors are witnesses to a coherent series of events ultimately authored by God. This series of events involves both divine words and divine deeds and, as such, is both revelatory and redemptive.

6. *The Old Testament testifies to the same drama of redemption as the New, hence the church rightly reads both Testaments together, two parts of a single authoritative script.*

Again, this hermeneutical thesis follows from the preceding theological claim. What unifies the canon is divine providence, and this in two senses: formally, the Bible is the product of divine authorship; materially, the subject matter of the Bible is the history of God's covenant faithfulness. It is the story of how God keeps his word: to Adam, Noah, Abraham, Moses, David, and so on. It follows that the Old and New Testaments are connected at a profound level, for the one story of God's faithfulness to his covenant promise is told in two parts.

7. *The Spirit who speaks with magisterial authority in the Scripture speaks with ministerial authority in church tradition.*

We owe the insight into the unity of the Old and New Testaments to precritical readers — Fathers and Reformers — who developed and maintained the Rule of Faith that generated in turn a typological Rule for Reading, in which earlier events and persons prefigured later aspects of the person and work of Christ.

8. *In an era marked by the conflict of interpretations, there is good reason provisionally to acknowledge the superiority of catholic interpretation.*

The word of God addresses the one church, local and universal; we are not the first generation to receive illumination. It is a bold critic who is prepared to identify his own interpretation with "what the Bible says" even when it flies in the face of the Great Tradition. One need not conclude from the history of textual effects that the Bible's meaning has changed, only that communities in different times and places have searched the Scriptures from their respective situations, enriching our understanding of the literal sense.

9. *The end of biblical interpretation is not simply communication — the sharing of information — but communion, a sharing in the light, life, and love of God.*

We need to recover the practice of reading Scripture in order to renew our mission and reform our habits. The theological interpretation of the Bible is as much if not more a matter of spiritual formation as it is a procedure that readers work on the text: "God's employment of the words of Scripture to be an instrument of his own communicative presence, by which process they are made holy, has its goal and essential counterpart in God's formation of a holy people."[35]

10. *The church is that community where good habits of theological interpretation are best formed and where the fruits of these habits are best exhibited.*

The church is not just another interpretive community with its own set of idiosyncratic interests, but the divinely appointed context wherein God ministers new life via his word and Spirit. Strictly speaking, "Scripture" makes no sense apart from the community whose life, thought, and practice it exists to rule and shape. And this leads me to my next point.

A More Enviable Union? "Exegesis Benedict"

Evangelicals have spent a disproportionate amount of time fretting about end-times and times-tables. It would be ironic if evangelicals were indeed "left behind" — not by Christ at his return but by other biblical interpreters who are running the Pauline race better and faster. Perhaps the following example will spur evangelicals on to greater things. To paraphrase the apostle Paul: "Theological interpretation has come to the Romans (i.e., Catholics), so as to make Israel (i.e., evangelicals) jealous" (Rom. 11:11).

The subtitle of Scott Hahn's *Covenant and Communion* is "The Biblical Theology of Pope Benedict XVI."[36] Evangelicals apparently are not the only people interested in renewing their biblical mission. Surely a pope who identifies his own theology as "biblical" and who is working hard to integrate biblical studies, critical scholarship, the history of in-

35. Murray Rae, "On Reading Scripture Theologically," *Princeton Theological Review* 1 (2008): 23.

36. Scott W. Hahn, *Covenant and Communion: The Biblical Theology of Pope Benedict XVI* (Grand Rapids: Brazos, 2009).

terpretation, and theology should make us sit up and take notice?[37] How, then, does Benedict conceive the union of biblical studies and theology?

Benedict acknowledges that the Bible comes from a real past; everything that helps us better to understand what was said in that past is worthwhile. Yet, because the Bible ultimately comes from the eternal God, "[e]verything that shrinks our horizon and hinders us from seeing and hearing beyond that which is merely human must be opened up."[38] Benedict complains that historical-critical exegesis "can never show Christ yesterday, today, and forever, but only (if it remains true to itself) Christ as he was yesterday."[39] It is not the historical method that is at fault as much as certain epistemological and metaphysical assumptions that reduce the mysteries of the faith to material things.

Biblical studies alone can never show what makes the individual texts in the Bible into a single book. One needs to appeal either to the church or divine authorship to do that. Benedict opts for the former option: "Without faith, Scripture itself is not Scripture, but rather an ill-assorted ensemble of bits of literature that cannot claim any normative significance."[40] For Benedict, then, the faith of the church alone [*sola ecclesia!*] makes the disparate texts into a single Bible. Protestants demur, claiming that God's inspired word is prior to human faith.[41]

In October 2008, Benedict addressed Roman Catholic bishops gathered from all over the world for a synod on Scripture. His thesis: "When exegesis is not theological, Scripture cannot be the soul of theology, and vice versa; then theology is not essentially Scriptural interpretation within the Church, then this theology no longer has a foundation. Therefore . . . it is absolutely necessary to overcome this dualism

---

37. For one biblical scholar who sat up and took critical notice, see Richard Hays, "Benedict and the Biblical Jesus," *First Things* 175 (August/September 2007): 49-53.

38. Joseph Ratzinger, preface to Holden, *Interpretation of the Bible in the Church,* p. 3.

39. Joseph Ratzinger, *Truth and Tolerance: Christian Belief and World Religions* (San Francisco: Ignatius, 2004), p. 133.

40. John F. Thornton and Susan B. Varenne, eds., *The Essential Pope Benedict XVI: His Central Writings and Speeches* (San Francisco: HarperSanFrancisco, 2007), p. 146.

41. Nicholas Wolterstorff argues for the unity of the canon in terms of God's authorizing it as a single work ("The Unity Behind the Canon," in *One Scripture or Many? Canon from Biblical, Theological and Philosophical Perspectives,* ed. Christine Helmer and Christof Landmesser [Oxford: Oxford University Press, 2004], pp. 217-32).

between exegesis and theology."[42] Amen. Evangelicals may not be able to meet in synods, but there is a long tradition of tent meetings.

Toward a New Federalism: Open Letter to Evangelical Biblical Scholars and Theologians

We, the evangelical people of God, in order to form a more perfect Union, establish justice, ensure domestic Tranquility — not least in our theology faculties — provide for the common defense, promote the ecclesial Welfare, and secure the blessings of liberty in Christ to ourselves and our posterity, do call for a canonical convention. In particular, we ask for a ruling on the following question: "whether a scholarly reading of the biblical materials should in some crucially important way be shaped by the Christian conviction that God speaks in and through these texts."[43] If you believe in canon clap your hands!

The original Federalist Papers were written to secure ratification of the Constitution and ultimately for the good of the federal whole and the state parts. Evangelicals stands at a similarly fateful moment: will we read our Constitution "federally," as displaying covenantal unity (*foedus* = "covenant"), canonical authority, and christocentrism, or will we read it according to the prevailing rules of the academy, like any other document of the university? The most important form of the church's public witness is its biblical interpretation: being biblical is the main concern *(res)* of the people of God *(publicus)*. To renew the evangelical mission we therefore need to form *a new theological republic of biblical letters, a people who represent the gospel of God because they are able imaginatively to indwell the society of biblical literature.*[44]

---

42. Cited in Hahn, *Covenant and Communion,* p. 43.

43. Rae, "On Reading Scripture Theologically," p. 13.

44. Some readers may detect an allusive reference to the federal or covenant theology of seventeenth-century post-Reformation Reformed dogmatics. The covenant motif, arising organically from the biblical texts themselves, provides an important integrative theme linking biblical studies, biblical theology, and systematic theology. However, my appeal to the analogy with the Federalist Papers does not require subscription to covenant theology.

The Goal: A Republic of Biblical Letters

We may, as a canonical community, have something to learn from another republican of letters, Martha Nussbaum, who like us has had to struggle with a disciplinary divide — in her case, between philosophy and literature. The prevailing academic culture of her graduate program refused this unequal disciplinary yoking; she was forced to choose between philology and philosophy, her love of words and her love of wisdom. This "ancient quarrel" between poets and philosophers parallels our topic, the ugly ditch between biblical studies and systematic theology.

Nussbaum holds that both dramatic poetry and philosophy are after the same goal: *eudaimonia,* human "flourishing." In *Poetic Justice,* she uses literature as a tool for training the minds and the emotions of the gatekeepers of public morality.[45] Instead of exiling the poets from the Republic, as Plato wanted, Nussbaum assigns them a key tutorial role. She enlists poets to present a *literary* vision of a just society to the corporate leaders of America. In her distinctly liberal political vision, literature teaches and cultivates empathy, tolerance, and compassion.

Evangelical exegetes and theologians pursue a similar goal: understanding not generic goodness but Godness, together with the gospel and its bearing on human righteousness, salvation, and *shalom.* Whereas Nussbaum uses literature to inculcate tolerance, biblical literature inculcates the knowledge, and love, of God. Apprentices to Scripture will learn not only bits of information but also, more importantly, habits of judgment — in a word, the mind of Christ, the *phronesis* or practical reason of God.

The Means: Tearing the Disciplinary Curtain in the Ivory Temple in Two

The way forward is to tear the disciplinary curtain that divides biblical studies from theology in the ivory temple in two. For between the exegete's focus on words, grammar, and historical background and the theologian's interest in concepts, doctrine, and system, there lies a rela-

---

45. Martha Nussbaum, *Poetic Justice: The Literary Imagination and Public Life* (Boston: Beacon, 1995).

tively untapped area of interest, at least as concerns theological interpretation: the various forms of biblical literature. The literary forms of
the Bible are lenses that school our imaginations to see and grasp
things as wholes: the individual books as a whole, the intertextual connections between the various books and, most importantly, our own
world in light of the world of the biblical texts. This is where the real
work still needs to be done, and it brings us back to David Wells's concern with the cultural captivity of the evangelical church.

The challenge is to read the Bible in such a way that we neither
learn merely *about* it (as in much biblical scholarship) nor merely *use* it
to substantiate our doctrinal claims (as in much systematic theology)
but rather learn *from* it in order to be changed *by* it.

To renew the evangelical mission we need to become a more liter-
ate people of the book: we must conform our hearts, minds, and wills to
the forms of desiring, thinking, and acting inscribed in Scripture. Being
biblical involves more than intellectually grasping propositions. It is
rather a matter of learning certain cognitive, volitional, and affective
dispositions that are part and parcel of what the Bible communicates. It
is through having our imaginations transformed by dwelling in the society of biblical literature that we can rightly order our lives before God.
Call it canonical catechesis.

In seeking such wisdom (for this is what we should call it), it is
never a good idea to look exclusively at either the parts or the whole. Exegesis and systematics here keep one another in check. We need to enter into a new hermeneutical circle in which commentaries and doctrines are mutually informing and illuminating, where systematicians
encourage exegetes to relate biblical texts to ever broadening contexts
and exegetes encourage systematicians to ground their conceptual
schemes in the particulars of the biblical texts.

The Result: Theological Exegesis and Exegetical Theology

Scholars know deep down that they can and should do better than stay
within the safe confines of their specializations: "For I have the desire
to do what is right, but not the ability to carry it out. For I do not do the
interpretive good I want, but the historical-criticism or proof-texting I
do not want is what I keep on doing. Now if I do what I do not want, it is
no longer I who do it, but interpretive habits that have been drilled into

me. Wretched reader that I am! Who will deliver me from this body of secondary literature?" Thanks be to God, there is a way forward: the way, truth, and life of collaboration in Christ, where sainthood and scholarship co-exist, and where theological exegesis and exegetical theology are mutually supportive and equally ultimate.

Theological exegesis is not less but more than grammatical. Meaning occurs not only on the level of the sentence but also of the genre as a whole, which is why our interpretation must be "lettered," adept at interpreting the whole panoply of the Bible's literary forms.

Theological exegesis is not less but more than historical. Everything depends on exegetes having a theologically "thick" view of history as the field of God's communicative activity. It is precisely because of this broader divine economy "that the ultimate meaning of texts cannot be simply handed over to the critical biblical scholar."[46]

Theological exegesis aims for both understanding and communion with God. Understanding without communion is empty; communion without understanding is blind. Joel Green's comment continues to haunt: "no amount of linguistic training or level of expertise in historical and textual analysis can supersede the more essential 'preparation' entailed in such dispositions and postures as acceptance, devotion, attention, and trust."[47]

The chief end of biblical studies and theology is to minister understanding of God's word. At its best, systematic theology is no more removed from Scripture than is exegesis. In the words of Murray Rae: "I understand the task of doctrinal formulation to be the specification of what we take to be true in light of the biblical witness."[48] Call it biblical reasoning: thinking *with* and *through* the Bible, not merely *about* it. Biblical reasoning is father to the Christian imagination, the means of viewing our world in terms of the strange new world of the Bible. An exegetical theology reasons biblically about the present, "figuring" the contemporary church situation into the drama of redemption.

Biblical reasoning requires canon sense. By "canon sense" I mean three things. First, the ability to locate a given biblical passage or event in light of the canonical whole and the entire drama of redemption.

---

46. C. Stephen Evans, "The Bible and the Academy," in *The Bible and the University*, ed. David Lyle Jeffrey and C. Stephen Evans (Grand Rapids: Zondervan, and Milton Keynes, UK: Paternoster, 2007), p. 310.

47. Green, *Seized by Truth*, p. 65.

48. Rae, "On Reading Scripture Theologically," p. 17.

Second, the ability conceptually to unpack the story line of the Bible in doctrinal terms. Third, the ability to see/feel/taste the truth/goodness/ beauty borne by Scripture's diverse literary forms. We find here potential common ground with biblical exegesis: in exploring the poetic lay of the biblical land.

Biblical reasoning requires catholic sensibility. Biblical reasoning also requires catholic sensibility, an awareness of how believers at other times, places, and situations have interpreted the word of God. The Republic of biblical letters is global and intercultural.

Biblical reasoning requires contextual sensitivity. Finally, biblical reasoning requires contextual sensitivity, an understanding of the present situation.

The Shared Mission: Leading Out (and Onward) the *Plain Canonical Sense*

To speak of "the" Bible is already to make a theological judgment about what holds the various books together, one that "places the interpreter (whether self-consciously or not) within a community of interpretation that evaluates positively the theological decision to read these disparate documents together."[49] This same judgment allows us to hold biblical studies and systematics together too: "The exegete concentrates upon the refraction of the subject matter through particular witnesses, thereby penetrating more deeply into the particular shape of the subject matter and helping to avoid banal theological generalities. And the theologian concentrates more upon the whole of the subject matter as it is expressed through the understanding of scripture in the dogmatic tradition, thereby helping to avoid the tendency toward fragmentation in exegesis."[50]

Over this sunny collaboration there hangs a dark hermeneutical cloud: does the divine authorial intent coincide with that of the human author without remainder or surplus? That the human authors say more than they could know best comes to light in canonical context,

---

49. C. Kavin Rowe and Richard B. Hays, "Biblical Studies," in *The Oxford Handbook of Systematic Theology,* ed. John B. Webster, Kathryn Tanner, and Iain Torrance (Oxford: Oxford University Press, 2007), p. 451.

50. Rowe and Hays, "Biblical Studies," p. 452.

where we see that Jesus Christ stands at the center of it all: "And beginning with Moses and all the prophets, he interpreted to them in all the Scriptures the things concerning himself" (Luke 24:27). The so-called "spiritual" sense is located here, in the text's *telos* or end in Jesus. One might describe the literal and spiritual senses in terms of the text's archaeology and teleology respectively. To invoke Benedict once more: "Certainly texts must first of all be traced back to their historical origins and interpreted in their proper historical context. But then, in a second exegetical operation, one must look at them also in light of the total movements of history and history's central event, Jesus Christ. Only the combination of both of these methods will yield a correct understanding of the Bible."[51]

Benedict's two exegetical moments are in fact aspects of a single interpretative task: that of expounding what we might call the "plain canonical sense." It all comes down to the question of proper context: is the meaning of Scripture exhausted when we have described the discourse in its original historical context, basic though it be, or may we go on to read the parts in light of the whole, as elements in a unified divine discourse? This is too important a question for any one individual to pontificate on, which is precisely why I am calling for a canonical convention of evangelical biblical scholars and systematicians.

The "plain canonical sense" demands both inward and outward looking exegesis. By inward looking, I have in mind how the Old Testament authors' words take on additional significance in light of the event of Jesus Christ. C. S. Lewis calls this a "second meaning," though, strictly speaking, the first meaning is already "in touch with that very same reality in which the fuller truth is rooted."[52] The New Testament authors are not foisting something alien into the words of the Psalmist, says Lewis, but are rather "prolonging his meaning in a direction congenial to it."[53]

Theological exegesis discerns the plain canonical sense. Exegetical theology then seeks to indwell it and to look out through it at everything else. We need to discern what the human authors were saying and then to indwell what God is saying via the human authors. Both discerning and

51. "Biblical Interpretation in Crisis," in *The Essential Pope Benedict XVI*, p. 256.

52. Lewis, *Reflections on the Psalms* (New York: Harcourt, Brace & World, 1958), p. 102.

53. Lewis, *Reflections on the Psalms*, p. 102.

indwelling require imagination.[54] The overall aim is to extend the plain canonical sense into our present situation. Following Lewis Ayres, we might call this "grammatical-figural" interpretation.[55] "Figural" means that we will use the text not only as a window into past history but into our own ongoing history as the people of God. It involves *extending the literal sense* so that we come to see the scenes of our everyday life as caught up in the same drama in which the biblical authors play their own respective parts. We are not very good at this; Reno likens us to stroke victims who must rehabilitate our exegetical imaginations.[56] Yet we may hope and pray for a full recovery . . .

Exegetes must be willing to make even thicker descriptions that elaborate the "plain canonical sense"; systematic theologians must be willing to be guided (and perhaps corrected) by the literal sense of the text (i.e., what the text communicated to its original authors and readers) even as they seek to extend it into the present. Both must change. Theological interpretation of Scripture names the joint exegetical-systematic project of holding the "original," "canonical," and "extended" senses in productive tension, which is the very point of invoking the federalist analogy, with its system of interpretive checks and balances.

Conclusion: The Courage to Be Evangelically Protestant

Our story seems to have concluded in the traditional manner, with a picture of the more perfect union we have been pursuing, namely, the wedding of biblical studies and systematic theology, where the dogmatic lion shall lie down with the exegetical lamb. The academy, however, is not yet that peaceable kingdom. The prevailing disciplinary winds continue to blow against the good ship theological interpretation. Could it be that interpreting the Bible theologically requires a new, counter-cultural practice?

The new Federalism that I have proposed here — the working part-

54. So Nicholas Wolterstorff, "Reply to Trevor Hart," in *Renewing Biblical Interpretation,* ed. Craig Bartholomew et al. (Grand Rapids: Zondervan, 2000), p. 335.

55. Lewis Ayres, "Patristic and Medieval Theologies of Scripture: An Introduction," in *Christian Theologies of Scripture: A Comparative Introduction,* ed. Justin S. Holcomb (New York and London: New York University Press, 2006), p. 15.

56. "Series Preface," Brazos Theological Commentary.

nership of theological exegesis and exegetical theology — may well require a cultural change in our theological faculties. If we are serious about renewing the evangelical mission, then we must produce theological interpreters of the Bible who are public intellectuals, first and foremost in the church, but also secondarily in the academy.

In the Academy

To Sir Edwyn Hoskyns's rhetorical question, "Can we bury ourselves in a lexicon, and arise in the presence of God?" we may respond with a resounding "Yes!"[57] It begins with a belief that God speaks to us in and through the human words of the Bible. Can we really read the Bible *as Scripture* in the academy? What if they deny us accreditation? In the light of church history, this is a rather mild form of persecution: "If in countries where seminaries are losing their accreditation for retaining a distinctively ecclesial raison d'être and pedagogical *telos* this means that Christians need to learn to train and educate people without accreditation, then that is exactly what it means."[58]

What if they laugh at us? So what? Let us continue to uphold standards of research and protocols of argument. Evangelicals, of all scholars, should display the intellectual virtues without which academic debate degenerates into grandstanding or mud-slinging. Intellectual humility, patient study, honesty, and consistency: against such there is no law.

Perhaps theological exegesis and exegetical theology will find no secure place in the academy. Even so, seminary faculties should stand against the prevailing modes of academic and popular culture to the extent that these fail to cultivate kingdom values. Overcoming the divide between biblical studies and systematic theology may well require curricular change. So be it. Perhaps this is the form our witness to the gospel must take. And we would not be the first to suffer a kind of martyrdom for doing so.

This is not to say that there is no place for evangelical biblical scholars in the academic guild. There is a continuing need for salt and light

---

57. *Cambridge Sermons* (London: SPCK, 1938), p. 70.
58. C. Kavin Rowe, euangelizomai.blogspot.com/2009/08/interview-with-kavin-rowe -on-luke-acts.html.

in that context too — for exemplars of "believing criticism" who write the kind of scholarly monographs that cannot be dismissed, because they display excellence in spite of what some may regarded as their "retrograde" theological presuppositions. They also serve who stand in, and up to, the academy. My one plea is that we not let this kind of scholarly witness become the de facto template that shapes our Bible college and seminary curricula. Yet I also want to acknowledge that, at its best, biblical scholarship overturns false interpretations and turns up new insights that become exegetical grist for the theological mill, further fuel for *semper reformanda.*

. . . and in the Pulpit

Seminary faculties need the courage to be evangelically Protestant for the sake of forming theological interpreters of Scripture able rightly to minister God's word. The preacher is a "man on a wire," whose sermons must walk the tightrope between Scripture and the contemporary situation. The pastor-theologian should be evangelicalism's default public intellectual, with preaching the preferred public mode of theological interpretation of Scripture.

Creating communities of embodied theological interpretation of Scripture is, I submit, the principal educational responsibility of the church today, and of the institutions that serve her. We gain neither wisdom nor holiness without submitting ourselves to the corporate discipline of interpreting the Bible in the church. Academic disciplines have only ministerial authority over what matters most, namely, the ecclesial discipline of teaching disciples how to read, and indwell, the Scriptures.

The Acts of the Desert Interpreter-Saints

In conclusion: interpreting the Bible theologically may be subversive of much contemporary practice. Those who reason about, and with, Jesus Christ from the Scriptures may find themselves, like the apostle Paul, being accused of turning the world — or at least theological curricula — upside down (Acts 17:2-6). Those who indwell the world of the biblical text do indeed bear strange new gifts to culture. Those who interpret the Acts of the Apostles must be willing to become part of its world-subverting action.[59]

Paul Ricoeur once spoke of the challenge of biblical hermeneutics in terms of wandering in the "desert of criticism."[60] Some fifty years on, the situation has changed. Evangelical biblical scholars and theologians have settled in populated areas, gained tenure in universities, held forth in the city gates and electronic villages. We have arrived in the academy, and it feels good. But there is a price to pay for this success. Are we willing to continue pursuing our academic specializations in isolation from one another, and from the church, separated by a dividing wall of disciplinary hostility (cf. Eph. 2:14)?

We need to bring down the Berlin Wall that compartmentalizes the work of biblical scholars and theologians. Perhaps we should leave our safe academic havens and sojourn out into the postcritical wilderness with the Desert Fathers: "Because there was so much emphasis in the desert on practice, on living with integrity, the monks interpreted Scripture primarily by putting it into practice. In the desert, Scripture's surplus of meaning endured not in the form of commentaries or homilies but in acts or gestures, in lives of holiness transformed by dialogue with Scripture."[61] May the fruitful union of biblical exegesis and systematic theology beget many more such saints — pastor-theologians who can make the Bible bloom in the desert of criticism and turn the empire of worldly desire upside down.

---

59. For an example of theological exegesis that also bears excellent academic witness, see C. Kavin Rowe, *World Turned Upside Down: Reading Acts in the Graeco-Roman Age* (Oxford: Oxford University Press, 2009).

60. Ricoeur, *The Symbolism of Evil* (Boston: Beacon, 1967), p. 349.

61. Douglas Burton-Christie, in his book *The Word in the Desert: Scripture and the Quest for Holiness in Early Christian Monasticism* (Oxford: Oxford University Press, 1993), p. 20.

Can We Say Very Much?
Evangelicals, Emergents, and the
Problem of God-Talk

ADONIS VIDU

I

The question of the current condition of the evangelical mission cannot avoid reckoning with a significant recent trend among a number of influential theologians who have been making a "postmodern turn" over the last decade. While this is a group of scholars who sometimes write very dense academic prose, often focusing on issues of epistemology, the critique of metaphysics, and the philosophy of language, they take these apparently arcane topics to be of utmost relevance for our understanding and transmission of the gospel. So much so that instead of the name by which this movement is identified, the "emerging church," many of these leaders prefer to describe themselves as "missional" theologians. Their revisioning of our deep seated assumptions about the meaning and the communication of the gospel is anchored not in a traditional understanding of the church, but in a theologically revised understanding of the mission of God, as well as a fresh awareness of the global shift of Christianity's center of gravity to the majority world. However, what gives particular force to this new movement (at least in the West) is its coupling with a number of epistemological perspectives, so much so that one cannot understand the "emergent church" apart from its roots in a postmodern critique of epistemology. Thus, the de-centering of global Christianity both reinforces and is being explained by a Western postfoundationalism. One of the areas of immediate impact is the teaching about the knowledge of God. Emergents create fresh spaces for theological pluralism by

226

claiming that (a) there is a legitimate openness to different religious conceptualizations of the divine, and (b) no particular religious conception is singly adequate to the being of God, because (c) words and concepts do not discover "facts" about the world, or God. Thus, lying at the very root of this new evangelical perspective on global mission is a particularly disputed understanding of the problem of theological knowledge, partly based on recent epistemology.[1]

This essay discusses precisely this underlying theological epistemology. Several sub-themes constitute the problem of God-talk, including intelligibility (meaning), success (reference, ontology), and rationality (justification). Neither of these can be approached in isolation from the others. I will therefore treat them together, as a cluster of concepts. What is the intelligibility proper to theological language, and what is its relation to the meaning of normal (observational) language? Can language refer to God, and if so, in what way and under what conditions? And as for the last theme, can faith be justified and in what manner?

Obviously these are not recent questions. Neither has the stream of possible solutions dwindled down. Yet there is something of an urgency attaching to these issues within present-day evangelical theology. Its recent turn toward postfoundationalism, espoused in particular by these "emergent" theologians, brings to the foreground these perennial issues. If there is such a thing as "emergent church" or "emergent theology" (a claim in which I have no stake), there certainly is an emergent consensus on postfoundationalism. Moreover, this philosophical and theoretical choice does have an emergent cash value. Indeed, the particular practical application of this epistemological turn is precisely what seems to bother so many critics of the "movement." Labels such as "relativism," "anti-realism," "liberalism" have become missiles, as well-meaning "traditionalists" fear that this new stance is utterly devoid of Christian convictions, fails to uphold historic orthodoxy, and ultimately consorts with "the world." As it most often happens in human relationships, before these missiles have a chance to explode (read: before the accusations are reckoned with) they are thrown back with matching rhetorical sting: it is the "traditionalists" who are concubines

---

1. I do not simplistically claim that this position is exclusively motivated by philosophical concerns. There are legitimate theological concerns that make such a philosophical position particularly tempting, as I will point out. This should not prevent us from evaluating whether particular philosophical tools adequately serve theological purposes.

of "the world" of modern epistemology. Sadly, more often than not, both sides fail to listen to one another.

My focus in this essay will be on the emergent position. I will suggest that emergent epistemic modesty rests upon a flawed understanding of the predicament of God-talk. In many ways this will be an appeal to temperance. It will be suggested that a proper understanding of postfoundationalism, one that does not buy into the notion that we are trapped within language, will not lead to fainthearted attitudes to conviction and doctrine. This will serve to protect those right "traditionalist" intuitions, even while it may challenge their own theoretical framework and explanation (isomorphism, metaphysical realism, foundationalism). The second section grants that there is indeed a problem of theological language, and it has a long and impressive pedigree in Christian theology. This observation will disassociate our problematic from the (important) debate over orthodoxy. This is not what is at stake here, at least primarily. Emergents are drawing on a respectable and mainline stream of the Christian tradition, the tradition of negative or apophatic theology. Moreover, the challenges brought by atheism, linguistic analysis, and deconstruction have the force that they do because of something, which Christians would assent to, namely the ontological difference between God and creation. Epistemic consequences flow from this distinction. There is a real problem of the meaning, reference, and rationality of our God-talk. The third section looks into the "emergent solution" to the problem of God-talk. It does not mean to engage with all relevant authors, but will focus on John Franke and Peter Rollins, since both have written monographs on this very topic. Finally, the last section outlines my own proposal.

II

To ask the question of why there is a problem about theological language is to risk opening a Pandora's box that cannot possibly be closed within the confines of this essay. I will thus restrict my inquiry to those aspects of the question which are proving to be foundational for the emergent solution. There are two sub-themes here. First, what are the conditions of intelligibility, reference, and justification in general? That is, what is the determination of human knowledge? What does it mean to know a thing, to say something intelligible about it, to be able to successfully refer to it and, finally, to be able to provide a justification for that belief? These are all central questions in epistemology. We will analyze the "postfoundationalist" approach to these issues and then move on to the second issue: what bearing does the fact that God is not a being like other beings have on the question of whether we can know him? In other words, what is the epistemic significance of the ontological difference?

The meaningfulness of our concepts has a double derivation. On the one hand, we can use our concepts confidently because they play a logical part in a so-called conceptual scheme. They belong to a catalogue of concepts that is constituted by logical relations between concepts. Definitions and rules of inference are an important part of the very nature of that catalogue. Some philosophers have called this a conceptual framework, or a conceptual scheme. A conceptual scheme is much like a language, though it cannot be identified with natural languages. There is no time to get into the complexities of these relationships at this point. Suffice it to say that in order to be able to meaningfully hold a concept, that concept must first of all be part of a conceptual scheme. There are no such things as atomistic concepts, concepts that stand on their own. Their very identity is given by the service they do in a conceptual system.

Not only is meaningfulness a question of integration in a conceptual scheme, but reference to things in the world always already presupposes the existence of a conceptual vocabulary of the sort described above. To refer to a thing is to bring that thing within the scope of concepts. It first of all means that I am able to *intend* that thing. But to intend a thing is to first of all know *what* thing one is intending. That is, one must be able to integrate that thing into a catalogue of concepts. To refer to something is not merely to point in its direction, for that has no ability to single out *the aspect* under which I am intending that thing. So, for instance, I may be pointing to a chair and saying "blue," "chair," "heavy," and so on. That is, I require such concepts as "object," "color," "weight" in order to refer to it properly.

The catalogue of concepts, the form under which we "take in" experience, is constructed through engagement with the world. Repetition is essential for the very formation of these concepts. Concepts such as "weight" have been able to be formed because we regularly experience something similar, which we find useful to identify by the name "weight." The confidence with which we use our language depends in large measure on the fact that, inter-subjectively, we apply that language as we inhabit a common world.

229

Now, empirical experience, our being related to "middle sized dry goods," as some pragmatists like to refer to observational reality, seems to be what anchors our language. It is what makes it possible, for instance, to translate radically new cultures. It is our inter-subjective sharing of a world that provides stability to our concepts. But this raises a huge problem for religious language, since it seems to have but the most tenuous of links to observational reality. If the intelligibility of our concepts is given by (a) the place they have in a conceptual scheme and (b) by them (or the scheme) standing in some kind of transparent relation to empirical, observable reality, then on both those counts religious language is deficient. On the one hand, religious language purports to be a language of faith, but it is very tempting to describe faith in private fashion. This loosens the link faith might have with any kind of logical system (the question of coherence). On the other, the religious object is by definition unconstrained by a kind of human experience. God remains good for religious people despite any amount of evil there might be in the world. God remains just despite any amount of suffering experienced by the world. Such is the grammar of religious language as such. And in fact this is precisely one of the key questions for this essay: in what ways is God related to that which might be experienced empirically, by the natural senses? And if God cannot be "reliably connected" to such experiences, does that mean that we cannot talk meaningfully about him?

A dilemma arises: we could conceive of God as being in some kind of linkage with created reality. This is a well-known tradition in Christianity, especially in its Thomistic strand: natural theology. God is conceived as the "cause" of this world. The temptation here is to select a concept from our own, mundane and observational language or conceptual framework and apply it to God. This is the temptation of idolatry. And, in fact, this is the temptation that terrifies emergents. But what is the alternative? The relationship between God and observable human experience (including the history of salvation) could be so weakened that we risk being unable to say anything substantial about God. That, I think, is the temptation which emergents are unnecessarily and unwittingly being forced toward by some of their theoretic/philosophical choices.

I will explore this dilemma as I turn to second aspect of the problem of God-talk. If, in order to talk about some thing I must first be able to *intend* that thing, which means to be able to have a concept of it, or to know *what* it is, then it is not difficult to see how this raises a problem for theological language. To know God means that I must first be able to intend God, which means that I must first know what kind of thing God is. It would thus seem that a condition of successful reference and intelligible belief about God is the fact that I am able to inscribe God on some chain of being, mapped by my (theological) concepts. But, as the Christian tradition in its entirety has held, *Deus non est genera*. God cannot be subsumed under any genus or species. This is the classical doctrine of divine simplicity, which also holds that there is no composition in God: there is no distinction between subject and predicate in God. God is his own attributes and these are one: himself.

Thus, not only would it seem that, since God does not fall into any class, we cannot (naturally) have him in mind, but also, since the only way to refer to something is by predicating something of that thing, neither can we refer to him. Since language works by way of composition and distinction, and God's being is absolutely simple, it follows that we cannot predicate anything of God, and thus that we cannot speak of God, since we cannot have him in mind.

Victor Preller[2] reflects on this fundamental limitation of knowledge when it comes to the being of God: "All existential references — in order to be significant for us — must be identified by reference to our experience of 'the world.'" But "can we intelligibly relate 'God' to 'chair,' 'person,' 'electron,' or to conceptual frameworks in which such intentions occur?"[3] Preller can only imagine this as a rhetorical question, unless one is prepared to accept the "horrendously naive attempts" of Thomists in the tradition of a natural theology that tries to graft God onto human concepts. Since God is wholly other, any relation in which he might engage with creation, thus any divine presence in human experience, would by definition be unique. The required repeatability which we identified as a condition of the meaningfulness of language in relation to the world would not obtain. From which it follows, for Preller, that "no language or science can be about God in the way in

---

2. Although the focus of this essay is not Preller, he is one of the main discussion partners. His 1967 book, *Divine Science and the Science of God: A Reformulation of Thomas Aquinas* (Princeton: Princeton University Press), has been pivotal in effecting a sea change in Thomistic interpretation, which brought Thomas in the proximity of the linguistic turn. I read Preller as supplying the intelligibility for much emergent thought, even though emergent thinkers themselves do not necessarily engage with him.

3. Preller, *Divine Science*, p. 19.

which any other language and science is about its object."[4] If, that is, it can be about God at all.

To sum up, the problem of God-talk stems from the combination of two factors: the intelligibility and reference of human speech depends on the way in which language connects to observable reality through repeatable experiences. A conceptual system is drawn on in the act of reference. However, since God is *ganz anders,* we do not have the required conceptual system that would make our talk about God intelligible. Every act of knowledge is partly receptive, partly creative (leaving undecided for now the result of that interplay). We draw on our so-called *spontaneity* and we passively take in the contents of experience. We have a spontaneity that *on the whole* seems to work for observable, macroscopic reality, even while we quarrel over the best theoretical explanation of that reality at a microscopic level. Our concepts have a certain mediated directedness to reality, in virtue of the conceptual scheme. The applicability of these concepts is indelibly tied to the role they play in a conceptual scheme. But, as Preller points out, we do not possess God's conceptual scheme.

Is there a way out of the dilemma? One might also ask: is this a compelling dilemma? Perhaps we have been forced into this corner by some bad decision somewhere along the line. I believe something like this to be the case. But an explanation will have to wait. D. Stephen Long writes that "Modern theology finds itself swinging between two equally unpalatable poles. Either God is turned into some kind of mythological creature who begins to resemble us: God suffers, God changes, creation affects God, God is finite. Or God becomes an ineffable sublime about whom nothing can be reasonably said, so that any speech is just as good as any other."[5] Either we think that God is commensurate with our conceptual scheme — and thus we have turned our concepts into idols, forgetting the fact that we have made them — or we give up saying anything at all about God — and thereby transform him into utter mystery. It is quite easy to see how, if we take the second route, it will become quite natural to weaken one's convictions. In what follows I will turn to the emergent "solution" to this predicament.

4. Preller, *Divine Science,* p. 21.
5. D. Stephen Long, *Speaking of God: Theology, Language, and Truth* (Grand Rapids: Eerdmans, 2009), p. 15.

III

Ceasing to talk about God is not an option. Emergents, together with the rest of the Christian tradition, insist on the necessity of bearing witness to God in human speech. But what is the kind of this witness? How might human speech have anything to do with God, given its apparent inherent limitations? In what way does it refer, what is its proper intelligibility, how might it be judged? The very fact that one can ask this question demonstrates that some kind of cognition of God is accepted. I mean "cognition" in a sense different than knowledge, which as was pointed out, requires an intentional object that can be inscribed on a conceptual scheme. Cognition is something like a pre-conceptual apprehension, or a pre-apprehension, much (but not exactly)[6] like my non-focal awareness that there are objects in my field of vision.

Up to this point the whole discussion has been construed in terms of natural reason, that is, reason unaided by anything coming from the divine side. But ought we not reasonably expect revelation to make a difference to this picture? It might be the case that we have so allowed a description of the natural limitations of language and knowledge to block our awareness of a revelation from God in the historical person of Jesus Christ. Moreover, does faith not constitute a kind of knowledge that is gifted to us by God? Indeed, special revelation, both in its scriptural mode as well as in its incarnational focus, plays a prominent part in the "solution" to the epistemic question. But, as we shall see, it does not simply defuse the problem.

I have identified three aspects to the emergent "coping" with the problem of God-talk. This is what I have earlier called the cash-value of their specific epistemological position. In the first place, both linguistic analysis, but especially the notion of ontological difference fund an *epistemic pluralism.* No single theological framework (one may read conceptual scheme) is adequate as witness to God. Secondly, revelation itself does not provide an easy way out of the dilemma, given its *indirectness.* Neither the meaning of scriptural revelation nor the divinity of Jesus Christ can be read off the pages of Scripture and the human nature of Jesus, respectively. Instead, these are given through them as free gifts. The letter mediates the spirit, but without the latter being ratio-

6. The equivocation results from the fact that I am betting on these to be "objects," so it is minimally conceptual.

nally tied (in exegetically significant ways) to the former. Humanity mediates divinity without becoming divine. Finally, since no discernible rational linkages obtain between the natural (Scripture, Christ's humanity, religious experience, natural world, etc.) and the supernatural (God), we have no way of moving rationally from the former to the latter. In what sense, then, can we ascertain whether our interpretations of Scripture, our doctrinal affirmations, our creeds and convictions are "about" the divine? Can we confidently ascribe truth to them? This brings us to the third aspect of the emergent response, which I have called the anonymizing (or hypernymizing) of truth. Emergents will claim that the truth of our theological statements is something that transcends our ability to justify and know it. Each of these specific strands in the emergent response is motivated by both theological and philosophical factors. Each explains the logic behind some of the emergent stances on doctrine, tradition, and convictions.

Epistemic Pluralism

John Franke, one of the most significant emergent theologians, arrives at the notion of epistemic theological pluralism from two directions. On the one hand, the inherent limitations of human language make any single reference to God inherently suspicious and potentially idolatrous. This is the mythical side of Long's dilemma of modern theology. To think that a single theoretical explanation, for instance the Chalcedonian definition, can capture divinity is to suppose that one humanly constructed conceptual framework — involving such concepts as *physis* and *hypostasis* is isomorphic to the divine conceptual scheme, that is, to the way in which God would understand himself. The obvious reason why this would be so damnable is that one would elevate a human creation (a linguistic/conceptual scheme) and map divinity onto it. This is nothing less than idolatry which is defined by Peter Rollins, an increasingly popular emergent theologian *cum* philosopher, as "any attempt that would render the essence of God accessible, bringing God into either aesthetic visibility (in the form of a physical structure such as a statue) or conceptual visibility (in the form of a concept such as a theological system)."[7] Idola-

---

7. Peter Rollins, *How (Not) to Speak of God* (Brewster, MA: Paraclete Press, 2006), p. 12.

try is in the eye of the beholder. The Exodus calf was not inherently idolatrous, but it was the people's attitude to it that made it so. Neither did the people regard the calf as being somehow divine, but only that it somehow stood for the God who took them out of Egypt.[8] Similarly, when a single concept or conceptual scheme arrests one's gaze in such a way that it claims to be uniquely appropriate to divinity, it amounts to conceptual idolatry.

It is important to understand that this awareness of the idolatrous temptation is what motivates emergents to take their particular stance with regard to creeds and convictions. Attachment to a single tradition and confession, with dogmatic certainty, they argue, tricks the mind into believing that this particular conceptualization of God, that this particular bringing into language, is uniquely sufficient. What is being forgotten is both the human contribution in the formation of those concepts, as well as the ontological difference, which precludes the transformation of God into an object of knowledge.

Epistemic pluralism surfaces as the answer to two simultaneous questions: negatively, what can be done to avoid such conceptual idolatry while, positively, continuing to say something about God? "This understanding," Franke writes, "affirms the incapacity of human language as a finite creaturely medium to refer directly to God in ways that correspond to the knowledge of God that is possessed by God. Thus it respects the inherent mystery and otherness of theology's subject matter. At the same time, it also preserves the possible occurrence of genuine and proper reference to God by the miracle of ongoing divine self-revelation, which allows humans to speak in an authentically informative way about God."[9] The Scriptures themselves give us this mandate in virtue of the plurality of their own witness to Jesus Christ, in the synoptic gospels and elsewhere. For Franke, the human response is included in the very act of revelation, resulting in a "differentiated unity expressed in plurality."[10] This yields "multiple perspectives within a set of possibilities."[11] As a consequence of the differentiated unity of the Scriptures themselves, theology should make room for such a plurality, again *within the range of a set of possibilities.*

---

8. Jean-Luc Marion, *The Idol and Distance: Five Studies* (Bronx, NY: Fordham University Press, 2001), pp. 1-9.

9. Franke, *Manifold Witness: The Plurality of Truth* (Nashville: Abingdon, 2009), p. 15.

10. Franke, *Manifold Witness,* p. 88.

11. Franke, *Manifold Witness,* p. 88.

Thus, revelation is not a matter of laying bare the structure of reality, or giving us the language of God. Revelation remains human, it presupposes and requires natural human powers of comprehension and expression. Moreover, because God is wholly other, mystery is not abolished but expressed in language as dialectic of veiling and unveiling. He remains "a reality that is tantalizingly and frustratingly both known and within reach as well as hidden and beyond our grasp."[12] Epistemic pluralism means to re-perform the plurality inherent in Scripture itself, in new settings, within the range of what is possible. This takes care of the negative aspect of the conceptual idolatry temptation: it ensures that we do not cling to any single theological framework and declare it absolute and adequate to expressing the mystery of God. No such framework can claim such accolades. But what about the positive aspect of the question?

This is where I think Franke has run against a problem: if any single conceptual framework (whether Chalcedonian orthodoxy, personalism, Tillichian theology, or what not) is inadequate because it cannot capture the divine conceptuality, then what sense will it make to say that a number of these schemes will? I doubt that Franke will explain the success (or advisability) of pluralism in terms of capturing the divine conceptuality, but then one has to ask what a plurality of inadequate schemes provides, what epistemic function does it fulfill, that a single scheme doesn't? Franke, as well as many other emergent theoreticians, has trouble explaining the precise function of this plurality, or its precise superiority.[13] He has managed to establish its superiority in virtue of the fact that it prevents fetishizing any single conceptual scheme, but he seems to want much more than that. His theological epistemology feeds on an optimism that *somehow* through the process of employing a variety of models, adequate reference to God is achieved and we can be in possession of informative knowledge of God. I will return to this optimism and this *"somehow"* toward the end of this section.

I now have to rehearse the argument according to which the scheme is thought to be inadequate. This is an important bit of detail, since the emergent solution hangs on a particular construal of the

12. Franke, *Manifold Witness*, p. 104.
13. I think this is one of the single most important challenges facing emergent theologians, namely, whether they are able to follow up on their critique of epistemology with similar positive construction. Can they rebuild the walls they have torn down?

problem. However, it is precisely in light of that analysis of the problem of reference that their own suggested solution of plurality does not make sense, as I've intimated.

The reason why any single conceptual scheme is inadequate to reality is, to put it very briefly, that it cannot mirror the very structure of reality. Emergents accept postfoundationalism, with its critique of the myth of the Given. There are no bits of uninterpreted experience, which we can use to justify our beliefs, concepts, and conceptual schemes. Since we have no God's eye view on reality, we cannot "get out of our skins" and analyze the relation between our conceptual schemes, concepts, and beliefs, on the one hand, and the very structure of reality on the other. The conceptual schemes we construct are shaped according to the purposes and interests we have with respect to the world.[14] Emergents are not alone in adopting this epistemology. If Preller is right, Aquinas himself accepted something like a critique of empiricism in that he understood our active contribution to knowledge. For Preller, there are possible variations in conceptual schemes. This involves the particular way in which a framework maps the world, the structure it assigns to it (whether we should talk about such things as natures, hypostases, subsistent relations, and so on). Moreover, we should also be open to the noetic effects of sin, which might induce a distortion of man's conscious apprehension of the nature of the real. Thus, writes Preller, "the actual form taken by our conceptual system is in some sense determined by the pragmatic concerns of human society-in-the-world."[15]

Now Preller has read a lot of Sellars and quite a bit of the pragmatists. Whether Franke and Rollins have read the same sources, their conclusions are very similar. We have no way of telling whether our conceptual system is correct because we have no independent way of verification whether it maps the world out correctly. We cannot check its isomorphism to the world. Vector in the problem of reference to a simple God, and it seems academic that any such conceptual scheme fails. But notice the reason why Franke (and Preller) think it fails: because it cannot ensure isomorphism. Because it cannot represent God (or the

14. Evidently, I am simplifying the debate horrendously. My intention is to provide a map of the emergents' engagement with postfoundationalism, which consciously underemphasizes much of the terrain in order to leave room for other aspects that will be dealt with.

15. Preller, *Divine Science,* p. 78.

237

world) on a conceptual scheme. Both Franke and Preller seem to parse the potential success of language in terms of how well it represents an independent object (whether the structure of the world, or the structure of the divine conceptual scheme). They are both unable to countenance a linguistic success that trades on something besides representation. Linguistic malfunction follows in the train of a failure of representation. That is an assumption that I do not think postfoundationalism ought to make.

One last item having to do with plurality before I move on to revelation and Christology. Part of my proposal will be that Franke, Rollins, et al. exaggerate the extent of the plurality (and incommensurability) that obtains between conceptual schemes. It will be up to me to demonstrate that, but now I want to suggest that they are enticed into that position by what D. Stephen Long labels as the designative understanding of the linguistic turn. Conceptual frameworks, they hold in similar fashion to a whole host of authors from Kuhn to Quine, divide the world differently. They each "slice the dough" in significantly different ways and the problem is that we do not have a non-conceptual access to the world itself so that we may judge them against it. Each concept, in virtue of its belonging to such a system, has its own peculiar way of being "about" the world. In Thomistic and Aristotelian categories, each concept has its own *modus significandi*. But because such schemes are formed with different interests and purposes in mind, because they are the result of specific cultures and historical ages, they divide the world so differently as to be incommensurable with each other. Here incommensurability is a name for our failure to judge between schemes. We have no way of translating one scheme into the conceptuality of another because there is no independent access to the world that would provide the common denominator for such a translation. An irreducible plurality seems to characterize our relation to the world. The point I wish to make is that Franke, Grenz, Rollins, and others simply buy into this outlook. But, as I will hope to show, it is a dualistic outlook, which thinks it can reflect about the meaningfulness of our concepts and their frameworks independently from reflecting about the world about which they are. More on this later. For now, let me rephrase an earlier question: If language fails because of a failure of representation, mapping, correspondence, why should we expect that the sum of all these failures somehow constitutes a success?

Revelational Indirectness

The second part of the emergent response to the problem of theological knowledge is incarnational. An immediate objection to the initial discussion of the problem of God-talk might be to point out the reality of the incarnation. Has God not become an "object of knowledge" in the person of Jesus Christ? While it might be true that natural theology's arguments for the existence of God risk becoming idolatrous by inscribing God within a causality and on a chain of being, doesn't Christology imply that God made himself available to our gaze, within a cause-and-effect world? One might be forgiven to think that certain optimistic epistemic consequences flow from the fact of the incarnation.

However, Franke points out that a Chalcedonian understanding of Christology precludes any such facile drafting into the service of such an epistemic optimism. The hypostatic union imagines a union without confusion between the human and divine natures of Jesus Christ. The *homoousion* does not mean that the human nature has been transformed into the divine, neither that it has been mixed with it. Reflection upon the humanity of Jesus is not ipso facto reflection upon his divine nature. We do not see Christ's divinity directly in his humanity. Revelation is, according to Franke, *indirect*. The eternal word remains transcendent even while it is incarnate and enculturated.[16] Franke reads revelation along the same lines with Barth, as a dialectic of veiling and unveiling. Thus, "revelation does not become a predicate of the human nature of Jesus. It is not something that is part of the natural created order and therefore may not be read directly from the person of Jesus apart from the grace of God."[17] This brings us to the crux of the issue, which is the connection that exists between the content of revelation (the divinity of Jesus) and that which is epistemically available to us, that which can figure in a human experience, in this case — as Franke reads it and I will contest it later — the humanity of Jesus.

So we seem to be back at square one. Even special revelation does not place God at our epistemic disposal. Under its scriptural aspect it doesn't because scripture is itself a plural human response to revelation and its meaning is not collapsed into its written form. As incarnation it doesn't because humanity does not become divinity. The human

16. Franke, *Manifold Witness*, p. 65.
17. Franke, *Manifold Witness*, p. 68.

nature of Jesus does not acquire the properties of his divine nature. Both Barth and Long see the Lutheran doctrine of the *communicatio idiomatum* as an important turning point in modern theology, opening the way to Feuerbach's critique of projectionism. Luther was wrong to think that the finite is capable of containing the infinite and thus opening up a way from humanity to divinity. But then, as Long points out, neither is Barth's dialectical method able to do justice to the Chalcedonian formulation.[18] Nevertheless, both Barth's and Franke's actualism requires that revelation needs something more, namely grace. The divinity of Jesus is not read off the face of his human nature, but it is something discernible by grace, through faith.

The significance of this move is monumental. Franke and Barth create such a gap between the humanity of Jesus and his divinity that one wonders how the two can be at all ever united. Moreover, in terms of the intelligibility of religious speech, both weaken the links between divinity (the content of revelation) and humanity (the means of the revelation, namely the history of Jesus, religious experience, etc.) that a *tertium* is required to provide that link. That third is supplied by the free activity of the Holy Spirit, which creates faith in us, which makes our judgments about the human nature of Jesus adequate to his divine nature. But the point is that this "epistemic bonding," which may or may not be seen as a continuation of the transcendent mission of the Holy Spirit, is not publicly available. Again, it is not an object that we can gaze upon and bring our concepts to bear upon it. It is something that *happens to* our language about God, not something that we bring about. But it is essential that it bears no intrinsic link to the *content* of that which is experienced by us, whether the history of Jesus, or religious experience, of knowledge of the natural world. The deliverances of that activity of the Spirit remain secret, non-public, and non-epistemic. God is not an object, but he remains subject in that activity. We are the objects, as we are drawn into a process of divine communication.

Rollins too stresses the fact that we are objects in revelation and God remains subject. The point of revelation is not knowledge, but transformation, and love. We ought to be transformed by revelation, rather than seeking to correctly interpret it.[19] Theology is the place where God speaks in human discourse. But crucially, this happens non-

18. Long, *Speaking of God,* pp. 93-109.
19. Rollins, *How (Not) to Speak of God,* p. 17.

epistemically, that is, without our being able to verify how and in virtue of what human content that happens. God, as it were, hijacks human speech and renders it applicable to him. But we do not know how! Theology is the site of revelation; it is worshipful testimony in the aftermath of God. But it does not testify to God in virtue of its content, but only in virtue of its existence.[20]

If, however, revelation is mediated through faith, but this faith is something not rationally connected to what is epistemically given to us, i.e., that which we can intend in light of a conceptual scheme (the human history of Jesus, his resurrection, creation, religious experience) it seems that faith slips out of the realm of intelligibility, reference, and justification. What is the new content of faith, that surplus deliverance of grace? Moreover, if faith does not stand in rational, but only in a quasi-causal links, with the objects of our experience — which, as we saw, anchor our language to reality — how shall we be able to discriminate between good and bad enculturations of the gospel, as both Franke and Rollins want? I will return to these and other questions about revelational indirectness in the final section of this essay.

Anonymity of Truth

The reader might have discerned the *passive* cast of emergent imagery. We are the "objects," the Spirit "causes" the success of our theological affirmations as they are brought before God in faith; theology is the "site" of revelation. God remains subject. This aspect of emergent epistemology could be described as the "anonymizing," or, as Rollins calls it, "hypernymizing"[21] of truth. While there is no space in this essay for a full-blown discussion of the theory of truth, I should point out that truth is no longer understood propositionally, but more along the lines of a transformation and a process. Truth as the discovery of adequate propositions is no longer the point, partly because such an adequacy of human languages to God is impossible. Instead, truth is that which happens to us when we make our fallible and plural judgments about God. More exactly, it happens to us as the Spirit graces our theological activity. Such is the epistemic authority of the Spirit. It is not that the

20. Rollins, *How (Not) to Speak of God,* p. 22.
21. Rollins, *How (Not) to Speak of God,* p. 25.

content of our confessions is right, but that truth *somehow* emerges, or rather envelops us, as the Spirit draws us to him. Faith is that disposition of receptivity for this action.

There is something undeniably right about this. It recognizes that God is always in excess of our language and that we stand in need of the gift of grace in order to say anything about him. Moreover, it disenchants us from the idea that there is only one right approach to reality, only one proper *modus significandi.* There is nothing in Christian theology to commit us to the notion of a single right description of the real, while there is quite a clear scriptural indication that the ultimate structure of the real is tied with the purposes of God, which will be perfected eschatologically.[22] Thus, to conceive of truth as being *exclusively* propositional, defined in terms of a correspondence between language and reality, is to forget that (a) language never stands separate from the world, so as to be compared with it, and (b) the structure of the world itself is something that God brings about *(creatio continua).* Franke et comp. are on the right track when they reconnect truth to soteriology.

But the propositional still matters, and propositional language gets is meaning from being reliably connected to things in the world. This is the weakness which I have tried to highlight in this essay: emergent (but also Barthian) theology loosens the rational links between our judgments about everyday experience, religious experience, and the history of Jesus to such an extent that we are then unable to see why these were necessary in the first place. What is the point of a historical revelation, if the *real* content of that revelation, i.e., the divinity of Jesus, does not stand in any discernible rational links to his humanity, to his resurrection, life, and ministry? Such an application to postfoundationalist epistemology to God-talk risks losing the intelligibility of the latter altogether. The following section addresses this mistake and how it might have been prevented.

IV

The predicament is generated by the way in which the theologico-linguistic dilemma is perceived. The second section explained that inter-

---

22. Franke labels this "eschatological realism" and alludes to, among others, 1 Corinthians 7:31. The *esse* of this world is not something given, but in the process of becoming under God's providential care.

pretation of the linguistic turn. The limitations of theological language are traced back to the fact that it is unable to map itself unto the divine being. Language operates through the creativity of the human mind, which structures its sensorial perceptions. The undeniably creative and human elements make it impossible for a single human language to adequately represent God. We lack sufficient repeatability in terms of the availability of God in our experience, to be able to abstract out of that experience a conceptual scheme adequate to God. And we can only know and say something about God by first having him in mind, that is, by first intending him. That presupposes a whole conceptual scheme — but then we would risk turning God into an idol, into a human creation.

This apparent problem is then given the solution of epistemic pluralism. Any single theological conceptual scheme is unable to mirror God, but somehow, God blesses the shuffling of a great many conceptual schemes. Similarly, when it comes to biblical interpretation, truth emerges as we imaginatively experiment, in midrashic manner, with possible meanings of the text. The truth is not in a single set of propositions, rather the truth is being epistemically adopted by God.

I am not convinced by the diagnosis of the problem. We are being told that there is a problem of theological language because of the clear inability of language to map divinity onto itself. But that is nothing to be ashamed of. If one was able to map divinity onto anything, then quite clearly this would not be the simple God of Christian orthodoxy. As Long astutely points out, isomorphism is precisely what we do not want and cannot have.[23] Since God is simple, he is not composed of parts, whose structure we can then map onto a linguistic scheme. More careful thinkers such as Preller are aware of this distinctive aspect of the Christian understanding of God, so they are re-casting the sought-after isomorphism. The correspondence has to be one between the structure of our language and the structure of a divine intentionality, of a divine language. Here again, our language fails miserably, since we have no experiential access to God's own self-description, except one mediated through historical revelation — but as we saw that doesn't solve as much as one would have liked.

All of the above betray a fundamental assumption about the conditions of the success of language: if only it *represented* adequately, either the being of God (not a very careful desire), or the mind of God (better, but

23. Long, *Speaking of God*, p. 175.

I think still unconvincing), then we would be satisfied. But there is a fundamental inconsistency in the program at this point. There is a quiescent assumption that non-religious language, either observational or theoretical, can be used with much more confidence. It is thought that while we can have such serious reservations about religious language, ordinary language does not suffer the same fate. What justifies such a preferential treatment? Nothing! Postfoundationalism, in fact, claims that "middle sized dry goods" are (technically speaking) just as much (partly) constructs of spontaneity, as are gods. One ought not think that the isomorphism which always eludes us for religious entities non-problematically applies to the objects of our mundane experience. The whole point of postfoundationalism is that the structure of the world itself is not something we can discover, and use to justify our conceptual schemes.

But then why do we assume observational language to unproblematically work? What kind of explanation can we adduce for this success? To suggest correspondence is again to go back to the myth of the Given, to go back to a Cartesian epistemic dualism between mind and world. Ironically it is precisely such a dualism that was inherited by those in the emergent camp. Correspondence, representation, isomorphism only works on the assumption that we can *first* outline the structure of our language and conceptual system (their meaning being unproblematic) and *only then* test their correspondence to the world. Such a dualism does not take into account a fundamental factor about meaning, namely that while meanings are partly learned by learning a language, they are also fixed by their use in practical life situations *in the world.* The referential success of our concepts is not something determined solely in virtue of their meaning (their place in the scheme, the *intension*),[24] but equally in terms of their being reliably used to do things in the world. The life-setting of concepts is an undeniable fact. Emergent postfoundationalists should have learned this from Wittgenstein.

If that is the case, then it appears that our concepts work not because they are able to mirror some depth structure of a reality independently discovered, but because they are useful tools in our life in the world. Skeptical worries about the links between our concepts and the world are born precisely because of the adoption of a dualistic framework, which counsels us to reflect on the meaning before we ask about

24. That is Preller's preference, although he puts it in terms of a preference for "referential opacity" v. "referential transparency."

the truth. Frederick L. Will[25] prefers to talk about conceptual schemes in terms of maps. The analogy allows some room for representation, but it is a conventional one, as maps use conventional symbols to refer to the terrain. "What is explicitly represented, drawn on a map is a basis, a skeleton of information defining, but not fully defining the feature of the quadrant, continent or whatever is its object. It is not inconsistent with its character as a map, but rather essential to it, that it leave room for refinement, detail, and even in some cases revision of basic outlines."[26] But the point of a map is that it orients one *within* the terrain. It is intended for use on the ground, so that it is able to be corrected when it fails. And the fact is that sometimes words do fail us — but we are able to tell those cases because language does not insulate us from the world, but *minds* our access to it.[27] As Kenneth Westphal insightfully comments, "Our cognitive predicament is not one of establishing a link between our thoughts and their supposed objects, it is instead one of exploiting the links our thinking does and must have with things in order to discriminate the genuine characteristics of things."[28]

If it is the case that words work because they are being reliably applied to things — and that we need no further explanation for that — it then follows that the discrepancy between theological and mundane talk is potentially smaller. Furthermore, if the meaningfulness of our language is only in part determined by the intrasystematic function of concepts (intensionality), but most importantly because language is a function of our being in the world, then the threat of incommensurability is largely defused. We can mean the same things because we inhabit a common world. It is our being in the world that anchors our language in reality. Incommensurability does not even make sense, because an incommensurable language would be an untranslatable language. But we would not even be in a position to recognize it as a language, unless we are able to translate it.

25. F. Will is a philosopher unfortunately neglected by theologians. His books *Induction and Justification* and, of particular interest for this essay and my project, *Pragmatism and Realism* offer a balanced approach to the idea of realism. I draw substantially on his work, but also on Donald Davidson and John McDowell.

26. Frederick L. Will, *Pragmatism and Realism,* ed. Kenneth R. Westphal (Lanham, MD: Rowman & Littlefield, 1997), pp. 31f.

27. This is part of a larger project, for which I draw mainly on the work of John McDowell and Charles Taylor, but also Hegel and Dooyeweerd.

28. Westphal, introduction to F. Will, *Pragmatism and Realism,* p. xxiii.

The implication of this for our discussion is that while there is a place for plurality of interpretation, it mostly applies to the theoretical and abstract aspects of reality. Since our languages are anchored largely in observational reality, utter differences will not apply at that level. To work with a dualism of mind and world is to think that the world impacts our mind only causally. Yet in the absence of *rational* links between mind and world, we are unable to justify our beliefs. But that goes against the right intuition that our conceptual scheme must have *friction* with the world. To give up the quest for rational friction between our beliefs and the world, as Franke does,[29] is only to make the question return in the form of anxieties about our coherent, but possibly false, systems of belief. An unconstrained coherentism should be out of the question. But how are we to think about the "interface" between mind and world without inventing dubious notions of epistemic intermediaries?

John McDowell argues that this apparent dilemma is rooted in a deep-seated mental block. It involves a dualism between nature and spirit. One conceives of nature as the realm of cause and effect, the space of law. On the other hand, there is the space of reasons, and thus of freedom: spontaneity. Once we start with such a dualism, it becomes difficult to connect the two realms again. But McDowell argues that "We can dismount from the seesaw if we can achieve a firm grip on this thought: receptivity does not make an even notionally separable contribution to the cooperation [between sensibility and understanding, or receptivity and spontaneity]. The relevant conceptual capacities are drawn on *in* receptivity."[30] To cut a very long story short, what our spontaneity does is that it actualizes aspects of the world, it brings these to light. Our conceptual schemes, thus, can be understood as being second-natures. They are not simply created in limbo, apart from our dealings with nature, but they in fact actualize nature.

It seems to me that this model opens up a real space for epistemic pluralism, but (a) one that is tempered by the realization that plurality extends primarily to theoretical issues; and (b) one that insists on the rational/justificatory links which remain between the theoretical aspects discovered by a cultural spontaneity and the observable language

29. Franke belongs to an important analytic tradition, stemming from Sellars, Quine, Davidson, Rorty.

30. John McDowell, *Mind and World* (Cambridge: Harvard University Press, 1996), p. 9.

of everyday experience. Pluralism is mandated not because *somehow* a greater number of failed conceptual schemes will round up the picture, or become fragments in a repaired mirror. It is legitimized by the fact that reality is possessed of a plenitude of aspects, because it was created by an infinite intentionality, and that we have a mandate to discover this richness by being open to what different languages and conceptual schemes might bring to light as real aspects of the world. But these differences obtain primarily at highly theoretical levels. Even so, they remain in rational links with the lower observational levels, without thinking that they can be reduced to these or translated into one another without loss.[31]

God remains wholly other, and there is no temptation of idolatry when we confidently affirm our creeds and confessions, as long as we understand that their *modus significandi* is not that of mirroring God, but that of bringing out aspects of our relationship to him. We can and we should be similarly confident in our theological judgments as we are in our talk about chairs, people, and particles.[32]

If we understand the fact that our humanly constructed languages and theologies may bring out real aspects of God's being, of his relationship to the world, that they discover a depth to our experience, then we will want to insist on the justifiability of these aspects (brought about by faith) in terms of mundane experience. This brings me back to the question of Christology, with which I will end.

Barth, Preller, and Franke have severed the links between the deliverances of faith (divinity) and the content of sense experience. For Barth, grace breaks into the circle of human rationality from above, as it were. For Franke, although the movement remains from God toward us, there is a sense in which this happens through our being open to a plurality of frameworks. But then the obvious question is, why would any kind of revelation be required? Preller makes a minimal concession that "the propositions of the language of faith must contain at least one straightforward and nonproblematic empirical referent."[33] The resurrection it-

31. My position is related to though not identical with Alister McGrath's conception of a "stratified reality" (*A Scientific Theology, Volume 2: Reality* [New York: Continuum, 2007], pp. 195-245). See also the works of Roy Bhaskar.

32. In a sense, my position is that all language is analogical, or at base metaphorical, not just religious language. There remains a difference of degree, not kind, between theological talk and observational language.

33. Preller, *Divine Science*, p. 246.

self is an act of faith and cannot be seen, but only believed. What faith does as *fides infusa,* for Preller, is that it provides the intellect with a new apprehension. Thus, the object of faith is not the history of Jesus, but what one apprehends as the salvific nature of those events. While the humanity of Christ is the indirect object of faith, included in the reference of faith, it is nevertheless "subordinated to the mystery operative in that humanity — the efficient causal order of salvation."[34] Thus, what faith does for Preller is that it renders a depth to those historical events of revelation, but crucially a depth that can only be sensed by faith: "The application of the light of faith to certain empirical events, however, makes present to the intellect non-empirical aspects of those same events, their soteriological efficacy."[35] But Preller is unwilling to allow for any rational way of connecting those aspects sensed by faith with those other aspects, sensed by natural reason, since "we do not know the mechanism by means of which we find ourselves informing certain events in terms of the language of faith."[36] In which case, the question is, how do we know that we have indeed discovered real aspects *of those same events,* once we sever the rational and justificatory links with them? This is exactly McDowell's concern about coherentism: if our beliefs (spontaneity) are only in a causal, rather than a rational relation to the world (receptivity), then we lose the very content of those beliefs, indeed, we lose the very notion of belief (which implies "aboutness").

Franke and Rollins are just as willing to cast the Spirit in a non-epistemic, causal role. The Spirit causes us to be in the truth, quite apart from our natural ways of telling truth from fiction. Yet both are at aware of the risks of relativism and self-deception. Both accept the difference between valid and invalid enculturations of the gospel.[37] But by denying themselves the ability to justify the deliverances of faith in light of accessible historical experience, they cannot help themselves to such notions.

34. Preller, *Divine Science,* p. 249.

35. Preller, *Divine Science,* p. 252.

36. Preller, *Divine Science,* p. 252. Long is superior to Preller at this point because he does not envision faith as supplying something private: "We need neither a different set of eyes than Feuerbach had, nor some private theological language, but only to see the things he rightly saw and those he said under a different formal object. The 'illumination' that comes is not some special privileged epistemology, but a way of recognizing a depth to our everyday natural vision that need not conflict with that vision" (p. 58).

37. Rollins, *How (Not) to Speak of God,* p. 18; Franke, *Manifold Witness,* p. 119.

I find it quite puzzling that both Franke as well as Preller seem to consider the only option to be that of moving rationally from the human nature of Christ to his divine nature. I am happy to concede that this movement is not warranted by the Chalcedonian definition. On the other hand, neither countenances the fact that we might move not from human nature, but from the historical hypostasis of Jesus — in which both his human as well as divine natures are manifested — to his divine nature. The first option would be impossible anyway, since we do not have an access to an abstract human nature (no *physis anhypostatos*), but only as it is manifested in the historical existence of Jesus. In that historical existence God has made himself an object for our nonsalvific, natural knowledge, and this is an act of grace. Faith grasps the divinity manifested in that hypostasis as a depth of that historical existence, the kind of depth not present in any other hypostasis. But it needs to be possible to tie that depth rationally to other dimensions (aspects) of that existence, perceived by other conceptual schemes. Unless we are able to connect faith to other such dimensions of experience, our faith will remain without any kind of relevance to life. No suggestion is made here that natural reason alone can ascend from the historical Christ to the Christ of faith, but that, as we reflect on the Christ of faith, i.e., the Christ whose identity is rendered by the scriptures, we can and we should find analogues with historical descriptions of the same event. Faith opens up a depth, but it must be *recognizably a depth of those same events.*

This means that the contents delivered by faith is neither reducible to reason, nor contrary to it, but it represents an intensification of human natural powers. This continuity validates the possibility of distinguishing between good and bad interpretations and contextualizations of the gospel. While an epistemic pluralism is encouraged, it makes better sense of it as the bringing to light of potentially valid aspects of reality. The same continuity justifies having a strong sense of conviction and doctrine: theological concepts can be successfully employed to *mind* our relations with the divinity manifested in an historical hypostasis, just as observational concepts similarly mind our engagement with an empirical world. The difference that remains between them is a matter of degree, not of kind. We only have one *kind* of knowledge, a human kind, even as we apply this knowledge to radically different ends.

The Only Mediator: The Person and Work of Christ in Evangelical Perspective

Bruce L. McCormack

IN HIS MOST RECENT BOOK, David Wells has offered an acute analysis of the decline of distinctively Protestant doctrine in shaping evangelical identity in this country. He holds that doctrinal theology was a central preoccupation of that "classical evangelicalism" which was born of the fundamentalist-modernist controversies of the 1920s and 1930s. Over time, however, fundamentalism became increasingly defensive. The oppositional attitude which was basic to the fundamentalist way of being Christian led to schisms within church bodies and isolation from the surrounding culture. In the 1950s and 1960s, fundamentalism gave way to a new way of being evangelical. "Neo-evangelicalism" was a loose coalition built around "two core theological beliefs: the full authority of the inspired Scripture and the necessity and centrality of Christ's penal substitution."[1]

The leaders of this new form of evangelicalism were Harold Ockenga, Carl Henry, and Billy Graham in the United States and John Stott, J. I. Packer, Martyn Lloyd-Jones, and Francis Schaeffer in Europe. What kept the coalition together was its willingness to live with diversity around the edges of the two core beliefs. As a consequence the evangelical movement of those years was able to include folks who came from a wide range of Protestant denominations. They may still have disagreed on the doctrinal issues which had always divided their denominations, but they knew themselves to be one on the two core beliefs —

---

1. David Wells, *The Courage to Be Protestant: Truth-lovers, Marketers, and Emergents in the Postmodern World* (Grand Rapids: Eerdmans, 2008), p. 5.

which also placed them at odds with the liberal-wing of their own churches and led them quite often to feel greater solidarity with evangelicals from other denominations than with liberals in their own.

The seeds of decline were sown in the 1960s and 1970s. Gradually, evangelicals were "losing the capacity to think doctrinally," as "the leadership of the evangelical world shifted from the older pastor theologians to the newer entrepreneurial organization builders. . . ."[2] Toleration of differences of opinion on matters not belonging to the evangelical "core" gradually became *indifference* to doctrinal questions. And with that, attachment to the "core beliefs" which once unified evangelicals also began to erode. What follows is a dismal picture of an increasing cultural captivity on the part of the churches and their theologians.

I think the historical narrative set forth in Wells's book contains more than a grain of truth and I am very grateful to him for sounding the alarm where the loss of Protestant identity in particular is concerned. I share his concern completely. But there are sources of the current shift on the part of many evangelicals to what we might broadly describe as an "evangelical Catholic" consciousness which are not adequately captured by words like "emergent" — which is the master-heading Wells employs to describe this aspect of the current identity-crisis in evangelicalism. Many, probably the greater majority, who now possess this consciousness have nothing but disdain for the emergent church movement. The resources they have turned to are many and varied and some of them quite formidable, ranging from Athanasius to Cyril, Augustine to Thomas. The list would also include Henri de Lubac, Hans Urs von Balthasar, Alasdair MacIntyre, and Benedict XVI on the Catholic side and John Howard Yoder and Stanley Hauerwas on the Protestant side.

Many have also done serious reading in the field of philosophy, having read some in the works of the ancients as well as the works of recent postmodern philosophers. So-called "Radical Orthodoxy" has also been a major influence upon many. Baylor University, to give but one example, has become something of a stronghold for self-styled "Bapto-Catholics"[3] — an intellectual movement which is somewhat analogous

2. Wells, *Courage to Be Protestant,* p. 8.

3. The movement was born with the publication of a "manifesto" in 1997. See "Revisioning Baptist Identity: A Manifesto for Baptist Communities in North America," *Perspectives in Religious Studies* 24 (1997): 303-10. For the history of the movement, see Cameron Jorgenson, "Bapto-Catholicism: Recovering Tradition and Reconsidering the Baptist Identity," Baylor University PhD dissertation, 2008.

to the older "evangelical catholicism" found among the Lutherans, though their inspiration seems to have come (variously) from Thomas Aquinas, Alasdair MacIntyre and/or John Milbank's "Radical Orthodoxy" rather than the Finnish School of Luther research as has been the case with a number of Lutherans.[4]

Of course, not all "evangelical Catholics" are as vehemently anti-Reformational as those nourished by Radical Orthodoxy tend to be. The majority might even want to retain the word "Protestant" as a descriptor of what they have become. Nevertheless, it is a Protestantism largely stripped of the forensic element which they now wish to defend. "Union with Christ" has largely supplanted forensic justification as the principal theme of "subjective" soteriology and divinization theories (or an ill-defined "Christus Victor" motif) have supplanted a forensic understanding of the atonement.[5] Among those who function in this way,

4. For the importance of Radical Orthodoxy for one of the leading figures in the movement today, see Barry Harvey, *Can These Bones Live? A Catholic Baptist Engagement with Ecclesiology, Hermeneutics, and Social Theory* (Grand Rapids: Brazos Press, 2008). Others associated with this movement at Baylor include theologians Ralph Wood and Peter Candler as well as the philosopher Scott Moore (though, it has to be said, Wood and Moore seem to have little interest in Radical Orthodoxy). Given that there were 55 signatories to the '97 manifesto (including such well-known names as Stanley Grenz, James McClendon Jr., and Roger Olson), it is hardly surprising that the movement has representatives at other Baptist-related institutions, such as Beeson Divinity School. See Steven R. Harmon, *Towards Baptist Catholicity: Essays on Tradition and the Baptist Vision* (Milton Keynes, UK: Paternoster Press, 2006). [It should be noted that Beeson is actually interdenominational, though located on the campus of a Baptist university.] For the Finnish reading of Luther, see especially Tuomo Mannermaa, *Christ Present in Faith: Luther's Doctrine of Justification* (Minneapolis: Fortress Press, 2005); idem, *Two Kinds of Love: Martin Luther's Religious World* (Minneapolis: Fortress Press, 2010). The American reception of Mannermaa's work began in earnest with the publication of Carl E. Braaten and Robert W. Jenson, eds., *Union with Christ: The New Finnish Interpretation of Luther* (Grand Rapids: Eerdmans, 1998). It should be noted that the Finnish interpretation of Luther's soteriology contributed in important ways to the "Joint Declaration on the Doctrine of Justification" signed by delegates of the Lutheran World Federation and the Roman Catholic Church on Reformation Day, 1999.

5. For a critical analysis of attempts to read Calvin as providing grounds for a divinization theory, see Bruce L. McCormack, "Union with Christ in Calvin's Theology: Grounds for a Divinisation Theory?" in *Tributes to John Calvin: A Celebration of His Quincentenary*, ed. David W. Hall (Phillipsburg, NJ: P&R Publishing, 2010), pp. 504-29. For other views on the subject, see especially J. Todd Billings, *Calvin, Participation, and the Gift: The Activity of Believers in Union with Christ* (Oxford: Oxford University Press, 2007); Julie Canlis, *Calvin's Ladder: A Spiritual Theology of Ascent and Ascension* (Grand Rapids: Eerdmans, 2010).

many began with Karl Barth — but have moved on now to Athanasius or to Thomas and are now lifting up those aspects of Barth's thought which are most compatible with the one or the other. In the process, even Barth himself has come to look less and less Protestant.

My point is that the word "emergent" conceals a great deal more than it reveals and it does not help us to understand the full dimensions of the problems we face. The situation today is chaotic and most certainly fluid. Everything is in flux and new developments emerge almost daily. The question is: what, if anything can be done about it? My special concern in all of this is one I share with Professor Wells — the need to explain and defend a robust version of Protestant faith which will appeal to young evangelicals who are still trying to find their "center" theologically. If we could convert a few of those who thought their minds were already made up, all the better. But how to do this?

I am not persuaded that the solution lies in an attempt to go back to the 1950s in an effort to expand the list of originating "core beliefs," so that they are now seen in their broader doctrinal interconnections. In fact, it I believe that it is precisely the doctrines to which a "core belief" like penal substitution — the subject of this essay — *was attached* which made it impossible, in the long run, to defend it.

Let me put my cards on the table. If you took penal substitution to mean that God tortured and put to death an innocent human being (as has been done by many a popular preacher), then you would have very serious problems on your hands. From the Socinians on through to present-day feminists, the charge of injustice and, indeed, immorality brought against a God who would do such a thing has proven insuperable where this crude picture has been allowed to stand.[6] The only remedy for it, in my view, is to understand the outpouring of judgment and wrath in the event of the cross in terms of *an event in God's own life* — and not as an action performed either by God or by God's human proxies on an innocent human as such. But to make this move, to make God Himself the subject of the human experience of suffering in the event of the cross, would require that we surrender the ancient concept of divine impassibility. And that is something the Reformers themselves were unwilling to do.

I hope you are beginning to see what I mean when I refer to the nexus of doctrinal connections in which the idea of penal substitution

---

6. See Section V, below.

was originally embedded. It simply will not do to try to restore the fortunes of the original doctrine in its innerconnectedness to other doctrines. On the contrary, great harm is done in making the attempt. The Reformation simply did not go far enough.

My thesis, in what remains of this essay, is this. *Commitment to the twin ideas of divine impassibility and divine simplicity constitutes the single greatest impediment to the full coherence of the traditional penal substitutionary theory of the atonement. Failure to address this problem results in an inability to respond effectively to current moral challenges to the idea of penal substitution — which is now having a negative impact on evangelical mission.* My argument will be developed in five stages. At each stage, I will begin by announcing a series of sub-theses and will then proceed to explain them. All of the sub-theses taken together, along with the supporting arguments for them, function *cumulatively* as the argument for my main thesis. That is to say, my case does not rest on any one set of sub-theses, considered in isolation from the others. I will conclude with some implications for the mission of the evangelical churches today.

I. A commitment to divine impassibility in any meaningful sense would entail the belief that God cannot suffer and, hence, cannot be the subject of the human sufferings of Jesus.

"Impassibility" is the English translation of the Greek word *apotheia,* from which we also get the word "apathy." Of course, etymology alone does not decide the meaning of the term. It is the actual use made of it by the Church Fathers which is most important, though they themselves did like to play with etymologies from time to time in defining terms. In its actual use, to speak of God as "impassible" was to express belief in the *non-affectivity* of God. As G. L. Prestige put it in his classic work, "impassibility means not that God is inactive or uninterested, not that He surveys existence with Epicurean impassivity from the shelter of metaphysical isolation, but that His will is determined from within instead of being swayed from without."[7] So God is not cold or indifferent to human suffering; the true meaning lies elsewhere. What then? In human beings, "the rational mind is dependent upon a fleshly instrument, and consciousness is mediated through the senses. Perfect mental and moral stability is thus impossible to us in this life."[8] With God,

---

7. G. L. Prestige, *God in Patristic Thought* (London: SPCK, 1952), p. 7.
8. Prestige, *God in Patristic Thought,* p. 6.

however, there is no fleshly instrument. God's "passions," if such there be, do not reflect variation in mental states. A grief or joy which was conditioned by anything taking place outside of God would have to be excluded. And the reason, finally, why God cannot have such "physical passions"[9] is that God does not have a body or a soul. Therefore, even if He did have mental states (and most Fathers were confident that He did), He could not have them as humans have them. He could not be moved *by* what He "sees" — for that would imply that God had been conditioned by something external to Himself. And, in any event, God knows all things from the beginning; His foreknowledge is exhaustive. So He could not be moved to do something by the plight of His people, for example, because He possesses a perfect knowledge of this plight from all eternity. Hence, conditioning from without is an impossibility from at least two angles of consideration (i.e., His lack of body and soul and His exhaustive foreknowledge).

In sum: when the Westminster Confession says that God is "without . . . passions"[10] it does not mean that He has no emotional life whatsoever. It simply means that His emotional life (whatever it includes) is conditioned by His eternal being and willing alone. With respect to all else, it is completely unconditioned.

Impassibility, so understood, is a close corollary of an alleged divine simplicity. "Simplicity" means that God is without parts or composition. For the ancients, that which is divisible into parts is also corruptible. Only that which is created is divisible into parts. God is "altogether one and simple"[11] — a truth that was thought to remain unqualified by the triunity of God (which was carefully interpreted so as to preserve the divine simplicity). In any event, the key point here for our purposes is that God lacks a body and a soul; *that* was the belief which safeguarded the commitment to both impassibility and simplicity.

It should go without saying that if God lacks a body and a soul, He could not suffer or experience death, either physically or spiritually. And so the ancient commitment to the twin ideas of impassibility and simplicity would have to have raised serious Christological questions sooner or later. That it did for at least one truly great Church Father,

---

9. Prestige, *God in Patristic Thought,* p. 8.

10. Westminster Confession of Faith, II.1, in Philip Schaff, *The Creeds of Christendom,* vol. 3 (Grand Rapids: Baker Book House, 1990), p. 606.

11. Prestige, *God in Patristic Thought,* p. 9.

Cyril of Alexandria, is a point to which I will return (it is the subject of my second sub-thesis). For now, I wish to say one final word about impassibility.

Impassibility is *not* the same thing as immutability, though these terms are often confused. That God is immutable means that He does not change. An alleged non-affectivity on the part of God is one possible way of explaining changelessness in God. But there are others ways of accomplishing this end, as we shall see. And the fact that there are other ways of accomplishing it means clearly that the relation of impassibility to immutability is not a necessary one. It is not *necessary* to conclude from the biblical witness to divine immutability (e.g., Mal. 3:6) that God is also impassible. And yet, in many of the books and essays I read, the attempt to offer a Scriptural defense of impassibility has recourse again and again to immutability. My point is this: if there are other ways to explain immutability, then an appeal to those passages which bear witness to immutability will not be sufficient to guarantee the biblical character of the idea of impassibility. What would be needed in that case is an *explicit* acknowledgment of impassibility. But that, it seems to me, is not something which Holy Scripture provides.

II. Logically, there are at least four Christological models which might serve the interests of preserving divine impassibility (defined in terms of non-affectivity). The first would be to restrict suffering and death to the human nature in such a way that it is hermetically sealed off from impacting the divine Word. Such an attempt was made by Nestorius in particular but it required, for its success, the supposition of a "two-subjects" Christology (a divine subject indwelling a human subject from whom He remains ontologically distinct). Where a "single-subject" Christology is upheld (as was the case with Cyril of Alexandria, for example), the situation was far more complex. For if the "person" of Christ is understood to be a single subject — and that subject is directly identified with the eternal divine Word — then it would seem to follow that He must be the "subject" of human experiences (including suffering and death). For those ancient theologians who adopted a single-subject Christology, efforts to preserve the divine impassibility took three forms (forms often found in the same theologian). Either one said that human suffering is rightly ascribed to the Logos because the human nature in which suffering takes place was "His" (in a possessive sense) — in which case the Logos is not seen as the subject of human suffering at all. Or one accepted the possibility that the Word "receives" what comes to Him through

His human nature but immediately added that He "transforms" it, render-ing it harmless to the divine impassibility. Or one so instrumentalizes the human nature that the divine Word is seen as the effective agent of all that takes place in and through that human nature. This third option would mean that the Logos is omnipotently and unceasingly active in and through His human nature so that He never allows Himself to be truly receptive. The best solution to the dilemmas created by these four options is to take the road not consistently traveled until the modern period, viz. to understand human attributes and experiences as really (and not merely figuratively) communicated to the divine Word.

Where the first option just described is concerned, a two-subject Christology was not a live option after the Council of Chalcedon for those who desired to measure their orthodoxy by its Definition. But there was another way to achieve what Nestorius had wanted to achieve (viz. a strict "separation" of the natures) without departing from the single-subject Christology which had been declared orthodox. One could simply take the communication of attributes to the person of the union as figurative, rather than real. This was the move made by John Calvin. He approached the subject of the "communication" as an exegetical problem, rather than a metaphysical one. "But the communi-cating of characteristics or properties consists in what Paul says, 'God purchased the church with his blood' [Acts 20:28], and 'the Lord of glory was crucified' [1 Cor. 2:8]. John says the same: 'The Word of life was handled' [1 John 1:1]. Surely God does not have blood, does not suf-fer, cannot be touched with hands. But since Christ, who as true God and *also* true man, was crucified and shed his blood for us, the things that he carried out in his human nature are transferred *improperly,* al-though not without reason, to his divinity."[12] What Calvin is saying in this passage is that the "communication of attributes" is only a figure of speech — and, indeed, a synecdoche (a speaking of the whole in terms of what is proper only to a part). This is an understandable position, in-tellectually respectable in its way. The problem is that Calvin under-stood penal substitution to be real — and given his treatment of the "communication," the penal sufferings of Christ had to be restricted to the human nature alone.

---

12. John Calvin, *Institutes of the Christian Religion,* ed. John T. McNeill and trans. Ford Lewis Battles (Philadelphia: Westminster Press, 1960), II.xiv.2, p. 484 (emphasis mine).

The remaining three options were devised by Church Fathers who were committed to a divinization soteriology. That is an important point to remember. Where supporters of penal substitution have taken any interest in them at all, they have done so only as an *independent* interest a doctrine of God which is grounded finally in cosmological speculation, rather than in God's Self-revelation in Christ. That is the source of the classical Reformed commitment to impassibility and simplicity. It followed then that Christology, the "person" of Christ, was treated metaphysically as well. That this should have created problems for integrating a metaphysical conception of the "person" of Christ with an understanding of the work of Christ along the lines of penal substitution should not be surprising. I will return to this problem under the heading of my next sub-thesis. For now, we will stay with our description of the three strategies for preserving impassibility employed by the orthodox Fathers.

It was Athanasius who took the lead in formulating the three strategies for preserving divine impassibility which were adopted by those affirming a single-subject Christology. ". . . [T]he Word is not able to die, being immortal and the Son of the Father — therefore he took to himself a body which could die. . . ."[13] In the early phase of his career, Athanasius had little need for the human soul of Christ. The point of his soteriology was to explain the overcoming of that corruptibility which is natural to the flesh as created. His explanation found its center in the thought of the joining of the incorruptible Word to corruptible flesh. Klalid Anaṭolios puts it this way. "The conjunction of activity and passivity already indicates a certain conception of the unity of Christ by way of a unified dynamic by which the divinity acts upon the humanity. Within this unified dynamic, the contrast is strictly maintained between the impassible and immortal Logos and the passible mortal body."[14] So the Word is purely active in relation to the flesh (indeed, omnipotently active); the flesh is purely receptive. The flesh is the instrument and object of the divine activity. So when Athanasius ascribes suffering to the Word, he means simply that because the body in which this suffering takes place *belongs* to Him, it is — in this sense — *His* suffering. ". . . He, although He

13. Athanasius, *De Incarnatione* 9, in idem, *Contra Gentes* and *De Incarnatione*, ed. and trans. Robert W. Thomson (Oxford: Clarendon Press, 1971), pp. 153, 155.

14. Klalid Anatolios, *Athanasius: The Coherence of His Thought* (London and New York: Routledge, 1998), p. 79.

was God, had His proper human body, formed and organized as ours, and made for our sakes and salvation. And on account of this, the properties of human nature are said to be His, because He existed in that nature, and He hungered, thirsted, suffered, laboured, and was perfectly sensible of these infirmities, of which our flesh was capable. On the other hand, those powers and operations, which were peculiar to Him as Divine, such as raising the dead to life, restoring the blind, and giving health to the sick, are ascribed to Him, because He did them by the instrumentality of His own body."[15] On this passage, E. P. Meijering comments as follows. "The divine activities, He Himself accomplished; the human activities are His only because it is His body."[16] Finally, the sufferings of Christ cannot truly "reach" the Word. "Wherefore, as nothing of imperfection can touch the nature of the Word of God, so He abides forever the same infinite immutable being. And so little do the frailties of the manhood molest or discompose Him, that they are obliterated before His Power, and they disappear at His presence. Our weaknesses and infirmities, which He admitted into His own Person, were so vanquished and extinguished, that we were delivered from those evils which had encompassed our nature since the fall. . . ."[17]

Thus, all three strategies for preserving divine impassibility are already present in Athanasius. The instrumentalization of human nature, the idea that human suffering may rightly be ascribed to the Word in a possessive sense only, and the thought that human infirmities are "obliterated" in the presence of His person — all of these ideas are found at a fairly early stage in the development of the orthodox Christology. And really, all three belong together, since they are mutually interpreting.

Now it is quite possible that the early church knew of one grand exception where the affirmation of an "unqualified impassibility" (or, as I prefer, the understanding of impassibility as non-affectivity) is concerned, viz. Cyril of Alexandria. Paul Gavrilyuk has arged that the starting-point for Cyril's doctrine of the incarnation was the idea of kenosis, found in Philippians 2:6-11.[18] Gavrilyuk cites a passage from

15. Athanasius, *The Orations of S. Athanasius Against the Arians* III.31 (London: Griffith Farran & Company, 1893), pp. 216-17.
16. See Meijering, *Athanasius: Die dritte Rede gegen die Arianer, Teil II: Kapitel 26–58* (Amsterdam: Verlag J. C. Gieben, 1997), p. 71.
17. Athanasius, *Against the Arians* III.34, p. 220.
18. Paul L. Gavrilyuk, *The Suffering of the Impassible God: The Dialectics of Patristic Thought* (Oxford: Oxford University Press, 2004), p. 150. It should be noted that Gavrilyuk

Cyril's writings in which the great Alexandrian says the following: ". . . when he [the Logos] enclosed himself in our flesh he was 'tempted in every respect.' We obviously do not mean that he had been ignorant before, but rather that to the God-befitting knowledge that he already possessed was *added* the knowledge gained through temptation."[19] Gavrilyuk's commentary on this is as follows. "In this passage Cyril speaks of God *gaining experiential knowledge* of human misery that was known to him before in a less direct, non-experiential, although no less perfect way."[20] What we catch sight of here is the idea of a real *appropriation* of human experiences by the Logos. Such an appropriation is made possible, according to Gavrilyuk, by divine kenosis — a "self-emptying" which Gavrilyuk defines as "a temporary restraint of divine power and other perfections."[21]

Now if Gavrilyuk is right about all of this, then Cyril did attain to the thought of a "qualified impassibility" — though it is hard to see what the difference between this and "passibility" would be. But the crucial point is that Cyril, on this reading, understood the Logos to be receptive to that which came to Him from His human nature. Far from "obliterating" the human experiences of joy, grief, suffering, etc., the Logos made Himself open to them and embraced them.

But not all specialists in the theology of Cyril come to the conclusions that Gavrilyuk has. John McGuckin explains Cyril's Christology this way. "The human nature is . . . not conceived as an independently acting dynamic (a distinct human person who self-activates) but as the manner of action of an independent and omnipotent power — that of the Logos; and to the Logos alone can be attributed the authorship of, and responsibility for, all its actions. This last principle is the flagship of Cyril's whole argument. There can only be one creative subject, one personal reality, in the incarnate Lord; and that subject is the divine Logos who has made a human nature his own."[22] For McGuckin, "ap-

---

himself does not regard Cyril as exceptional but rather as the embodiment of patristic theology more generally (at least among those acknowledged by the churches as orthodox). That is something I am not convinced of, quite obviously. But I am fascinated by his treatment of Cyril.

19. Gavrilyuk, *Suffering of the Impassible God,* p. 150 (emphasis mine).
20. Gavrilyuk, *Suffering of the Impassible God,* p. 150 (emphasis mine).
21. Gavrilyuk, *Suffering of the Impassible God,* p. 158.
22. John McGuckin, *Saint Cyril of Alexandria and the Christological Controversy* (Crestwood, NY: St. Vladimir's Seminary Press, 2004), p. 186.

propriation" is the expression on an instrumentalizing of the human nature in Christ which results in benefits for it — rather than the addition of anything to the Logos. ". . . The divine Logos appropriates human nature. This human nature becomes none other than the human nature of the one who is God, and is thereby lifted to an extraordinary glory. More than this, it becomes the economic instrument [*Organon*] of the divine Logos. . . . The human nature of the Logos is, therefore, an instrument of the divine energy."[23] And again, ". . . the human nature of the Logos thereby becomes the instrument of omnipotent power. . . ."[24] McGuckin understands kenosis in Cyril to reflect a change in the way God's glory is expressed, rather than in an Self-limitation. "The subject is unchanged, the divine Logos, but that subject now expresses the characteristics of his divinely powerful condition in and through the medium of a passible and fragile condition."[25]

This is not the place to seek to resolve a conflict of interpretations among specialists whose knowledge of the subject exceeds my own. I will simply say that *if* Gavrilyuk is right (and I rather hope that he is), this would only make Cyril to be the exception that proves the rule. In the main, early church reflection on Christology sought to preserve a doctrine of divine impassibility understood as non-affectivity. This was achieved primarily through an instrumentalization of Christ's human nature (which was wholly consonant with the divinisation soteriology which it also served).

Taking a step back, the most obvious problem with the instrumentalization of Christ's human nature — from the standpoint of New Testament theology — is that the Synoptics, in particular, understand the work of the Mediator to have been performed in the power of the Holy Spirit. One need only read Sinclair Ferguson's treatment of the Spirit's ministry in the life of Jesus in his fine book *The Holy Spirit* to convince oneself that this is true.[26] The problem that this creates, however, is this: Why should the Father have poured out His Spirit upon the man Jesus, to empower Him in His works of love, His performance of miracles, etc., *if*, as a consequence of His hypostatic union with the *second person of the Trinity*, He was *already*, from the moment of His conception on-

23. McGuckin, *Saint Cyril of Alexandria*, pp. 184-85.
24. McGuckin, *Saint Cyril of Alexandria*, p. 185.
25. McGuckin, *Saint Cyril of Alexandria*, p. 186.
26. Sinclair B. Ferguson, *The Holy Spirit* (Downers Grove, IL: InterVarsity Press, 1996), pp. 35-56.

ward, the instrument of omnipotent power? If the divine Logos has made this human nature to be the medium through which He exercised His omnipotent power, what need is there for an outpouring of the Spirit upon Him? Would this not make the Spirit's ministry in the life of Jesus superfluous to requirements? Why then do the Gospels take the Spirit's ministry in the life of Jesus so seriously?

I would like to suggest that the best resolution of these difficulties would be a pneumatologically driven two-natures Christology. Such a Christology would remain within the bounds of orthodox doctrine as defined by Chalcedon, but it would give greater scope to the Spirit's ministry in the life of Jesus by making the *kenosis* to consist in the understanding that the Logos relates to His human nature in the modality of pure receptivity, rather than (as occurred in Athanasius) activity. This would also mean that if the "person of the union" is rightly thought of as a single subject and if that single Subject were to be identified with the Logos, then it would no longer be possible to speak of a real appropriation of human attributes (and the experiences which they make possible) without surrendering the understanding of the Logos as an utterly *simple* Subject. What we have before us is a most complex Subject which cannot be described in terms of divine simplicity. Moreover, the idea of a *temporary* restriction of divine power and other perfections would have to result in change on the part of the Logos, thereby calling into question His "immutability." The only way to preserve immutability while affirming possibility is by making the appropriation that occurs in time, in the incarnate state, to be the result of an eternal "determination" of the Person of the Logos precisely *for* this appropriation. If the Logos is a composite subject in time, He must already be so in Himself in eternity.[27] The humility and obedience which make appropriation possible must be "personal properties" of the Second person of the Trinity.

III. In classical Protestantism, the two-natures Christology was regarded as a necessary pre-requisite to the work of Christ. But this "necessity" was consistently undermined by the fact that neither the divine nature nor even the Logos Himself played a role in that work. Suffering and death were restricted to the human nature alone. The divine element in the God-human

27. For more on this point, see Bruce L. McCormack, "Karl Barth's Christology as a Resource for a Reformed Version of Kenoticism," *International Journal of Systematic Theology* 8 (2006): 243-51.

was brought into play solely at the point at which the problem of an equivalence of the penalty paid (i.e., three days in death) with the penalty owed (i.e., eternal separation from God) was raised. But the sought-for equivalence could never be established in this way, since the Logos had no part of the payment of the penalty beyond offering up His humanity. The problem here is that the Reformers failed adequately to integrate the person and work of Christ.

Neither classical Lutheranism nor classical Reformed theology was able to provide the kind of integration of the person and work of Christ which, in the long run, would make sense of the doctrine of Christ's penal substitution which they (largely) shared. Their unfortunate debate over the real presence of Jesus Christ's body and blood in the eucharist led the Lutherans to elaborate a Christology in which the predominant element was that of the "communication" of attributes proper to the divine nature of Christ to His human nature (the so-called *"genus of majesty"*). At the same time, they refused to allow for any traffic in the other direction. Human properties and experiences could not be ascribed to the divine nature (the so-called *"genus of humility"*). For their part, the Reformed rejected the inter-penetration of the two natures which would make the sharing of the human nature in the divine attributes of omnipotence, omniscience, and omnipresence conceivable in the first place. They argued instead (in good Cyrilline fashion) for a communication of the attributes of both natures to the person of the union (the Logos) rather than between the natures. What they failed to see was that a *realistically intended* communication of human attributes and experiences to the Logos was, in itself, enough to make of the person of the Logos a "composited unity." And if this "composition" was not to produce change in the Logos, then the composition in question could not be "new" to Him. It had to be eternally planned for and, indeed, *proper* to the Logos. But to admit that much would have meant the surrender of divine simplicity (in its traditional form) and, with that, divine impassibility. This they were not in a position to do. And so they waffled back and forth between a merely figural understanding of the communication of the attributes of both natures to the "person of the union" (Calvin's view) and a more realistic understanding (Heinrich Bullinger's view).[28]

---

28. In defense of this point, see Bruce L. McCormack, "For Us and Our Salvation: Incarnation and Atonement in the Reformed Tradition," in *Studies in Reformed Theology and History* (Princeton: Princeton Theological Seminary, 1993).

Clearly, impassibility and simplicity were, once again, controlling their thinking.

Pure activity on the part of the Logos on the Lutheran side, waffling on the Reformed side: neither was capable of addressing the problem of equivalence that lay at the heart of the penal substitution theory because neither was capable of producing an integration of the person and work of Christ which would make the Logos to be — in any sense — the subject of the human sufferings of Christ. The sought-for equivalence in the penal substitution theory was between the penalty *owed* and the penalty *paid*. The Reformed, especially, took up the problem. But their solution was no solution at all. They said that the union of the divine nature to the human nature in Christ gave infinite value to what was experienced in the human nature. The problem is that this could be true *only* if second person of the Trinity were in some sense the subject of the suffering and death which took place for us and in our place. To the extent that the Reformed kept the natures separate, however, and refused to allow the communication of human properties and experiences to the person of the union to be real, talk of the "infinite value" of a strictly human experience was rendered empty. What the Reformers generally were left with was a restriction of suffering and death to the human nature alone (with the notable exception of Luther). Penal substitution, interpreted against this background, could only mean that God had willed (and perhaps contributed directly to) the torture and death of an innocent human being. Again, what is playing havoc with the penal substitution theory here is the prior commitment to divine impassibility and simplicity.

IV. We have already taken the biggest step in rendering the penal substitution theory more coherent than had been the case historically. We have identified the commitment to the twin concepts of divine impassibility and simplicity as an obstacle to coherence, insofar as such commitments make it impossible to understand God as in any way the subject of the human sufferings of Jesus. Where the latter occurs, it also becomes impossible to address the problem of an equivalency between the penalty owed and the penalty paid. But the problem of equivalency is even more difficult than we have been able to indicate to this point. We must, therefore take one final step — which will require a reconfiguration of the doctrine of penal substitution as traditionally conceived.

The problem of equivalence is not finally resolved where it is treated solely in quantitative terms. The quantitative equivalence of "three days" with eternity is not even solved by making God the subject of the experience of death. That is, to be sure, a necessary first step. But it will not do to say simply that "being infinite, God can experience in a moment of time what it would take us an eternity to experience" — because He still experiences the just penalty upon sin *humanly* (in and through His human nature). And if humanly, then he would have to have precisely the same human experience as we would have had, had we had to pay the debt ourselves. But precisely here lies the problem. The debt we owe is the experience of "hell"; not a mere physical death, but the experience of a separation from God *in death* which holds forth no hope of coming to an end.

Part of the problem here, of course, is that "eternity" has often been understood along the lines of an endless duration of time. But if it is God's being which defines the meaning of "eternity" and God is able to enter into time without ceasing to be God, then "eternity" cannot simply be time extended infinitely — which would make God finite (since even a time which extends into infinity would still have had a beginning). Nor can it be the opposite of time (i.e., timelessness). No, "eternity" is a description of the "moment" which founds time, the "moment" which stands outside the definite sequence of moments which we experience as their ground. Such a relationship is wholly positive and helps us to understand how it comes about that God could enter time and live a human life. Time as we know it is not alien to the innermost being of God even though God Himself, as its Creator, transcends it.

In any event, the solution to the problem of equivalence is to stop trying to understand it in quantitative terms and to understand it instead in qualitative terms. What, after all, is the penalty due to us for sin? According to Jesus' own teaching it is *separation* from God. An abyss opens up between God and the sinner upon his/her death which can never again be bridged from the side of the sinner.[29] S/he who dies in God-forsakenness enters into the experience of separation. So if there is indeed an equivalence between the penalty owed and the penalty paid (as penal substitution surely demands), then God in Christ must allow Himself to be subjected to this experience; not to merely physical death but to *this* experience.

This is not the place to carry out the exercise — it would require far

29. Luke 16:26.

more space than has been allotted to me — but penal substitution can-not be finally made coherent where it is conceived of apart from the theme of Christ's descent into hell.[30] That God Himself pays our debt means that God is the Subject of precisely *this* human experience. Any-thing less would still be incoherent because the problem of equivalency would not have been given an adequate answer.

It is God Himself then, in the Person of the Son, who gives Himself over to this experience. In that He does so, He takes it into His own *be-ing,* wherein its power is fully expressed. He is the subject of the "living death" — a contemplation in pure receptivity of the absymal horror of a separation from God which the man Jesus can do nothing to bridge.[31] And when this terror-filled experience is brought to an end, it is brought to an end by the same Holy Spirit who made possible the miracles per-formed by Jesus in life, not by the Logos acting omnipotently through and upon His human nature. It is the Spirit which, as the power of the Father and the Son, raises the man Jesus from the dead.

On this showing, justice and mercy do not compete in God. God up-holds His own justice in that the debt is paid — and the sinfulness of sin is recognized for what it is and dealt with. The justification which al-ways lay at the heart of the traditional penal substitution scheme — viz. that simple forgiveness on God's part was not enough because the sin-fulness of sin would be ignored and, thereby, remain untransformed — has here been upheld and maintained. But God does all of this through an act of loving Self-giving, of Self-donation, in order to reconcile hu-man beings to Himself.

V. Already in the sixteenth century, criticism of the penal substitution the-ory focused upon the consequences which it would have upon human be-havior. The basic thought was: human beings are called to live lives pleas-ing to God. If, however, they conceive of God as arbitrarily choosing to punish an innocent human in the place of the guilty, they conceive of God as fundamentally unjust. The attempt to please this God, to be like this God, could only have disastrous consequences on the plane of human to human

---

30. I have, in any case, treated this theme elsewhere. See Bruce L. McCormack, "'With Loud Cries and Tears': The Humanity of the Son in the Epistle to the Hebrews," in *The Epistle to the Hebrews and Christian Theology,* ed. Richard Bauckham, Daniel R. Driver, Trevor A. Hart, and Nathan McDonald (Grand Rapids: Eerdmans, 2009), pp. 37-68.

31. Cf. Hans Urs von Balthasar, *Mysterium Paschale* (Edinburgh: T&T Clark, 1990), pp. 168-72.

relations. Such an argument cannot be adequately addressed until we cease understanding the self-offering of the man Jesus as "satisfying the wrath of God" so that it might be turned away from the rest of us (an idea which leads to pitting God's justice over against His mercy) and begin to understand God's judgment upon sin as something He takes upon Himself. United to the man Jesus, receptive to all that comes to Him through this man, He Himself is the sin-offering.

In the sixteenth century, the Socinian assault on penal substitution had three elements. First, they laid their finger on the weakest point in the theory, viz. that Christ's death is neither "eternal" nor can it be "for all" (i.e., have universal significance) since, according to the orthodox theory, the divine nature is untouched by what happens in the human nature. Second, God is clearly able to forgive sins without a satisfaction having been offered, since that is something that is frequently done by Jesus Himself who simply declared sinners He encountered to be forgiven. Third, "it is simply unjust to let the guilty go unpunished, and to punish the innocent in their stead."[32] This last point might have been mitigated had the first been adequately addressed. But as we have already seen, the Reformers were not in a position to address the first point. What later orthodox Protestants were able to do when faced with these criticisms was to suggest that the situation here was unique, that its meaning cannot be comprehended against the background of public law, because it is a private matter between God and human beings, the terms of which were established in the covenant of grace. In the eyes of the Socinians, however, such an appeal to a private law was simply a return to the Scotist emphasis of divine willing over against the necessities of divine being. If the saving significance of Christ's death could not be explained in terms of universally accepted public law, then it was a wholly arbitrary contrivance. The truth is that the Thomist emphasis upon universally accepted rational principles of moral judgment was already in the ascendency, even among the Reformed orthodox. So this appeal had to look self-contradictory and even self-serving.[33]

The solution to this conundrum lies, I think, in seeing essence and will in God as one rather than as sequentially (and, therefore, temporally) related. The determination which the triune God gives to His be-

32. Albrecht Ritschl, *A Critical History of the Christian Doctrine of Justification and Reconciliation,* trans. John S. Black (Edinburgh: Edmonston and Douglas, 1872), p. 300.

33. Ritschl, *Critical History,* p. 303.

ing in eternity (i.e., to do what He does in the Person of the Son in time) is a determination which "grounds" His own being, thus ensuring His changelessness in the "becoming" to which He subjects Himself in time.[34] To make this move is to establish the basis for a covenant ontology which would eliminate every last vestige of the arbitrary from divine willing.

The feminists of the twentieth century heightened the stakes where moral objections to penal substitution is concerned. For they advanced the astute observation that even if "punishment" were an event which takes place between the eternal Father and the eternal Son, it would still constitute a case of what they call "cosmic child abuse"[35] — which would give us a concept of a vengeful God to emulate which would lead to unhappy consequences on the plane of human-to-human relations. The solution here is to recognize that the Christian doctrine of the Trinity does not allow the kind of ontological differentiation that would allow the Father to act upon the Son as a subject distinct from Himself (in the sense that human beings are objects to one another's actions). God's experience of His own judgment upon sin is an experience that is appropriated by Him in His second mode of being but it is the one divine Subject who has this experience.

In any event, the conception of the penal sufferings of Christ argued for here would provide an adequate response to moral objections to the traditional form of the doctrine (old and new) because it would

34. It is, perhaps, well known that I have also made the suggestion that it is the Father, rather than the triune God, who is the "origin" of the divine act of Self-constitution. But that is a piece of theological experimentation and is not necessary for the success of the argument being developed here. It is sufficient to say (with Eberhard Jüngel) that election is an eternal act on the part of the triune God of "setting-Himself-in-relation" which looks in "an inward and an outward direction at the same time." And, therefore, ". . . as event, the being of God possesses *freedom of decision.* Decision does not belong to the being of God as something supplementary to this being; rather, as event, God's being *is* his own decision." See Jüngel, *God's Being Is in Becoming: The Trinitarian Being of God in the Theology of Karl Barth,* trans. John Webster (Grand Rapids: Eerdmans, 2001), pp. 83, 81 (respectively). For my most recent contribution to debates over the logical relationship of triunity and election, see Bruce L. McCormack, "Election and Trinity: Theses in Response to George Hunsinger," *Scottish Journal of Theology* 63 (2010): 203-24.

35. See Joanne Carlson Brown and Carole R. Bohn, eds., *Christianity, Patriarchy and Abuse: A Feminist Critique* (New York: Pilgrim Press, 1994). This criticism of the penal substitution theory has also been adopted by leading figures in the "emergent church" movement. See Steve Chalke and Alan Mann, *The Lost Message of Jesus* (Grand Rapids: Zondervan, 2003).

make the Self-giving of the Son in love to be the medium through which God's judgment upon sin is realized. Such an understanding of God could not, in the nature of the case, provide a model for any other human behavior other than that of humble, self-giving love.

Conclusion

I have assumed throughout that Professor Wells was right to make penal substitution a core belief of evangelicals. Penal substitution was central to the soteriology of the sixteenth-century Protestant confessions after the Osiandrian affair. And if "evangelical" is still today rightly understood, as it was originally (in the sixteenth century), as a synonym for "Protestant," then it must be a core belief of evangelicals as well.

The problem of course is that many evangelicals today have a very uncertain relationship to Protestantism. Hyphenated pieces of self-description like "Bapto-Catholic" are ways of saying that the old standards no longer hold. Confessional allegiances are now increasingly rare. In the midst of this confusion, divine impassibility and divine simplicity are making a strong comeback in evangelical circles. And if what I have argued here is cogent, the resurgence of interest in these ideas simply *must* come at the expense of a well-ordered, defensible account of penal substitution.

The crying need in evangelical theology circles today is for a theological ontology which is *fully* commensurate with the central doctrinal commitments of the Protestant faith. The Reformation did not provide us with this. Instead, they simply received the ancient metaphysically based ontology and taped their central convictions to it. Today, Protestantism can no longer survive if it tries simply to continue this practice. Before long, all that will be left are Catholic and Eastern Orthodox churches — and those non-denominational congregations which seek to feed their people with a theology patched together from a few leftover scraps of a moribund Protestantism and the living ideas of a vital and resurgent Catholicism and Orthodoxy. If that is the best we can do, it is not hard to predict the future.

Appendix: A Hymn in Honor of David F. Wells

THE FOLLOWING intentionally catechetical hymn was written in honor of David Wells — whose work and witness have provided the occasion for both the "Renewing the Evangelical Mission" symposium and for the present volume.

GARY PARRETT

There Is None Good but God Alone

There is none good but God alone.
Not one of us is righteous.
We spurned God's Way and sought our own,
and so have become worthless.
What hope, then, can we see?
Christ Jesus: only He
the path of life has trod,
to love both man and God.
Yes He alone is worthy.　　　　*(Mark 10:18; Rom. 3:9-23; Isa. 53:6; 1 John 2:1; Rev. 5)*

Scripture alone reveals these things;
thus do the Fathers witness.
Good News of life and light it brings
to those now lost in darkness.
For from this sacred Word,
what wonders we have heard:

God's grace in Christ revealed.
By His stripes we are healed.
We glory in the Gospel!

(2 Tim. 3:15-17; 2 Pet. 1:19-21; Luke 24:25-27, 45f.; Tit. 2:11; Isa. 9:2; 53:5; 1 Tim. 1:11)

In Christ alone is all our trust
for full and free salvation.
With His own blood He ransomed us
from ev'ry tribe and nation.
For us He lived and died.
Now, at the Father's side,
full knowing all our needs,
our High Priest intercedes.
He lives to make us holy.

(1 Tim. 5–6; Acts 4:12; 1 Pet. 1:19; Rev. 5:9; Heb. 2:11; 7:25; 9–10; Rom. 8:28-39)

And now by faith alone we stand
in Christ, our risen Savior,
who has fulfilled each just command
and made us just forever.
In Him is all our peace
and life that cannot cease.
By no work of our own,
but all of grace alone,
have we become God's people.

(Rom. 3:28; 5:1-2, 15-19; Eph. 1:4-5; 2:5-10; 1 Pet. 2:9-10)

For not by human pow'r or might,
but only by God's Spirit,
do we begin to glimpse the light
of all we shall inherit.
The new life He imparts
transforms our hardened hearts.
Our race, by faith begun,
in faith must still be run.
Christ set us free for freedom!

(Zech. 4:6; Eph. 1:13-14; Rom. 8:2, 11; 2 Cor. 3:17-18; Gal. 3:2-3; 5:1, 7, 16-18, 25)

Above all pow'rs abides the Word,
God's mighty Word that frees us.
Through prophets and apostles heard,
for us made flesh in Jesus.
No other word we speak,
nor human glory seek.
All earthly schemes must fail.
God's Kingdom shall prevail.
To God alone be glory!

(John 1:1, 14; Heb. 1:1-2; 2:1-4; 1 Pet. 1:23-25; Rev. 4:11; 11:15; Ps. 145:13; Rom. 11:36; Isa. 42:8)

Text: Gary A. Parrett, 2008/Tune: EIN' FESTE BURG
Common use of the tune: "A Mighty Fortress Is Our God"